In praise of CUSTOMERS RULE!

"In the wake of recent dot.bombs, Blackwell and Stephan rise to the challenge with much needed marriage counseling for the rocky, post-honeymoon relationship between business and the Internet. Let *Customers Rule!* show you how to deliver better shopping experiences and provide more value to your most valuable assets—your customers."
  —DON PEPPERS AND MARTHA ROGERS, PH.D., partners, Peppers and Rogers Group, and coauthors of *The One to One Future* and *One to One B2B*

"Once again, Roger Blackwell has used his marketing genius to show entrepreneurs the way. The technology revolution demands creative, innovative, and bold application of the Internet. His incisive and informative commentary can show you the way to success. Ignore it at your own peril."
  —JOHN KASICH, managing director, Lehman Brothers

"Roger and Kristina use experience from both the academic and the business worlds to understand what the future holds for successful firms. *Customers Rule!* will be an instant classic."
  —WALDEN O'DELL, chairman and CEO, Diebold, Inc.

"Roger Blackwell stands out as the voice of common sense and reason as he sees through all the e-commerce glitz and focuses squarely on the fundamentals that a company needs to survive in today's business climate."
  —OSWALDO CONTRERAS, president and CEO, CITGO

"Whether in the board room or from the stage, Roger preaches the necessity of understanding not just what customers want but why they want it."
  —DAVID PUGH, chairman and CEO, Applied Industrial Technologies

"Roger Blackwell has always taught that the customer is king, and his teaching has always been proven true in the marketplace. *Customers Rule!* will reintroduce readers to the time-tested principles of service and how they apply to today's marketing environment."
  —JIM OATES, president, Leo Burnett Company

"Roger Blackwell offers real-world insights that are invaluable to our people as he steadfastly preaches focus on the *customer* as the sustaining key to business success."
  —TOM MOSER, vice chairman, KPMG

"Roger Blackwell is in a class by himself when it comes to understanding consumer behavior. *Customers Rule!* takes his tremendous knowledge base of consumers, adds the e-commerce equation, and gives you a formula for success in the new century."
  —JACK KAHL, chairman, Henkel-Manco

"Dr. Blackwell has captured the essence of the dynamics that define the new winning ways of business. When 'customers rule,' business leaders will understand that it's not just their companies that compete—it's their supply chains that are battling."
—STEVE SASSER, CEO, Frontstep

"Once again Roger Blackwell has successfully surveyed the e-commerce/traditional business landscape and emerged with a pragmatic, insightful, and prescient guide for those who treasure the customer."
—ROBERT J. DANZIG, author of *The Leader Within You*

"Every distributor CEO ought to read this book. While others are focusing on direct to consumer models, Roger and Kristina analyze the evolving role of the distributor in the customer economy."
—DIRK VAN DONGEN, president, National Association of Wholesalers

"With their usual skill and aplomb Roger and Tina cut to the quick of the issue. . . the validity of the consumer proposition drives the validity of the business model. *Customers Rule!* is an entertaining and practical read."
—EMIL BROLICK, president and chief concept officer, Taco Bell Corp.

"Roger Blackwell's thoughts and strategies really represent the most clear-thinking approach to the Internet that I have seen. As the history of the Internet commerce landscape is being created, he sheds new perspectives on the fundamental business strategies for success."
—DON HALL, JR., executive vice president, Strategy and Development, Hallmark Cards

"Once again, Roger helps us understand that the customer truly is in charge of which companies win. In *Customers Rule!*, he points out that only those supply chains that adopt the tried and true commerce principles of the past, coupled with great technology and creative brand management, can best satisfy customer wants and needs."
—DIMON R. MCFERSON, chairman, Nationwide Insurance

"Roger Blackwell is one of the truly great minds in the field of consumer behavior. I've been involved in the development and introduction of over 60 new products generating billions of dollars during my career, and I can honestly say that Roger's theories and guiding principles remain at the forefront of the field of marketing. His ability to take the nuances of various retail trends and combine them into a cogent, executable strategy for executives is something I have always admired. You will always come away from the time you spend with Roger Blackwell, in person or in print, with a better way to look at your business."
—MARK GOLDSTON, chairman and CEO, NetZero, Inc.

CUSTOMERS RULE!

WHY THE E-COMMERCE HONEYMOON IS OVER AND WHERE WINNING BUSINESSES GO FROM HERE

Roger Blackwell and Kristina Stephan

CROWN
BUSINESS
NEW YORK

Published by Crown Business, New York, New York.
Member of the Crown Publishing Group.

Random House, Inc. New York, Toronto, London, Sydney, Auckland
www.randomhouse.com

Crown Business and colophon are trademarks of Random House, Inc.

Printed in the United States of America

Design by Robert Bull Design

Library of Congress Cataloging-in-Publication Data

Blackwell, Roger D.
Customers rule! : Why the e-commerce honeymoon is over and where winning
businesses go from here / by Roger Blackwell and Kristina Stephan.
1. Consumer behavior—United States   2. Internet marketing—United States.
I. Stephan, Kristina.   II. Title.

HF5415.33.U6 B58   2001
658.8'4—dc21
2001017343

ISBN 0-609-60865-7

10 9 8 7 6 5

First Edition

To Each Other

ACKNOWLEDGMENTS

When we first wrote the proposal for this book in early 1999, traditional business models and store-based retailing had all but been declared DOA, kaput, finito. Championing consumer-driven business strategies that generated profits rather than technology-based strategies that generated media attention was not "the place to be."

Laureen Rowland, editor turned agent extraordinaire, understood the significance of the message and believed in us from day one. So did Bob Mecoy, senior editor at Crown Business. Together, they asked the tough questions, demanded concise and focused answers, and helped us consolidate volumes of information and data to create this book. But *Customers Rule!* is not the product of just two authors, an agent, and a publisher; it is the culmination of ideas, facts, and observations discussed with business leaders in conferences, seminars, and boardrooms around the world. Listing everyone who has been a part of this project would be impossible.

We would like to extend special thanks to the following people who reviewed ideas and chapters and left their marks on the manuscript: Todd Mollenkopf, OnVentures; Anita Ward, Zefer; Ed Razek, The Limited; Lars Nyberg, NCR; Ajay Teneja and Bill Purser, Applied Industrial Technologies; and Ameet Patel, Chase Manhattan Bank. Nancy Kramer and Kelly Mooney of Resource not only contributed valuable comments but also allowed us to include information from Resource E-commerce Watch 2000. Joel Copeland assisted in developing an online, distance-learning course related to the topics in this book, which can be previewed at www.kmi.com. Many thanks also to Bob Mecoy, Will Weisser, Dorianne Steele, and the Crown Business and David Black Agency teams for their guidance and enthusiastic support.

The Fisher College of Business has also played an important role in *Customers Rule!*, especially Roger's M.B.A. and Honors students who reviewed and debated the issues, theories, and strategies described in this book. Among them are Jay Pauley and JR Ryan, who reviewed the manuscript from a twenty-something perspective, and Mazen El-Khatib and Ramesh Patibanda, who kept Roger's classes running flawlessly during hectic times. The Ohio State University is fortunate to have so many bright students contributing their ideas and forcing faculty members to push themselves to new levels of business acumen. We thank them for allowing us to see a glimpse of tomorrow before it happens.

Several individuals in academia affected the outcome of this project as well. Thanks go to Steven Burgess, professor of marketing at The University of Cape Town, former student, and trusted friend, for his support, especially during his assignment at The Fisher College when this manuscript was being prepared. Special thanks also to Joseph Alluto, dean of The Fisher College of Business, and Brit Kirwan, president of Ohio State University, for their encouragement to reach beyond the walls of the university and into the business community.

Special friends and colleagues not only make the writing process possible, but also fun. Though Jack Kahl has taught us much about retailing, branding, and entrepreneurship, his greatest gift to us has been the precious gift of friendship, for which we will always be grateful. A million thanks also go to Kelley Hughes and Mary Hiser for keeping the Roger Blackwell Associates office running smoothly during our writing hiatus and for their friendship and kind words during the process. And heartfelt thanks to Josette, Gavin, and Anna, whose visits let us flee the world of business and escape into a kinder world of hugs and laughter.

Most of all, we would like to thank our parents, Dale and Rheva Blackwell and Trudy and Al Stephan, for their unwavering support through this process. Since life doesn't stop while one writes a book, they did the daily chores that keep a household running and cooked meals to keep us "over nourished." We believe in the notion that children are products of their parents, and we hope they see a little bit of themselves in this book—Dale's ability to keep ahead of the times, Rheva's knack for turning a phrase, Trudy's "let's get it done" attitude, and Al's attention to even the most minute detail.

It is safe to say that this manuscript would not be what it is today without Laureen. We want to express our thanks and appreciation, not just for her professionalism and business relationship, but for the friendship and care she has given us. Our hope is that she never loses what makes her so special—her complete dedication to her "customers."

On a final note, authors always extend a special thank-you to their spouses—in this case, it would be to each other. As dedicated as we are to business, our personal dedication is to something much more significant. The ultimate goal of our work together is to create a marriage and partnership that is stronger than when we started. The reward is in the process rather than in the final product, which this time, happens to be this book.

ROGER BLACKWELL
KRISTINA STEPHAN
Columbus, Ohio

CONTENTS

CUSTOMERS
RULE!

CHAPTER 1

THE E-VOLUTION OF COMMERCE

RIGHT NOW, in technology hotbeds from Silicon Valley to Bangalor, India, young would-be Internet millionaires, armed with big ideas for business-to-consumer Web businesses, great domain names, and short-but-sweet business plans, are being turned down by the very same venture capitalists—the VCs—who brought you Amazon.com, Priceline.com, TheGlobe.com, CommerceOne, and Intel.

Why? It's not because these hopefuls have bad ideas. It's because the VCs have finally realized a basic truth of Internet business: Any pure-play business-to-consumer (B-to-C) Internet company that doesn't have a foot planted firmly in the real world—with experienced management teams, a physical presence, efficient distribution systems, and ability to make a profit—is doomed to fail. This is something we've believed almost from the beginning of the Internet explosion based on over thirty years of in-depth research of consumer behavior and a decade of work in the area of logistics. And this isn't exclusive to the business-to-consumer arena. A great majority of business-to-business (B-to-B) business plans and up-and-running commerce sites require the same foundation—at a minimum—for mass acceptance and long-term survival.

In short, the afterglow of America's brief but impassioned affair with dot-coms quickly gave way to the harsh light of the morning after, in which swinging technology investors find themselves murmuring the familiar phrase "What have I done?"

In the frenzy of the last few years, hundreds of new Internet start-ups have gone public—initially to great success on Wall Street. But how many have made good on their promises of soaring sales, retail revolution, and pie-in-the-sky returns? Nearly none! The exception to the rule may prove to be eBay, because it illustrates the most fundamental principle of commerce: customers rule! One of the fundamental keys to eBay's rapid growth is that it solves consumers' buying problems better than any solution available before its arrival on the retail scene, thus allowing it to attract and retain customers on a profitable basis. How many other dot-coms can say the same?

And what of the bricks-and-mortar enterprises, maligned for their slow service, complex logistics, and high costs, pronounced (prematurely) extinct as dinosaurs of the "old economy" at the glorious birth of the "new economy"? Ironically, following in these dinosaurs' footsteps is probably a dot-com's last chance for success. In the twenty-first century, it is the flexible, most agile dinosaur that wins—not just because of its power but because of how it does business. Traditional retailers and manufacturers that have survived the mass consolidation of the 1980s and 1990s have in place a host of consumer-driven strategies designed to grow profits quarter after quarter and enhance shareholder value year after year. Some of these strategies were designed to make shopping pleasant, efficient, and cost-effective for consumers; others were implemented to streamline the supply chain and continue economies of scale, brand loyalty, scalability (bizspeak for "big-time growth and acceptance by the masses"), and sustainable profit margins.

Yet not every dinosaur can survive. Evolution beckons only those companies that can adapt their bricks-and-mortar strengths to the warp-speed, borderless, instantaneous response–oriented new economy. This transformation can, and will, create a new breed of competitor—a truly new economy enterprise that combines the best of "e" (technology) and "commerce" (the exchange of goods and services). It is as inevitable and trackable as the evolution of biological life: The species that continue to evolve and adapt to consumer-driven, technology-fortified forms will most likely survive in the future. That's why we like to think of this era in business history as another evolutionary stage of commerce rather than a radical, revolutionary one.

We realize that our contrarian position may not be as heretical now as when we first advanced it in 1997, but it continues to go against the grain of net orthodoxy still found in business today. Onetime net-stock bull Henry Blodgett of Merrill Lynch has lately been telling anyone who will listen that he believes 75 percent of dot-com retailers will be gone in five years. Add Goldman Sachs & Company's report promising that more than half the public e-tailers will be gone by the end of 2001 and you begin to see that the rosy picture of the dot-com landscape has turned murky. Our prediction was that dot-com entrepreneurs and new-breed e-tailers would have to establish some form of a physical presence or risk becoming roadkill on the information superhighway, alongside such IPO notables as Toysmart.com, Ubid.com, and Boo.com. Be either one—a dot-com company with no bricks-and-mortar presence or a bricks-and-mortar firm sans an Internet presence—and you're destined for extinction in the e-volution of commerce.

GET OFF YOUR LAZY ASS(ET)S

Often, the greatest benefit of innovation is not the innovation itself, but the hand-wringing, head rubbing, and night sweats it causes among even the brightest thinkers and strategists. Rewind to the mid-1990s and the hoards of brash e-entrepreneurs taunting the most seasoned retail executives with an "I know something you don't know and it's going to take you down" chorus. At first, some retailers chose to ignore the threats, others responded without much long-term, strategic thinking, and some entered e-commerce cautiously, watched mostly from the sidelines, and took lots of notes. But the attention these e-businesses would gain in the next few pivotal years would stir the beehives at giants as mighty as General Electric and Wal-Mart.

Never has the adage "timing is everything" had more validity than when reaping the financial rewards of the record-breaking IPOs of the latter 1990s. One after another pure-play dot-coms popped up on the Web and quickly became the darlings of the financial community. Even the most successful, profitable, and established retailers, from Wal-Mart (or more recently Wal*Mart) to The Limited, temporarily fell out of favor with Wall Street, which cast its attention instead on newcomers TheGlobe.com, Amazon, Yahoo!, MP3, iVillage, and PlanetRx.com. Few traditional retailers could ignore the pressures of the financial community to expand into e-commerce, even though many of their strategies were half-baked and their execution lackluster.

Their CEOs had to answer to shareholders and analysts demanding strategies for e-tail and e-commerce retaliation even though those making the demands were often unsure what they were asking the CEOs to do. Many of these executives, wringing their hands, answered with strategies that were based primarily on technology for the sake of technology. Some companies hoped to get a stock boost from jumping on the e-tail bandwagon, such as Consolidated Stores' KBkids.com venture, which became a technologically sound site but had difficulty delivering products to customers in time for holiday gift giving or reaching positive profit margins. Others hoped to get a new-economy positioning, such as Banc One's

online banking venture, Wingspan, which was designed to update Banc
One's image with a new e-presence and online banking product. Each
strategy gave analysts a reason to pump up the parent companies' valua-
tions until dismal results were released.

For many traditional retailers, the e-tailing arena was entirely unfamiliar. With no experience and little research in hand, these retailers
jumped in more to satisfy the analysts who cover their stock than to satisfy their customers. And to accomplish this misguided effort, they spent
millions on e-strategies that resulted in profit drains and unsatisfied customers. Contrary to what financial types may believe, ultimately it is customers who create shareholder value, not financial analysts.

These same retailers would never spend millions on a traditional marketing program (such as revamping product lines and store layouts,
lengthening store hours, instituting toll-free customer service hotlines, or
increasing in-store promotions) unless it were entrenched in the desire to
serve customers better. The ability to tout technological advancement was
the driver that justified massive allocations and board approval for an
e-commerce initiative, but they forgot the simple lesson that customers
decide what will succeed and what will fail.

And that wasn't their only mistake: Driven by the dot-coms, retailers
underestimated how much profits count, regardless of the initiative. The
financial community was more forgiving toward the profit woes of
Amazon.com than those of such firms as Consolidated Stores, Banc One,
and other established organizations, even when many of their losses could
be traced back to their e-ventures. The punishment for missing their numbers, regardless of reason, was swift and certain: lowered ratings and
plummeting stock prices. On the other hand, e-businesses benefited from
news of increased hits and sales and partnership agreements between new
and old economy giants. Amazon's stock price climbed in 1999 despite the
fact that it reportedly spent an average of $113 to get each new customer
and its bottom-line deficit was growing dramatically. Analysts bought Jeff
Bezos's vision of dominating the future of e-tail, which at that time many
still considered the end-all, be-all of commerce. Amazon was proving it
could perform several commerce functions well (customer service, fulfillment, and branding) and that it had scalability. The Street saw Bezos as
the Henry Ford of the Internet, and analysts decided to bet on the inven-
tor rather than the meek also-rans.

Similarly, many early dot-coms and e-tailers (with roots in the physical world) raced to establish themselves on the Internet with a "throw cau-
tion to the wind" attitude toward their business models. "Whatever it
takes" was their motto, and for many, that attitude remains, seen in their

lack of concern for profitability. Their focus was on speed and mind-share—how quickly they could get their companies up and running and attract consumers to their sites.

The hype, however, was not all hype. In its purest form, the Internet offers different ways for customers to shop—anytime, day or night, from the comfort of their homes or offices—and for businesses to reach customers. Rather than be limited to the items retailers make available at local stores, consumers can shop the global marketplace for everything from the latest Paris fashions and fine art to celebrity autographs and gingerbread from a small Bavarian bakery. And beyond shopping possibilities, consumers can use the Web to search for information about the products they want to buy, the places they want to go, and the entertainment they want to experience whenever the mood strikes them. And the information is usually available at little or no cost. Internet applications also enable customers and consumers alike to trace and track their orders, and give firms entrée into consumers' buying preferences, patterns, and behaviors. The potential of the Internet seemed endless and the barriers to entry minimal, leaving the venture capitalists, the media, and strategists alike wondering if we were a few bangs short of securing the final nail in the coffin of traditional bricks-and-mortar retailing.

It would have made a great story—truly the end of commerce as we once knew it. But the financial world came to its senses, realizing that profits *do* count in the long-term viability of a firm and a business model. Corporate America's e-commerce honeymoon was over. Tech stocks tumbled, skepticism skyrocketed, and the media, which had profited from several years of hyping dot-coms, turned traitor, publicly bashing the previous dot-com darlings of the e-world for poor customer service records and lack of profits.

But the story has only just begun. It's becoming increasingly more complex as the Targets, Wal-Marts, Staples, and Nordstroms of the world launch their own strategic e-missiles, based more on research and operational systems to deliver good shopping experiences than on the desire to achieve first-mover status. From years of experience, these traditional firms understand that the priority must be the customer—connecting with the customer where, when, and how he or she desires. Add to that the fact that the flashy, glamorous elements of e-commerce are giving way in importance to the nitty-gritty elements of logistics and supply chain management, and it is apparent that e-commerce will evolve drastically in the coming decade. We believe the so-called chapter on e-commerce in the centuries-long book chronicling the evolution of commerce is only just now beginning to be written.

Perhaps most important, what these in-your-face e-competitors did was force traditional businesses to wake up and refocus on using the latest technology as a tool to satisfy better their core consumer groups. Even in today's digital age, understanding consumers, monitoring their lifestyles, and formulating strategies based on consumer behavior hold the key to success for traditional firms and dot-coms alike. Firms like Target, Wal-Mart, and Crate & Barrel can attest to the fact that giving customers what they want at a good value; delivering it in a timely, convenient fashion; and making money have never gone out of style. Companies that have paid close attention to the strategies employed by the few firms that have found success on the Web, such as Victoria's Secret and Dell, are pushing past the comfort zone their respective businesses once enjoyed.

JCPenney, for example, in another day and age, might have been complacent enough to fight its retail battles by revamping its stores and changing its merchandise strategy. But in today's environment, JCPenney has to think "out of the box" to capture attention, press, and hopefully sales. Watching the success of eBay and the online auction model, knowing that consumers spend more time at auction sites tracking bids, and recognizing the need to boost online sales, JCPenney.com joined with FairMarket, a developer of turnkey auction sites, to become the first general merchandise retailer to introduce an Internet auction component for consumers. Now consumers can bid on excess and overstock merchandise from its stores and catalog operations.

DOWN WITH THE DOT-COMS

Another adage says that *what goes up, must come down.* Riding the roller coaster of Internet stocks brought increases of 400 percent and more for many investors during 1999 and into early 2000. But by 2001, most Internet stocks had tanked, declining upward of 80 percent, with many liquidating and declaring bankruptcy. Pets.com, which sold for as high as $14 share and paid $2.2 million for a Super Bowl commercial in January 2000, had fallen to twelve cents by the time the next Super Bowl rolled around in 2001, selling its URL and technology to PETsMART. Other firms, such as eToys, teetered longer on the brink and then collapsed, and a lot of B-to-B dot-coms, although later in the e-commerce cycle, are now biting the dust as well. A few, such as eBay and Schwab, have retained much of their value, but even those with profits saw their stocks pummeled by the dot-com free-fall.

So what exactly is wrong with e-commerce today? For one thing, there is far too much emphasis placed on the "e" or technology component of the equation and not nearly enough on the "commerce" side of the equation. This could never be more apparent than in January 2000, when the 1999 holiday season numbers rolled in accompanied by horror stories of missed shipments, stock-outs, and order inaccuracies. With the logistical nightmares of returns still looming on the horizon, seasoned retail executives sat back after the holidays, put their feet up on their desks, laced their fingers behind their necks, and snickered, "Welcome to the real world of retail."

For many dot-coms, communication (or the lack thereof) throughout the supply chain created behind-the-scenes mayhem, reminiscent of the famous chocolate factory assembly-line scene from *I Love Lucy*, shown in reruns even today. Ironically, much of this trouble could have been avoided with the help of order-fulfillment companies such as SubmitOrder.com, which specializes in running e-fulfillment for its clients. Many dot-coms learned a valuable and expensive lesson to start the season: Great advertising only accelerates the demise of bad products or poorly executed services. Advertising helped dot-coms attract customers and get sales, but poor execution cost many of them future sales and potentially loyal customers.

Beyond current operational woes, the economics of e-only businesses are simply not capable of building or sustaining high scalability. While Webvan and Pets.com may have appealed to specific segments of consumers, these segments (a subset of the total number of people shopping online) are not large enough to foot the bill for marketing and operations programs or to sustain the long-term market growth required to keep the Street interested. In addition, cost-laden fulfillment strategies, consumer delivery and service challenges, and staggering marketing and promotional expenses make it difficult for e-tailers to make money. In addition, despite how large their advertising and marketing budgets have been in the past, dot-coms simply don't have the money to spend to acquire mass-market customers and hang on to them. Their budgets are dissipating rapidly due to a dearth of new capital for B-to-C and B-to-B applications that have no immediate hope of profits.

Regardless of how great a new concept is or how cool its Web graphics are, if a company doesn't create and keep customers and make money in the marketplace, it will die. Research indicates that for now, most consumers still shop in brick-and-mortar stores—they may search on the Internet, but for the most part, they are pretty satisfied with their current shopping solutions. Unless e-tailers can improve on the things most important to customers and overtake the strides made by retailers in their stores, e-tailing will forever lag behind its brick-and-mortar predecessor. To succeed, e-tailers must focus on how to capitalize on the information, knowledge, and motivational aspects of e-commerce to build brand dominance while streamlining behind-the-scenes operations such as procurement, inventory control, and billing.

Does this mean that every dot-com that longs to see a new day should set up a retail store? No. Retail space is expensive and not a cost-effective extension for all firms. It does, however, mean that they require a physical presence that would offer myriad opportunities, such as getting closer to the customer—beyond data mining to providing great service and convenient pickups and returns—not to mention establishing a greater brand awareness. Today, even diehard "netizens" are forced to live in the real world, and no one can dispute the efficiency of a Gateway storefront in cutting through the traditional advertising clutter. Even if you don't actually purchase a computer there, you can run your fingers over the keyboard, see how the computer really looks, place an order, and talk with a real, live human being about just how easy or hard it is to set up and use.

So how would an innovative dot-com go about establishing a physical presence? Take Amazon, for example. Like most other retailers, many of its problems live in "the last mile"—that place where costs skyrocket and the customer's last impression is formed. A strategic alliance with a company like Mail Boxes, Etc., BP/Shell, or Exxon could establish a drop-off and pickup depot for bundled shipments and reduce Amazon's shipment-and-delivery charges. Done correctly, creating a brick-and-mortar presence for a dot-com company like Amazon would increase convenience to consumers, eliminate the hassle of return postage and insurance, and provide a high-touch, face-to-face opportunity for consumer learning and feedback.

While this alliance might be difficult to accomplish with BP/Shell or Exxon because of limited space in their existing facilities, it is easy to see the potential for an alliance with Mail Boxes, Etc., with its three thousand plus stores. Kinko's would also be a great partner for Amazon or AOL, which now controls over 54 percent of all Internet access. AOL would benefit greatly from partnering with Kinko's one thousand strategically located stores—most are open 24/7, boast spacious and well-lighted facilities with technologically savvy and customer-friendly personnel, a mailbox service, and daily deliveries from FedEx and UPS. We'd have to predict that a person as savvy as Steven Case at AOL could see the potential of an alliance with Kinko's as of much strategic value as an acquisition of Time-Warner!

AND THE WINNER IS . . .

Coach Woody Hayes was once asked who he thought would win an upcoming football game between Ohio State and Michigan. Without hesitating he answered, "The team that scores the most points will win the game." Ditto for the game of commerce. In order to win the battles for precious market- and mindshare and the revenues that accompany each, you've got to score big with customers. Debates that focus on who will win, traditional businesses or dot-coms, focus on the small picture. The big picture is what is the nature of the game and who can score the most points with customers.

The battles of the future are not likely to be between traditional brick-and-mortar retailers and online e-tailers. Nor are they likely to be between off- and online wholesalers and manufacturers. Most of those contests have already been won. The battle will be fought supply chain against supply chain, fortified with consumer-savvy facilitating organizations and multichannel retail, distribution, and marketing activities. And, right now, the best teams are actively choosing up sides, all with the goal of satisfying the customer better than their competitors. Ultimately, customers choose the winners—voting with their dollars and their loyalty for the business that best satisfies their needs and wants.

Brick-and-mortar retailers that have adopted an effective Internet strategy will battle those who haven't. And distributors and manufacturers who have correctly anticipated the evolution of e-commerce and incorporated it into their strategies will follow suit. For good investments in the technology and business solutions arena, look primarily to those who help the Wal-Marts, General Electrics, and smaller but successful firms build their Internet solutions. Forget most of the pure dot-coms; they'll never make the transitions needed for survival! Only supply chain partners who adopt the tried-and-true commerce principles of the past—give customers what they want at the time, place, and price that creates loyalty—can rack up points on the scoreboard.

Can existing firms discount the impact of the Internet? Absolutely not. There is no debating that, as a means of communicating, the Internet has changed the way we live, relate, and work. In the realm of retail, wholesale distribution, manufacturing, and many other forms of organization, the Internet is a very effective marketing tool. No, it is not the Internet and the application of technology that are the losers in this game; that title is reserved for a majority of e-only enterprises.

What is important to understand is that the key to survival in the short and long run is a blended strategy. Described throughout this book, blended strategies may take many forms, but at the core of each is a particular business model's inherent strengths. Traditional retailers and e-tailers alike must adapt to the realities of the consumer marketplace in order to compete effectively and profitably, capitalizing on the strengths inherent in a firm's current business model and formulating strategies to alleviate its weaknesses. For traditional firms it means developing e-technology strategies that complement current marketing and business strategies, just as Wolf Photo attempted with Outpost.com, in which kiosks were placed in some of its seven hundred stores to allow Wolf's customers to buy computers, games, and other products sold by Outpost.com. For e-commerce firms, it means developing marketing, operations, logistics, and distribution capabilities similar to the partnership between Amazon and Toys 'R' Us, in which Toys 'R' Us took charge of both buying and virtual merchandising, admitted areas of weakness for Amazon.

Regardless of how creative and popular their virtual sales methods, e-tailers have to operate in the real world, in which distribution and operating efficiencies count and the customer comes first.

In order to create an operating model, which will survive in the consumer marketplace for the long term, significant shifts must occur in the dot-com portion of any business model. Without the shifts shown below, the e-tail model is doomed to the fate of CB radios, Quadraphonic Hi Fi, and Beta VCRs.

Necessary Shifts in the Current E-tail Model

Hits	to	Sales
Sales	to	Profits
Free	to	Fee
Trials	to	Habit
Customer attraction	to	Customer retention
Technology focus	to	Consumer focus
How to buy	to	How to fulfill/deliver

Most dot-coms and some e-commerce divisions of traditional firms will never make these transitions because they lack the funding, time, or vision required. Blended retailers, fortified by profitable in-store retail divisions, will best be able to withstand the profit drain of these ventures. Best-of-breed dot-coms may survive these transitional years, provided investors don't pull the plug on their funding first. To survive, many e-entrepreneurs will turn to the same MBAs and corporate executives they disparaged a few short years ago, assembling their own teams of commerce experts who understand profitability, shareholder value, marketing, merchandising, logistics, and the operations theories that have evolved over the years. Their mission will be to introduce old-economy efficiency to the commerce functions required to operate in the virtual world.

The winners of the future will need to steal a page from the playbook of the winners of the past, who have an abundance of experience gained from having already successfully adapted to waves of customer-driven change in the past. They understand why consumers buy and use products, how business functions shift (but are never eliminated) between channels, and how to structure and manage organizations.

As the inevitable shakeout unfolds, the big fish will step up to the dot-com smorgasbord and eat the little fish for lunch. Some companies will snatch them up, benefiting greatly from information technology (IT) resources, establishing a cyberpresence, and acquiring systems for pennies on the dollar, just as Wal-Mart did with HardwareWarehouse.com and Ahold did with Peapod. Others will hire experts to develop it for them. Regardless of method, companies of all sizes will have to adapt to the changes in the environment around them, to consider the needs of consumers, and to develop innovative ways to solve their problems.

EDISON, BELL, GATES, AND BEZOS

Commerce has evolved over time by adapting to changes in the environment and admitting that customers do indeed rule the future of business. What was possible in the past often becomes mandatory in the future, as environments and circumstances change. Take, for example, telephones and electricity. Merchants during the early 1900s would have scoffed at the notion that these modern-day conveniences were necessary to run a successful store.

To believe that a retailer can succeed in the long run without a good e-commerce strategy is just as absurd as believing that it could survive without electricity and a good phone system.

Disruptive innovations can revolutionize an industry, but acceptance, utilization, and introduction of the innovation is more successful if it isn't disruptive to the customer. Electricity and phones affected a company's *ability* to serve its customers, not its *need* to do so. The need existed earlier. The technologies did not change why people buy products and services; they only changed the method of meeting those needs—with extended evening hours, refrigerated display units, freezer storage, and answering customer inquiries by phone. On a macro level, technologies such as electricity and telephones, along with the automobile, changed which cities could support retailers and which could not. For adaptive firms, capitalizing on the Internet's inherent ability to improve customer service and continuing success is no different from capitalizing on the advantages of electricity and the telephone. E-commerce is the electricity of the twenty-first century, but how it is incorporated by companies and individual consumers will determine its ultimate role in supporting and helping businesses serve customers better.

THE OLD IS NEW AGAIN

Just as bell-bottom jeans and a host of 1970s accessories found their way back onto New York's fashion runways and the pages of magazines in the late 1990s, so, too, will tried-and-true business theories and practices become the focus of business publications and corporate strategies in the early 2000s. During perceived revolutionary times, the traditional often becomes the radical. Those who throw open their arms and adopt a pure "out with the old, in with the new" philosophy rarely survive the transition to the new unless they operate antiquated, unsuccessful firms to start.

Make no mistake, new technologies rarely change the mission or values of the organization; they just offer new ways to carry out the strategies designed to fulfill company goals. Basic corporate missions, such as increasing customer satisfaction and enhancing shareholder value, will continue to serve as strategic lighthouses—guiding companies through smooth and rough waters to their ultimate destinations. New technologies, the Internet included, just provide new instruments to navigate the journey, but the lighthouse never moves.

The concepts of customer service and profitability are constants in the game of commerce. As online pioneer Levi's discovered, if selling your products online decreases customer satisfaction and profitability, don't sell online. Levi's launched its first site in 1994 but couldn't figure out how to run it profitably. The company soon found itself in the uncomfortable position of competing against the retailers that accounted for about $6 billion in annual revenue. It also made some mistakes with customers: It didn't offer its popular 501 brand until many months after launch, and the Levi's stores didn't accept online purchase returns. After failing to attract customers to its site, Levi's agreed to allow JCPenney and Macy's to sell some Levi products on their sites. Today, Levi.com offers information about its fashions and an opportunity to view its Super Bowl commercials but guides customers to brick-and-mortar stores and to other websites to make their purchases.

If you look at the mission statements and corporate goals featured in the annual reports of today's stellar retailers and compare them to the results of their online ventures, it can raise questions about the motivation behind rapid e-expansion. Sure, business models evolve, and venturing into online shopping to some degree might satisfy some consumers' needs, but rapid expansion should never carry the price of long-term profit devastation or jeopardize the rest of the firm.

As for pure-play e-tailers, how do their business models fare in the creation of satisfied customers, delighted shareholders, and profits? They provide many of the advantages that already exist in a variety of forms, including multichannel selling (connecting with consumers through a variety of ways, from one-on-one personal contact to mail-order sales), customer service centers, toll-free phone numbers, and personal selling and communication.

A case in point is the catalog, a close cousin to most e-tail websites. After years of experience—with the Sears catalog dating back one hundred years—mass acceptance and profits continue to elude even the best-known catalog brands, such as Spiegel and JCrew. Combined industry-wide catalog sales still only account for less than 3 percent of total retail sales. And yet for the most part, catalogers operate efficient warehouses, offer exceptional customer service, and have perfected consumer delivery—claims few dot-coms can make.

Executives and managers at online retailers might be better served to review classic articles and books written by Peter Drucker, Ted Levitt, and Joseph Shumpeter on the theories of management, marketing, and economics than recent issues of business magazines focused solely on technology. In doing so, they may conclude, like we do, that the Internet, though full of possibilities, is nothing more than a marketing tool—a new delivery system of ideas, information, and relationships. As such, its emergence and integration into business mark another era in the evolution of commerce rather than the revolution they've been touting. For most, the "honeymoon" is over!

THE RACE TO INTEGRATE TECHNOLOGY

The businesses that failed to understand and adapt their strategies to the evolutionary changes in technology didn't make the cut into the latter half of the twentieth century, similar to onetime computer leaders Wang and DEC. The competitors in the race to embrace revolutionary technologies, not limited just to e-tailing, are opting for one of several strategies to incorporate technology into their arsenals of competitive weapons.

First, we see firms adopting technology-driven and technology-focused strategies—that is, they incorporate technology for the sake of technology. These strategies often satisfy the needs of a firm to ring its bells and blow its whistles more than they solve the problems of customers better than existing solutions. All too poignant while preparing this manuscript are the hundreds of features available on Microsoft Windows; studies show that up to 95 percent of them are unused by consumers. And when was the last time you sat and watched a prime-time news show only to have the anchors tell you to leave your television set and "log-on to our website" to monitor the broadcast from the computer. Why? Because it's technologically possible. Yet viewers opting to turn off their sets and go online are likely to log on to other websites, play games, enter chat rooms, or check e-mail. Can you imagine Wal-Mart announcing in its stores that customers should go home and log on to its website, especially knowing they will pass a Kmart and Target on the way home?

Contrast that strategy with one that is technology-driven *and* customer-focused—one in which the customer shares center stage with the technology. Target, and more recently Wal-Mart, expanded the use of scanner technology in their stores. Known primarily for their role in speeding up the checkout process, scanners have been placed throughout the stores to allow consumers to check the prices of misplaced or sale items for themselves. In the past, consumers had to find an employee or wait until checkout to learn the price of a product. And if either of these options were not convenient, they often put the product back on the shelf. Consumers like the scanner price-checking system because it works better for them and decreases the likelihood of their dissatisfaction in the store, as well as decreasing labor costs for the store.

Finally, some progressive companies develop customer-driven and customer-focused strategies, in which they actually develop new technologies that they think will better satisfy customers and/or increase profitability. For example, Dell allows its customers to configure the specific computer system they want, matching their specific needs. Similarly, Echostar and Americast developed special customer management and billing solutions that allows their pay-TV consumers to tailor their program-channel lineups. On an even more intimate level, personalization in the form of e-coupons and promotions that can be tailored to an individual consumer's product preferences and tastes is facilitated by the

Internet, making it possible for e-tailers to connect one-on-one with customers.

At the heart of any successful technology-based strategy is the motivation behind its development and implementation. After having been held to the fire by the financial community, company execs are rethinking the positioning of these strategies—away from a misguided financial community and toward consumers. In the last few years, we have seen hoards of technology-focused strategies designed to revolutionize the way people shop, yet people do not shop like machines. The best strategies are still those grounded in the principles of human behavior, the topic of Chapter 3. It is these customer-focused strategies, adopting technologies because they serve customers better than current systems, that establish a basis for a sound "marriage" between technology and profits.

TECHNOLOGY AND THE HUMAN FACTOR

Many facets of the study of biological evolution focus on the "missing link"—the element that explains why some biological species evolve and survive while others become extinct. The same principle must be considered in analyzing and predicting the evolution of commerce. The missing link in understanding the e-volution of commerce, however, is not about technology; it's about human behavior. Though entrepreneurs, stock analysts, and investors focus their debates on the role of technology, answers about the future evolution of business and life are better found in the realities of human behavior.

Raise all the capital you want from angels, venture capitalists, or initial public offerings (IPOs). Design the best website, buy the biggest servers IBM or Dell can produce, link them with Microsoft, Oracle, or any other technology provider, and you will still come down to the most basic principle of all: Technology determines what can be offered; consumers determine what will be accepted.

Our approach to understanding the missing link in the evolution of commerce can be described as the filter theory of the Internet. Regardless of which combination of new technologies, products, services, delivery systems, and marketing activities you develop, the final mix has to filter through a fine mesh of human characteristics, including people's emotions, decision-making activities, lifestyles, and openness to change. Only the product bundles that pass through the filter should ever make it to market. Even B-to-B products fall prey to the human characteristics of buyers and end users. That's why, regardless of industry, understanding the Consumer Decision Process (CDP) model in the following chapters is vital in evaluating the winner and loser applications of e-commerce.

Just as human behavior determines the future, so, too, do technologies and products affect the future of human behavior. As such, the Internet is about much more than commerce: It is really about life and the evolution of society. The Internet could provide a watershed among inhabitants of contemporary society, a digital divide that increasingly determines the "haves" and the "have nots" of corporate prosperity as well as the "haves" and "have nots" among nations. But just as connectivity will divide some, it will benefit others. India's citizens, many with math and computer backgrounds, have benefited greatly from the wave of e-commerce and information-based technology sweeping through the world. As firms outsource computer-related jobs and programming to countries with large, qualified workforces and less costly labor, India has enjoyed an increase of jobs, giving its citizens skills, incomes, and access to become consumers of the world.

We take long walks in neighborhoods throughout the United States as often as possible to observe the lifestyles of people in different life circumstances (a study in human behavior in itself). It fascinates us because it brings a fresh perspective to issues, including e-commerce, that most business executives won't get. Walking through a particularly disadvantaged neighborhood one day, we noticed that the women were taking their children for walks around the block in shopping carts "borrowed" from nearby supermarkets. The light bulb came on. If these Americans, who make up a substantial segment of the consumer base, can't afford baby strollers, do we really expect they will spend their money on computers and connections to the Internet? Frankly, electronic buying couldn't be farther from their minds.

A safe bet is that most Web entrepreneurs and their investors don't spend a lot of time in these neighborhoods. They should; you should. Understanding the "haves" is essential to building profitable Internet companies, but understanding the "have nots" may be just as important in understanding the future of a nation. It's not really about money or computer skills; it's about personal and cultural values, motivation, and the value placed on the kind of information the Internet offers.

As politicians debate what to do about the digital divide, the harsh reality is that the Internet has as much capacity for increasing inequality as decreasing it. If customers—whether they are consumers, business firms, or nonprofit organizations—can buy more efficiently electronically than from existing sources, then we effectively eliminate everyone who is not Internet-fluent from the "haves" of society.

SAVING THE MARRIAGE

By the time you finish reading this book, you may conclude as we do that the Internet is just another phase in the evolution of commerce. The Internet and websites are not "e-commerce"; they are *enablers* of e-commerce. The technology of the Internet and the methods of Web-based commerce will not replace the successful retailers, wholesalers, and manufacturers of today any more than electricity and telephones replaced those of the past. But it probably is no less important than those innovations.

Most organizations, during the past several years, have sought and married a partner to compensate for their inherent weaknesses. Dot-coms have married financially stable corporations for the money and credibility, while traditional firms enjoyed the attention from the Street when they introduced their new trophy dot-com partners. Call it blended strategies or multichannel marketing and selling, the fact is that both entities realized that at some level, they need each other.

Business leaders recognize that the Internet is not a fad. Firms that cater only to the Internet, however, will suffer a fate similar to that of the pet rock or the lava lamp unless they quickly learn the methods of commerce that created successful brick-and-mortar firms. In the new marketplace, all firms, regardless of size, industry, or technological orientation, must compete for the minds and wallets of consumers. There is no magic to making money on the Internet. Dot-com firms, at least the few that survive the massive shakeout, need to study and perfect the old-fashioned fundamentals that provide the winning edge that most of the dot-com firms lack. It is these fundamentals—capturing and retaining customers, building quality brands, amassing highly efficient logistics and distribution systems, and posting impressive growth rates and profits—that we describe in this book.

Retailers that adopt a blended approach to retailing (and industrial companies that adopt a similar B-to-B multichannel sales and marketing approach) will be the best positioned to satisfy customers in the evolving markets of the twenty-first century. A blended approach reaches consumers in a multitude of ways—with catalogs, direct sales, specialized broadcast media, location-based retailing, and the Internet to build strong brands and relationships with an increasingly valuable customer base. We believe:

1. Consumers override technology in importance—technology determines what can be offered; customers determine what is accepted.

2. Pure-play dot-coms that fail to offer something traditional retailers don't or can't—hard-to-find products, digital products, special values—will die unless they establish a physical presence to compete more effectively.

3. Few consumers do their shopping online, thus making online retail sales a small proportion of total retail sales. Expect the number of consumers whose buying decisions *will be influenced* by what they learn and find online to dwarf the number of consumers who will do *most of their shopping* online (relative to the total number of consumers).

4. For most firms, product categories, and consumer segments, the Internet is more important as a marketing tool and brand builder than as a sales channel. Customers will search for and evaluate products online more than they will purchase online.

5. Online retailing, even where it is most successful, can expect to achieve profitability levels similar to catalog operations because of the similar costs of performing essential business functions.

6. The businesses most likely to win in the future are those that belong to the most efficient supply chains, fortified by B-to-B Internet technology.

7. It is more important for winning organizations to master the "commerce" rather than the "e" of e-commerce.

Marketers often want a cut-to-the-chase, bottom-line answer to the strategic issues they face. The question "Will e-commerce last or not?" falls into the "I need an answer now" category. The key is that this is not a yes or no issue. For some firms, a higher proportion of customers will adopt online shopping, while for others, the diffusion rate will be low as shown in Chapter 7. Many consumers will migrate specific shopping activities to the Internet, but still buy in stores because of the advantages of bricks-and-mortar retailers, as is highlighted in Chapter 3. Many B-to-B customers already do much of their ordering online, yet they still turn to sales reps or customer service for assistance and relationship-building. In the long run, the answer will depend on individual firms' abilities to wed their "e" and "commerce" strategies and create a profitable union.

Ultimately, the answer to the question of how best to incorporate the Internet into a firm lies in its ability to develop customer-driven solutions, master the commerce functions required for profitability, and delight customers with new and existing sales and communication channels. All of these efforts exerted by retailers and manufacturers alike are designed in the hope that customers will like buying online, because if they don't, they simply won't shop that way.

The fact of the matter is that most firms today are married at some level to e-commerce. For some, the marriage is based on selling on the Internet, and for others it revolves mostly around marketing to and communicating with customers online. In either case, many of these marriages are in trouble. After a brief, albeit expensive, courtship and an impassioned honeymoon, corporate America's marriage to e-commerce is in need of some counseling.

So where will winning businesses go from here?

The remainder of this book focuses on what we believe companies can do to survive and thrive during this evolutionary stage of commerce. Some lessons will be gleaned from the triumphs and mistakes made by best-of-breed dot-coms, retailers, and industrial firms, and others will be offered up based on our research and experience in the marketplace. But at the heart of all winning strategies is the realization that customers decide which companies, retail formats, sales techniques, and strategies will survive in the long run.

And so, corporate America, the real work begins.

CHAPTER 2

THE "COMMERCE" SIDE
OF E-COMMERCE

OF THE COUNTLESS QUOTATIONS for which Sir Winston Churchill is known, perhaps few are as insightful as, "Those who fail to learn the lessons of history are doomed to repeat them." And in no industry is that snippet of wisdom (a verity that Churchill himself borrowed from numerous leaders of history) more true than in the world of commerce. IPOs decline, market shares erode, and bankruptcies increase because so many business leaders and entrepreneurs fail to learn the lessons taught by business history.

Just ask Boo.com founders Ernst Malmsten and Kajsa Leander, who discovered the hard way that it takes more than a cool website and hip products to create boom-times in the world of e-tailing. Much anticipated and publicized throughout 1998 and 1999, Boo.com set out to sell international sportswear brands around the globe via the newfangled Web. Promising to deliver "a gateway to world cool" on its website, it caught the attention of and a $125 million capital infusion from backers including Alessandro Benetton, son of Benetton CEO Luciano Benetton; Bernard Arnault, chairman of LVMH; J.P. Morgan; and Bain Capital.

Armed with ambition and come-hither sex appeal, the Swedish twentysomething cofounders—Malmsten, tall, stylish, and male; Leander, a former Elite model—assumed the persona of what e-tail might be. Boo's business model consisted of defining global style; connecting with rich, stylish people; producing an interactive magazine; hyping the company and concept; and, oh yes, selling fashion. But what Boo possessed in funding and ambition it lacked in business sense and management experience. The company spent its capital quicker than it could say *boo*, thereby breaking the number one lesson from business history for new start-ups: "Don't run out of cash." First class, not low overhead, was its motto in image and operations. It hired four hundred employees to staff six European and U.S. offices and spent its funds on board meetings in lavish hotels, extensive first-class travel, posh office suites, and flat computer screens for all employees. Malmsten and Leander should have invested in a diligent, tightfisted chief financial officer who would have quickly stopped the financial bloodletting. The history of start-ups reveals that the ones with the greatest chance of success are those that keep costs low.

The company also floundered in developing its website because it broke another commerce rule: It never understood its potential customer base. The way the site was constructed required users to have high-speed access, state-of-the-art browsers, and a Flash plug-in to get the full benefit of the site's spinning and zooming bells and whistles. Unfortunately, most folks with all these online bells and whistles are technology buffs rather than the cool and rich users targeted by Boo.com. Complications in developing the technology for this much-hyped shopping experience delayed launch of the site by five months, several months after a multimillion-dollar ad blitz hit the pages of fashion rags around the world. And even then, Apple users, who fit the profile of the stylish, independent-thinking person Boo.com had in its sales-sight, couldn't tour the site because of technology glitches.

The much awaited end result was a site that took too long to download and was difficult for consumers to use. So caught up in what might be possible technologically, Boo.com lost sight of what its customers really wanted—access to global fashion brands—thereby breaking another lesson from business history: "Give the customers what they want." Once on the site, consumers were greeted by Miss Boo, a sexy but virtual personal shopping assistant who really didn't do anything to ease the shopping process. Browsing was available in seven languages, indicating Boo.com's zealous strategy of marketing globally right from the get-go. To peruse product selections, consumers clicked on "Brand" to find Boo's highly touted fashion brands, including labels from Puma and Converse to DKNY Active and Timberland—all great brands but not exactly the cutting-edge fashion labels fresh from Paris runways that they'd promised and customers expected.

But it was Boo's failure to understand the challenges of the commerce side of fashion e-tailing that led to daunting obstacles in sourcing and reselling "really hot" designer fashions. The major fashion houses had agreements with physical retailers, and these agreements created a schism between Boo's marketing mirage and its ability to deliver. Designer labels are not sold through just any retailer—fashion houses select which retailers will represent and uphold the image and quality of the brand best and rely on them to sell and promote the brand to consumers. In turn, these selected retailers agree to carry a complete line of the brand, accounting for the majority of sales volume for these labels. Bypassing the retailers and selling directly to consumers via an online brand consolidator such as Boo.com might jeopardize brand image and existing sales agreements, both of which are important assets to the most exclusive fashion houses. Mass brands, with many channels of distribution, do not face the same risks and therefore are often more willing to sell online—unless their primary distribution channels object.

Boo was, however, forward-thinking in some of the consumer-friendly features of its system. First of all, shipping and returns were free—a perfect example of the "profits-schmofits" mentality indicative of many generously funded dot-coms. Second, consumers could manipulate product pictures, zooming in to get magnified images of fabrics and colors and rotating three-dimensional images to view products from all angles, which created a buying experience that rivaled reality as much as it could. And finally, the big innovation: Consumers could try on the garment. One click on the dressing room and a fit-and-trim silhouette appeared, ready to model consumers' fashion finds. Similar to a cyber version of paper dolls, consumers could then drag the garment to the mannequin. But why? To check fit? Did the clothes ever not fit the mannequin? Although a techno-fun feature that might better have been billed as a "mix-and-match accessories" feature, it demonstrated Boo's lack of understanding of one more lesson from business history: Add real value if you expect new products to succeed.

Following dismal first-quarter sales of $680,000, Boo-world officially closed on May 18, 2000, when the cofounders announced it would liquidate assets. The only remaining Boo.com staff member was Miss Boo. In a postpartum visit to its website, Miss Boo sent visitors to her new place of employment—FashionMall.com, which bought Boo's technology infrastructure shortly after it hit the auction block, and resurrected the brand in the fall of 2000. Its mission? To reestablish itself as a fashion portal with links to websites e-tailing the urban and active brands in demand among young, trendy, affluent fashionistas, such as San Francisco–based shoe retailer, Shoe Biz. The new Boo will not carry or sell any inventory as the old version did; it will, however, dole out fashion advice through advisers, editorial content, and a community site.

In its first go-around, Boo.com brashly took on the world and failed.

The scary thing is that investors bought the Boo.com concept from beginning to near-end, even though customers clearly did not. Analysts and financiers alike forgot to ask questions about sourcing abilities, distribution costs, technological feasibility, merchandising, and consumer insight—topics on which CEOs from Jack Welch to Lee Scott (CEO of Wal-Mart) would be grilled before getting any positive press.

The tragedy is that what today reads like a comedy of commerce errors might have really made a difference in the world of international retailing. It could have broken language barriers that sometimes stifle global selling and taken e-tail technology to a new level. It might have penetrated the inner sanctum of high-fashion retailing had it provided a one-stop shopping site (rather than buying site) for global fashion labels. It could have been the prototype for a truly global e-tail site. But instead of pioneer and leader, Boo.com was deemed loser—the kind of company people love to hate. Its failure gives credence to our thesis that *forward-thinking executives who know business fundamentals, like adding value for customers, establishing vendor relationships, controlling costs and conserving cash—all lessons clearly taught by business history—have a critically important role in this evolutionary stage of commerce.* It may be a new economy, but you still have to master the basics of business and play by the old rules, and ultimately it is customers who establish those rules. We'll see how they like the new Boo.com site and philosophy.

20/20 HINDSIGHT

Which entities and companies will emerge as the leaders of this new age of commerce? What "principles of commerce" must be mastered to succeed in e-commerce? Answers to these and other questions can be gleaned from studying solid, traditional business fundamentals. Unfortunately, many e-entrepreneurs failed to learn from business history, jumped into ventures hastily, and found themselves staring into their own rearview mirrors. Even Churchill's words don't stop Internet entrepreneurs from ignoring business fundamentals of margin, inventory turnover, and expense management—factors that determine which firms survive.

Whether you are an Internet pioneer or someone who was dragged kicking and screaming into the pick-and-click age of buying and selling, understanding how business worked (or didn't) in the past can help you formulate strategies for the future. A little history can reveal powerful truths about the future of commerce and give you the 20/20 vision you need to predict which business models will prevail.

A Picture's Worth a Thousand Words

If you've ever visited the museums of Europe, you probably remember the massive paintings of the seventeenth and eighteenth centuries. Their size reveal that only kings and the Church had the large spaces necessary to display them plus the wealth to buy them. But wander through the museums of Holland (including Amsterdam's famed Reiksmuseum) and you'll see a unique collection of "small" paintings by the same famous artists, created for the only individuals other than kings who could afford them—Dutch traders.

Why could Dutch traders afford them? Because they traversed the world to find products that others wanted ("sourcing"), loaded them on ships, transported them (logistics) to the people with enough money to buy them (market segments), and charged low fees (pricing), which they could do because of conservative policies and cost control (risk-taking and finance). These pioneer-merchants and logisticians became wealthy enough to own paintings by the masters, yet they lived in modestly sized homes beside the graceful, busy canals of Holland—hence the small-sized paintings that you rarely find in the rest of Europe's museums.

By building an empire mostly of trading ships rather than battle ships, this generation of Dutch entrepreneurs created massive global corporations built on serving customers and treating trading partners fairly, great but unpretentious personal wealth, and international influence based on making alliances instead of war. Study your business history carefully because the Dutch pioneered the skills that today are still the core requirements for success in business. If you recall your high school history classes, you'll also remember that the Dutch traded about $24 worth of shells, collected from the shores of the East Indies, with Native Americans for an island off the shore of America. Today that island is called Manhattan, with the former city of New Amsterdam renamed New York. Some of the East Indies (now Indonesia) shells used for global trade were quite unattractive, covered, as they were, with a black substance (oil), but the industrious Dutch turned that relationship into "Shell" Oil, a process described in *Prize: The Epic Quest for Oil, Money, and Power*, Daniel Yergin's Pulitzer Prize–winning history of oil.

The Netherlands has another claim to commerce fame: the "tulip markets" of the 1600s. Similar in scope and hype to the dot-com market of the late 1990s, investors throughout Europe clamored for the highly touted bulbs, causing prices to soar to unsustainable levels. Eventually the market collapsed, destroying the fortunes of many tulip speculators, bringing prices of tulip companies back to reasonable and sustainable levels.

Today, well-managed, professionally marketed tulip merchants thrive, making tiny Holland one of the agricultural and commercial powerhouses of the world. Even though it has little land, Holland adds high value to its products as one of the leading exporters (measured by monetary value) of bulbs, flowers, cheese, and other "value added" products, in contrast to economies mostly exporting commodities.

What's the lesson here for the e-commerce community? Well-managed e-tailing firms with profitable operations will be based on commercial skills similar to those of the Dutch traders and tulip merchants, not on speculative values based on future potential sales. If you have the opportunity to visit the Reiksmuseum in Amsterdam, look at the small but massively expensive paintings of the old masters and reflect on today's Internet firms. Which are built on the centuries-old skills and business acumen of Dutch commerce—the creators of Shell Oil, Royal Dutch Airlines (KLM), Breck's tulip company, and other commercial ventures—and which more closely resemble the speculation by European investors in the tulip markets of the seventeenth century?

Who's in Charge of Commerce?

Throughout history, various entities—traders, manufacturers, wholesalers, retailers, and marketers—have made advancements by capitalizing on and improving the products and processes of their predecessors, evolving commerce to higher levels of excellence and efficiency. This begs the question: "Who will be in charge in the next several decades?"

Business evolved beyond the trading empires of Europe and colonial America to encompass steam-powered manufacturing, first with firms from England and eventually the United States, where manufacturing existed only on a small scale until shortly before the Civil War. Excellence in manufacturing was not only the driving force for colonization by England, it became the primary reason why the North emerged victorious over the South during the American Civil War. Until the 1960s and the rise of chain retailing in the late twentieth century, commercial excellence in the United States and elsewhere was often based on manufacturing excellence.

Following World War II, mega-retailers captured the title of Who's in Charge of Commerce. These retailing superstars include global giants such as Wal-Mart and the French hypermarket chain Carrefour as well as many others—Kroger, Royal Ahold (the Dutch, again), Aldi (German), Home Depot, Lowe's, Gap, The Limited, and Toys 'R' Us. Fortified with economies of scale, bargaining power, and buying expertise, these retailers rewrote the rules of retail buying with coordinated logistics, collaborative forecasting, continuous replenishment, and Vendor Managed Inventories (in which the vendor decides what will appear on the shelf space provided by the retailer) performing the "buying" function more proficiently than independent retailers could have ever hoped. Inefficient retailers lost market share to these mega-retailers whose operating models boasted consistency, attention to customer value, and long-term supply chain relationships—those in which partners invest in and have a vested interest in the long-term success of each other. It's these efficiencies and supply chain relationships, owned by existing bricks-and-mortar mega-retailers, that govern commerce today. These efficiencies are also the primary reason why most dot-com firms quickly realize that their e-tailing businesses are dead on arrival.

Even more paramount to the question of who will be in charge of commerce in the twenty-first century is who will have access to consumers, and that's determined by who solves the consumers' problems well enough to earn their pay. Just as it's false to conclude that the Dutch succeeded because they had ships, the English succeeded because they had the steam engine, or Wal-Mart became the world's largest corporation because it has 200,000-square-foot superstores, it's false to conclude that the technology will dictate the future of commerce. While some wonder whether the future belongs to Amazon or Wal-Mart, the answer is no more dependent upon who has the best website than believing that the future of the Gap versus The Limited is determined by who has the best cash registers. If Amazon knows what products consumers want and how to buy them from vendors better than Wal-Mart, Amazon will win; but if Wal-Mart understands consumers and vendors better, it will conquer Amazon regardless of who has the better website. Technology plays a significant role in the evolution of commerce, but successful strategies are built on what really matters in commerce: the customer.

While the media and investors describe the twenty-first century as a new economy with a heightened focus on technology, we describe it as the Century of the Consumer. Consumers will determine the winners and losers in the new economy, just as they did in the old economy, and only firms—"e" or otherwise—with superior distribution, marketing, retailing, manufacturing, partnering, and general business prowess get to play the game with a chance to win.

Successful commerce is a team sport, a fundamental truth missed by too many B-to-C and B-to-B dot-com firms and their investors. Success depends heavily on a firm's ability to blend all business functions into a continuously evolving and coordinated group of organizations, originating around the needs, wants, and lifestyles of people. That's what we call a demand chain*—a nonlinear constellation of organizations (manufacturers, distributors, retailers, etc.) with boundary-spanning functional relationships, beginning with the minds of consumers.

Consumers form the core of the e-commerce model that will prevail in the future, dictating which business model will be profitable enough to sustain an e-tail business. If consumers enjoy shopping on the Internet, they will buy enough and be willing to pay enough for firms to be profitable. If consumers don't like buying on the Internet, they won't no matter how compelling the technology may be. The biggest mistake in evaluating the future of e-commerce is to assume that just because consumers use the Internet for e-mail, information searches, and to interact with each other, they will use it for shopping. The "e" technologies— whether EDI (electronic data interface), Internet, wireless, or whatever follows—are *not* commerce, they are *facilitators* of commerce.

The weaknesses of e-business, for the most part, fall into the "commerce" side of the e-commerce equation—areas such as interpreting consumer demand, creating supply chain relationships, and managing logistics, to name a few. In the rest of this chapter and the chapters to follow, we describe firms that are winning—and losing—in each area. Once the "glamorous" commerce functions of advertising, customer acquisition, and building brands are completed and the consumer places an order, the product must find its way through the supply chain and into the hands of the consumer, most likely via UPS, FedEx, or the U.S. Postal Service. To perform these functions well, most e-tailers will have to partner with experts in the areas of distribution, inventory management, shipping, and delivery in order to achieve the efficiency required to make this system financially feasible since they do not have the resources and years of expertise in each of these areas to perform them alone. Similarly, integration of the existing infrastructure of wholesalers, common carriers, warehouses, and logistics specialists will also attract more attention and more funds because of their critically important role in determining the success of B-to-B ventures and building the "railroad tracks of e-commerce," as you'll see in Chapter 8.

There's one area of e-commerce, however, where logistics realities help rather than hurt new competitors—digital products. Digital e-commerce involves products in which bits of information, and not physical molecules, are shipped. Digital products include financial products (stocks and mutual funds), electronic airline tickets, hotel reservations, online banking trans-

---

*Roger D. Blackwell, *From Mind to Market* (New York: HarperBusiness, 1997).

fers, computer software, music, and any other products that can be shipped digitally instead of physically. Because of the challenges physical distribution brings to the e-commerce table, the greatest successes and opportunities lie in digital products, and that's where the growth has been for E*Trade and Charles Schwab, Citibank, Travelocity and Expedia (and airline websites), Ticketmaster, and of course, Napster.

Firms selling molecular products on the Internet succeed only if they can overcome logistics issues described in this chapter, often with a strategy of shifting these important functions to logistics specialists. Too many e-commerce firms, both B-to-C and B-to-B, ignore the importance of e-fulfillment; without remedy, these functions can spoil future plans to run profitable e-ventures. That's why the rest of this chapter focuses on how to understand and solve the "commerce" part of e-commerce. You'll see here why, as GE's legendary chief executive Jack Welch said, "The Internet is easy; the fundamentals are hard."

FUNCTIONAL ANALYSIS: THE KEY TO BUILDING A BETTER MOUSETRAP

Regardless of what business you are in, certain marketing functions must be completed in order to move your products from inception to point of consumption. These functions, defined as *inescapable business activities required to get goods from producer to consumer,* can be completed by any channel member (manufacturer, wholesaler, retailer, specialized agency, or the customer), but they must be completed. These universal marketing functions may carry slightly different labels, but they always include the exchange functions (buying and selling), the physical distribution functions (transporting and storing), and the facilitating functions (standardizing, financing, risk-taking, and securing marketing information). Performing these functions well rests on a foundation of understanding why people buy goods and services and how to get them to buy from you— that is, the creation and stimulation of demand. Marketing functions can be shifted to more efficient channel partners, as shown in Figure 2.1, but they cannot be eliminated. An e-commerce firm that has not figured out how to perform these functions more efficiently than existing firms has little chance of enduring success, regardless of how advanced its Internet technology may be.

The world's most successful business models—firms such as Wal-Mart, GE, Sony, and Microsoft—have evolved over time by mastering efficiency in performing essential marketing functions, maximizing output, and minimizing energy, monetary, and human input. These organizations, and others like them, have prospered by figuring out which entities in their supply chains are best able to perform the functions required to conduct business.

If you look at the evolution of commerce, innovation and enduring success occurred by performing marketing functions more efficiently and serving customers better than competitors. That is also what all e-commerce firms must do to succeed. Consider, for example, the rise of department stores in the United States. Most started in the late 1800s and early 1900s and thrived for many reasons. Foremost among these was their ability to source products such as "ready made" apparel not usually available in the general stores they quickly displaced. Roland H. Macy searched the world, bringing apparel as well as crates and barrels of unique household goods to his emporium on Thirty-fourth Street in New York City. He performed the "buying function" more effectively than existing stores and introduced department stores, a new form of retailing, to the United States. Macy's new form of retailing thrived until after World War II.

During the late 1920s and 1930s, department stores, like many other businesses, ran into great difficulty obtaining the credit needed to finance inventories. Because of seasonal needs, credit is the lifeblood of retailers, but this part of the financing function was one manufacturers had often previously performed but were no longer willing or able to provide during the Depression. In a roll-up of stores that were relatively weak independently, a larger, more stable organization was formed with access to capital markets—namely Federated Department Stores, Inc. Capitalizing on collective strength and economies of scale, the finance function shifted to the fortified parent, organized by the Lazarus family, rescuing family-

FIGURE 2.1   Functional Shiftability in the Supply Chain

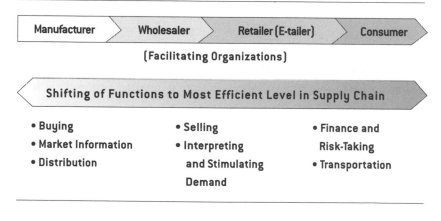

| Manufacturer | Wholesaler | Retailer (E-tailer) | Consumer |

(Facilitating Organizations)

Shifting of Functions to Most Efficient Level in Supply Chain

- Buying
- Market Information
- Distribution

- Selling
- Interpreting and Stimulating Demand

- Finance and Risk-Taking
- Transportation

owned and tightly stretched operations around the country. Original Federated stores included Bloomingdale's, Lazarus, Filene's, Abraham & Straus, and Shillito's and eventually grew to include Rich's, Burdines, Stern's, Macy's, and several other major regional nameplates across the country. Today, Federated boasts annual sales of over $17 billion. As you evaluate the future of e-tailers seeking success on the Internet, the question that must be asked about each of them is: "Does this e-tailer know how to perform essential marketing functions, such as buying and finance, as well or better than existing retailers?"

The discount retail scene emerged rapidly after World War II, first with names such as EJ Korvettes and Polk Brothers and later with Kmart and Target. They copied the buying methods of department stores but added a new dimension in efficiency by shifting from decentralized cash registers, common in most retail stores at the time, to self-service and centralized checkout. Self-service shifted part of the selling function from store employees to consumers; they in turn were rewarded with lower-priced products made possible by the cost savings of employing fewer salespersons. Shifting the function of service to consumers in this manner is part of the reason Kohl's experienced spectacular growth in recent years, robbing market share from JCPenney, Sears, and other department stores. Breakthroughs in performing marketing functions have occurred in discount retailing recently and they provide the models Internet retailers must meet and exceed if they are to survive.

It was during the last few decades of the twentieth century, however, that a truly revolutionary shift occurred in one of the most costly functions of marketing—transportation and distribution. Two retail masters performed the logistics functions in a way that essentially destroyed what remained of department store dominance. One of those retailers was Wal-Mart, which attacked department stores at their point of greatest vulnerability—price and value—especially in rural America, where Wal-Mart had its roots and where department stores believed the demand too small to be worth their attention. The other great retailer was The Limited (which eventually included Limited Stores, Express, Lane Bryant, Lerner New York, Victoria's Secret, Structure, and Bath and Body Works), attacking department stores where they had their greatest strength—selling fashion apparel with personal service.

Limited stores boasted an abundance of sales associates clad in Limited fashions and accessories so that customers could see how items looked on real people rather than just on mannequins. Both Wal-Mart and the Limited mastered functions that were important in the development of department stores but also achieved excellence in logistics, a function to which most traditional retailers had paid little attention. Department stores and both independent chain and specialty stores never regained the market share seized from them with the super-efficient supply chains of Wal-Mart and The Limited.

And that's where we were by the late 1990s, when e-tailing burst onto the retail scene with more fanfare than any innovation in the past. As you reflect on the concept of functional shiftability, one conclusion should stand out: If a retailer can't perform marketing functions—buying, selling, distribution, financing, marketing research, and so forth—with excellence, it will be replaced by retailers who can. The decision to sell on the Internet is, by itself, not a viable business strategy unless e-commerce firms can perform with excellence all the universal marketing functions. It's easy for Wal-Mart and The Limited to add the Internet to their arsenal of retail formats by simply buying software and ASP (application service providers) services or perhaps just buying one of the failed dot-com retailers. The existing retail giants already possess excellence in their consumer knowledge, vendor relationships, and logistics capability. If new e-tailers can't perform marketing functions better than Wal-Mart, Federated, The Limited, and other great retailers, they are as doomed as the Woolworth dime stores that once pervaded America.

At the heart of the matter is the creation of a superior business model, one in which business functions reside at their most efficient and cost-effective levels. Wal-Mart has honed its retail business model over the last thirty years, with small and large competitors snatching a page from the Wal-Mart playbook when possible. Though this model is admittedly not perfect, it comes closer to the pinnacle of perfection than a vast majority of others. Sam Walton, founder of Wal-Mart, used to tour the stores reminding associates that "the customer is the only one who can fire us all." In addition to location-based stores, however, there's another retail model that helps evaluate the future of e-tailing.

Apples to Apples

Imagine that your stockbroker calls you with information about a hot new IPO. The broker explains that the opening price is expected to be between $14 and $17 with the possibility of rapid rise. Sales are a few million with no profits yet, but the entrepreneur hopes to raise several hundred million dollars to fund a business that will sell apparel and other products to consumers. It is promised to revolutionize retailing as we know it. This direct-marketing approach, your broker explains, will be a new catalog. How would you feel about buying the stock? Yet that is what many people did when they started and/or invested in e-tail ventures.

The Street, the analysts, and most of the e-entrepreneurs missed the fact that, though the method of communication was different, the economic models for online retailing and catalogs are almost identical. When they started to figure it out, around April 2000, the collective gasp of brokers and buyers alike brought soaring stock prices to a screeching halt. Just watch how, when, and why consumers shop catalogs and you'll see that Web shopping more closely parallels the way consumers buy from catalogs than the way they buy from location-based retailers. And the ways of performing marketing functions and their costs for online retailers closely parallel the way those functions are performed by catalog retailers.

E-tailers would be wise to study the economic laws that pervade the successes—and the many failures—of catalog retailing. Know the present profits of successful catalog marketers and you know the pro forma profits of future successful Internet marketers, in part because the functions performed by online retailers and their costs are nearly identical to those of their catalog cousins. And catalog retailers such as L.L. Bean, Lands' End, Spiegel, and Sharper Image are a lot farther down the experience curve when it comes to understanding the challenges inherent to this retail model. Sure, even in apples-to-apples comparisons some differences exist—namely, e-tailers build websites rather than cut down trees to print catalogs—but both vie for the same consumer shopping niche, must perform the same marketing functions, and must deal with the same logistics and fulfillment issues. And unfortunately for the future of e-tailing, the costs of acquiring new customers is higher online than in catalogs.

E-tailers are not alone in their struggle to make the electronic catalog model profitable. The "greats" of off-line retailing—ranging from Bloomingdale's to Wal-Mart—face the same challenges with their e-commerce strategies that have plagued catalog retailers for the past century, including delivery, product sourcing, inventory management, and logistics. After decades of experience in the direct-to-consumer business, catalog sales still account for less than 3 percent of total retail sales. And yet because of their understanding of consumers and business functions, catalogers are, in fact, better positioned to win in the e-tail race than most of the new online retailers. Expect more traditional retailers with catalog operations—like Bloomingdale's By Mail and Macy's By Mail—to run their online strategies with the distribution systems already in place for their mail-order ventures, giving previously blended retailers the greatest advantage of all in e-commerce.

The Internet, as a retail model, is no more revolutionary than the catalog model. While Wall Street and the media most often evaluate the future of e-tailing by comparing it to physical retailers, they would obtain a much more accurate understanding of the future of e-tailing by comparing it with its much closer relative—the catalog. Understanding how catalogs function to satisfy consumers provides the best lessons and most useful strategies for e-tailers that hope to become profitable in the future.

HAVING WHAT CONSUMERS WILL BUY

The foundation for any successful retailing business is an in-depth understanding of consumers—why they buy, what they want to buy, and how their lifestyles are changing, all of which are discussed in Chapters 3 and 4. The focus here is on the process of understanding consumers so that retailers can buy (source) what will sell in their stores—the two functions go hand in hand. Understanding consumers usually arises from *experience* observing what people buy and don't buy, a *passion* for products or a lifestyle, and *market information* that helps managers make better decisions.

Predicting and Interpreting Consumer Demand

At most retailers, the locus of power and influence rests in the buying function, with the Chief Merchant sitting atop the hill. At department, value, and specialty stores, these are often the highest-paid, most traveled, and creative members of management. As a strategy, Internet firms should appoint an experienced Chief Merchant as their number two in command, ahead of even the Web-master.

Look at the well-established stores you visit and catalogs you receive from Bloomingdale's, Foley's, Marshall Field's, and Saks Fifth Avenue. More than good merchandise that is attractively presented, peek behind the collections and you'll find buyers who have been predicting consumer demand and buying clothing for decades, often missing miserably but learning from their mistakes. Buyers and merchandise managers know whether consumers are likely to buy white or red this season, what percentage of the sales will be size 6 or size 16, and what proportion will occur in March or December. They also know, in the best of firms, how to use mathematical models and other analytical tools to refine even further their judgment of which lines or designers and what clothes people will buy.

Online retailers, founded often by technology wizards, have the challenge of duplicating the knowledge base before they can predict consumer demand for specific products. Once easily lured away from established retailers with stock and options in e-tail hopefuls, good merchants are not a dime a dozen. Those who have grown up at Nordstrom may be working on the Nordstrom.com site today, wiping up the would-be e-tail competitors with knowledge about fashion trends and product display strategies, attempting to duplicate online the in-store shopping experience. Today, e-tailers have to offer a different carrot to lure these merchants or learn good old-fashioned retailing principles themselves.

E-tailers, however, have an inherent advantage over traditional retailers when it comes to connecting with consumers who harbor a fetish or specific passion. Home to many types of enthusiasts, the Internet provides a forum where snowboarders, toothpick-holder collectors, and golf junkies can kvetch and exchange ideas, all the time taking solace in the fact that there are others like them in the world. Developing a success strategy for online retailers may mean developing a sense of "community" among a narrow segment of buyers made possible because of the boundary-spanning geography of the Internet. AOL has been masterful at this, creating an online community through chat rooms, clubs, and interest groups.

Doug Young has been passionate, actually head-over-heels crazy, about hats for a long time. Founder of Noggintops.com, he took his passion and parlayed it into *the* Internet site for finding and buying high-quality men's hats.

An acknowledged hat fanatic, Young was constantly searching for high-quality, stylish hats that fit his active, outdoorsy lifestyle to little avail. In September 1999, he and his wife investigated starting their own e-business. It seemed like a great idea since the Internet not only let them connect easily to other hat-enthusiasts, it also allowed them to operate from Congerville, Illinois, a sleepy small-town American city. Home to only 350 residents, the town isn't large enough to support a grocery store, a coffee shop, or a gas station. But from a long-closed country store turned warehouse and command central, Young could satisfy penchants for the finest chapeaus and barrettes.

On December 1, 1999, the Youngs opened their cyber-doors and today average about three thousand hits and one hundred sales per week, selling to an eclectic cadre of customers from as far away as Japan and Europe. That might seem like a small business to IPO-oriented investors, but it's a good example of the power of the Internet to make small but economically viable e-commerce strategies possible for thousands of new entrepreneurs. Young knows there are people out there who want to buy the hats they see in old pictures or movies, but they don't know where to find them. Sourcing products from manufacturers on four continents, Young can find hats to satisfy even the most discriminating tastes and created a viable business in much the way small-business people have operated for centuries. It may not be a model to become wealthy, but it is a lesson on how to play the age-old game of retailing with the addition of Internet technology.

Sourcing Products

As Doug Young knows all too well, understanding what consumers will buy is only half the battle. Finding a source and negotiating successfully are even more difficult, especially when the manufacturer is domiciled in another country, which today is often the case because of lower production costs in developing nations. For specialty products that often have limited distribution, getting suppliers in other countries, who are seeking their own opportunities to grow, to work with small retailers is easier than flushing-out suppliers of well-known, widely distributed products who will do the same at equitable terms. Hiring buyers who can identify reliable and quality-oriented manufacturers, negotiate prices in foreign cultures, arrange letters of credit, forecast currency exchange rates, and arrange transportation and logistics routes in countries with poor roads—all at costs as low as those of competitors—is not easy. But it's what must be done to succeed in e-commerce.

Another problem faced by would-be competitors is that all the good suppliers may already be committed, and often with long-term relationships, to existing retailers. This was a problem for Boo.com. These barriers to entry make it difficult for new companies to find suppliers willing to sell to them. How can a new retailer compete against Wal-Mart, which enjoys bargaining power virtually no other retailer can duplicate, and retail's other big guns that have formidable economies of scale and experience in sourcing? Understand that the big guns will not hesitate to use the power their size and sales gives them. For example, when Rubbermaid sold to other retailers at lower prices than to Wal-Mart and was unwilling to change its materials to get the price down, Wal-Mart downgraded Rubbermaid's shelving position. Rubbermaid's outdated manufacturing, slacking consumer demand, and weakening sales through other outlets were not enough to make up for the sales lost on account of Wal-Mart's decision. Soon thereafter, Rubbermaid failed to make its numbers and was sold off to Newell.

On the other hand, catalogs, often riding on the coattails of their physical stores, entered the retail scene easier than their contemporary cousins because they inherited the buying expertise and resources housed within the company. Boo.com had to compete against established retailers' strength in buying; it failed, and many like it will suffer the same fate. E-tailers were first to the game of selling on the Internet, but they were prohibitively late to the game of procurement. Established retailers hold that advantage, giving them a leg up on pure-play dot-coms in the retail marketplace.

All is not doom and gloom—persistent online companies may overcome these barriers to entry and become successful, but most successes will be those companies that already operate in the old economy. One of the strategies we advocate is to rely on strategic alliances with physical-world distributors and manufacturers who depend on selling to small retailers, riding on their coattails, so to speak, by trading their experience for opportunities to increase sales on the Internet.

How can one do that? By knowing the answer to the question: "Why is Amazon based in Seattle, Washington?" Because Seattle provides ready access to the many computer programmers found in the Pacific Northwest? No—because Jeff Bezos wanted to be across the street from Ingram Book Company.

As America's largest wholesaler of books, Ingram's expertise is in getting books from publishers around the world, assembling the titles consumers are most likely to buy, managing its warehouses precisely, and shipping in small quantities to anyplace in the nation. Ingram, which for decades has performed these functions for thousands of independent and chain bookstores, has been one of Amazon's most valuable partners. Jeff Bezos recognized this and out-sourced these functions, most likely until he could develop similar capabilities to perform these marketing functions internally.

Marketing Research, Data Collection, and Information

The power of information has never been greater in the world of commerce. Information about customer wants, needs, habits, peeves, lifestyles, and behaviors is collected, mined, and discussed on a daily basis in marketing circles around the world. Marketing research still serves as a primary source of information for small and large firms alike. Whether a firm talks to customers informally or conducts focus groups, formal surveys, or carefully controlled experiments is not as important as what is done with the information once it is gathered. Before it can be useful to the company, it must be analyzed and interpreted—areas in which many firms fall short.

Retailers, both traditional and e-tailers, however, make a huge research mistake if they talk to their current customers—people buying in their stores, shopping their websites, and calling their 800 numbers—but forget to talk to noncustomers. It is the noncustomers' brains you have to pick if you want to figure out what you need to change in order to recruit these people as customers. Executives at Wal-Mart are known for spending time walking through and working in their retail stores. Perhaps less well known is that they also spend enormous amounts of time in other stores, both competitors and any retailer that may be a source of insight and innovation. That's an important lesson e-tailers should learn from the most successful of brick-and-mortar retailers.

Hewlett-Packard became a great technology firm, partly because many of their executives practiced MBWA—managing by walking around. These leaders spent lots of time talking to employees, listening to their needs and ideas, and managing accordingly. For retailers, online or off-, the strategy we recommend is much the same—marketing by walking around. If customer satisfaction is your vision for your business, spend time listening to customers and end users wherever they may be. That includes all types of retail stores, in homes where people use your products, in offices and leisure locations where people wear or use your products, and on other websites—anyplace that puts you in contact with noncustomers who might become customers.

This is where the Internet provides a real and enduring advantage to both B-to-C and B-to-B firms. Online retailing has the potential to conduct this type of marketing research, at least for current customers and browsers, faster and at less cost than any other form of retailing. When it comes to price flexibility and testing different price points, e-tailing is the clear winner over other retailers, especially catalogs. Once a catalog is printed, the price might as well have been chiseled in stone. Short of another mailing, it's almost impossible for a retailer to lower the price of a product that is not selling well or raise the price of a product in which demand is outpacing supply.

With bountiful applications, the Internet could rule consumer information unless consumers get too skittish about how much is known about them. With a consumer's Internet provider address and a "cookie" planted on their computer, companies can obtain a wealth of information about present and potential customers, from credit status and surfing activities to buying patterns and income (or a close proxy of it). Capture e-mail addresses, and you have access to distributing low-cost, tailored offers and messages. A successful strategy for traditional retailers and consumer products companies may also be to use a website, if enough consumers can be attracted to it, simply for the value it adds to the speed of collecting information about current style and color preferences, and price elasticity for products offered in stores.

How can start-up dot-coms afford the systems to do all of these things? The answer is that many can't. While working as an entrepreneur-in-residence at Institutional Venture Partners and Matrix Partners, Monte Zweben talked to hoards of dot-coms searching for money. A vast majority were looking for funding to build their own operating systems. This seemed like an enormous waste because the software was costly and time-consuming to develop—and it already existed. It was just that no one had yet packaged software for online retailers.

Zweben saw this as an opportunity and voilà, Blue Martini was born. Zweben's company specializes in software that lets companies capture buying patterns and shopping preferences, and allows firms to personalize sites to match the preferences of each customer. In short, Blue Martini's software lets retailers narrow the information and products offered to a specific customer based on information they know about that person—the ultimate use of information.

But Blue Martini, or any firm using the Internet for marketing research, faces challenges in the data collection arena. First, you have to buy into the assumption that customers want their options limited. Second, you have to believe consumers will not revolt against this type of snooping even as consumers are disabling cookies, buying software filters (from sites like Addsubtract.com), using fake or multiple e-mail addresses, and using sites and software that lets them surf anonymously. Although such efforts restrict data collection, e-tailers still probably have more research and information available about both their customers and their noncustomers than traditional retailers have ever had.

LOGISTICS CHALLENGES

Want to subdue even the most optimistic discussion of online commerce? Bring up logistics—the killjoy of Internet retail operations and strategic competitive advantage of profitable businesses such as Wal-Mart and P & G. Often overlooked in marketing discussions, this increasingly critical function can single-handedly shut down even the fanciest Web-retailers. Logistics is the design, implementation, and control of the physical movement of products from manufacturing to consumption, including materials management, transportation, warehousing, and distribution.

On average, marketing costs make up about half of the cost of consumer products, and about half of the marketing cost usually involves logistics. In today's competitive environment, businesses with inefficient logistics systems forfeit realistic expectations of becoming profitable and subsequently growing profits. Here is where the e-tailing model gets ugly.

Logistics functions are far more expensive for most online retail operations than for location-based retailers—no ifs, ands, or buts about it. Certainly, digital products such as stocks and electronic airline tickets move easily through cyberspace, but the logistics functions and costs of selling clothing, books, home products, and other "stuff" online mirror those of catalog retailers. Additional culprits of elevated costs are less-than-efficient picking and distribution models and costly returns. Even E*Trade sends out monthly statements on old-fashioned paper via the U.S. Postal Service. And chances are the more customers you have the worse it gets.

When Less Costs More

One of the basic principles of distribution is that it costs more per item to send small loads of product than large shipments. LTL (less than truckload) prices to ship a product across the country are greater than prices to ship the same product at TL (truckload) prices. If you can make it a large shipment and send it via water or rail, you can bank even more savings. "Piggyback" services are used to ship containers or entire trucks on barges and railways across long distances, then unloading the containers or hooking the trucks to tractors for final local distribution. Even heavy, bulky items can be sent across the nation to stores for pennies rather than the dollars per unit that it costs when individual units are sent from central warehouses to offices or residences.

Logistics all-stars, Wal-Mart and The Limited, are very proficient at matching supply from around the world with local demand. Supply, to be most efficient, occurs in large, homogeneous production runs, but demand occurs in small heterogeneous orders. Matching homogeneous supply with heterogeneous demand and using a combination of transportation modes, warehouses, inventory levels, and distribution points at the lowest possible costs and at the most dependable level is what logistics is really all about.

The Long Last Mile

"Going the last mile" is often the most expensive part of the logistics process. Stated alternatively, the costs of getting a purse on Monday and a jacket on Wednesday to an individual's home or office may cost considerably more than the cost of sending those items through the channel from a foreign manufacturer to a local store. A well-managed logistics system gets goods *to the store* at minimal costs, but even the best-managed stores can't lease or buy trucks and hire drivers to deliver goods to consumers' homes and expect to maintain low costs.

Fortunately, for traditional retailers, this all-important "last mile" of the delivery has been shifted to the most efficient member of the supply chain—the consumer, who "delivers" items to their own homes at no cost to the retailer. Consumers practice a sort of distribution consolidation program themselves by bundling errands and stops along their routes, either on their way home from the office or on designated shopping trips. Stopping by Kroger to pick up dinner on the way home from work adds very little marginal cost in terms of time or money.

Logistics costs are less prohibitive in the B-to-B arena. First and foremost, these sales are made to offices that are usually equipped and ready for their delivery anytime during business hours. Certainly, when UPS or FedEx contracts to deliver products the costs are substantial, but they are much less per unit when delivering to an office than to a home. As an official of one of these firms explains, "When we deliver a package to an office, we drive the truck one minute to the next office where we deliver thirty packages. When we deliver a package to a residence, we drive the truck thirty minutes to deliver one package. Which one do you think costs less?"

Yet one firm's problem is another firm's prayer. Can you think of an organization that is relatively efficient in last-mile delivery to both homes and offices? Although it is the butt of many jokes and has gotten a pretty bad rap, the U.S. Postal Service could be sitting in the e-tail fulfillment driver's seat—literally. By law, the USPS must make the trek to every home in America, in cities or rural areas, even in the most remote areas of Alaska, every day, come rain or shine. It keeps its costs low by consolidating packages into containers that may be shipped partially by rail or consolidation trucks over long distances. If you are an e-tailer whose product is light enough to fit into the postal carrier's mailbag, and if consumers are willing to accept vagaries in the timing of delivery, the Postal Service could be the lower-cost solution for you. Books are a good example of the type of goods that fit this logistics solution, and Amazon now uses the USPS for standard delivery service.

In March 2000, Federal Express announced the creation of a new program focused on B-to-C deliveries. Dubbed FedEx Home Delivery, the service will offer a host of premium services, such as scheduled appointments and evening deliveries, which have generally not been available to the consumer market. The program, to be launched in major metropolitan areas, however, does not solve the delivery problems for Web consumers living in Weaubleau, Missouri, population four hundred.

Another solution is to send products to intermediary pickup posts. In Japan, 7-Eleven stores have been transformed into order pickup centers to which consumers have Internet purchases sent (often after placing the order from the store's online computers). Albertson's, the U.S. grocery giant, has recently opened a new concept store that is half store, half "waiting area" for consumers to pick up their orders. While they wait for someone to complete the "shopping" for them, customers can read and have a cup of coffee to pass the time. The problem here is that consumers who purchase online want to avoid "wasting time" in stores. If the Albertson concept is to work, it should hope that it doesn't see too many customers lounging in the waiting area, unless the store creates a quasi "social" experience for consumers. Any retailer with a chain of stores can offer consumers the convenience of accepting delivery and storing customers' online purchases until they are ready to retrieve them. To do this retailers may have to set up an "inventory in waiting" space that is well organized and secure so that consumers can pick up their purchases quickly. For many e-tailers, however, their success strategy will need to include a place to pick up the goods rather than incur the costs and inconvenience of home delivery.

The "Picking" Problem

Warehouse management and inventory costs are a big part of the logistics function for any retailer, whether online, catalog, or store. A critical and costly function is "picking." Merchandise moves pretty efficiently around the warehouse on pallets, usually with forklifts, before someone "picks" the individual items to complete a specific order. Based on the nature of the order (small quantities and heterogeneous assortments), the function is costly in terms of labor cost and inaccuracy of fulfillment.

Similar to last-mile delivery, the "picking" function in traditional retailing resides with consumers, who walk through stores scanning thousands of items in a few minutes and picking the ones they want to buy—at no cost to the retailer or to the customer. E-tailers and catalog retailers are far less fortunate; they have to pay someone to "pick" the exact assortment of goods from large, case lots in the warehouse or in a store. And what happens in the case of a stock-out? Consumers can scan alternatives and make quick substitutions, but those decisions are nearly impossible for a third party to make. E-tailers need to tie inventory levels to their consumer-ordering platforms so that consumers know immediately if an item is out of stock. Getting an e-mail that says "By the way, the suit you ordered yesterday is out of stock or discontinued" doesn't foster great customer satisfaction, confidence, or loyalty.

Assuming consumers have perfect knowledge of what they want when they enter their order online or from the catalog, and that those items are always in stock and no substitutions are ever needed or wanted, the retail store still always has the advantage. Let's face it, most consumers don't want to incur substantial service charges to pay someone else to "pick" their groceries or socks from a local grocery or value retailer. To address these issues, Webvan's model focused on shifting these functions even farther down the chain to online warehouses. But lack of mass-market demand and the high costs of building warehouses to accommodate picking single items made Webvan's future uncertain at best by early January 2001. Significant external funding by the end of 2001 would be required to keep the business open.

Some firms predict that robots and automation technology will come to the rescue of ailing picking systems. On a theoretical basis, they're great. But if you've ever examined the warehouse automation systems of the most sophisticated distribution firms, which have invested huge amounts of capital into automated picking with decades of experience, you know that it is extremely difficult or impossible to do. Those that have achieved some success usually pick relatively few items and in large quantities (normally cases of products).

Reverse Logistics

When consumers pick items from a catalog or online, what they see isn't always what they get. The flattering fashions they see often turn into garments that are less than flattering. They also may miss-click on a color or size option and get a size 2 red shirt instead of a size 12 blue skirt. Whether it is their mistake, a problem with the quality of the garment, or a result of a can't-touch, can't-feel evaluation process, the only solution is to send it back. Consequently, return rates for online and catalog retailers are higher than for retail stores. And the costs of returns, sometimes called "reverse logistics," are much higher than for direct logistics.

One major problem is order accuracy. Bar coding revolutionized inventory management, making it possible to trace and track inventory in the warehouse and throughout the supply chain. Look for new, automated (and expensive) systems to be introduced to the marketplace in the next decade to increase order accuracy even more. Using voice recognition software in warehousing and for inventory control can increase accuracy to about 99.9 percent, which means fewer returned items and happier customers. Also, it becomes valuable when returns come back to the warehouse without bar codes. Not only do these need to be re-sorted, but the reason for the return and the item's condition need to be recorded. The problem with voice recognition is "garbage in, garbage out." If an employee says he is picking five sweaters and is really picking seven, recorded inventory levels will be off.

Retailers with a presence both on- and off-line will be best positioned to deal with returns. If consumers have problems with their purchases, they should be able easily to return them to a branch store even though this would require a shift in policy among retailers that sell different products in their stores and through their other sales channels. In fact, returning products often stimulates sales for firms with consumer-friendly policies because the visit to the store is likely to stimulate an exchange for the same product or something similar. With a catalog, the sale is often lost because consumers ask for a refund and avoid the uncertainty of another try, which results in a sales deduction instead of an exchange.

What strategies can online retailers use to accomplish e-fulfillment at a competitive level? The answer most likely is to outsource this function to e-fulfillment firms that are experienced in handling call centers, picking, and transportation functions. Some may be able to perform these functions as effectively as experienced catalogers, who currently provide the benchmarks for efficiency and costs. Firms such as Fingerhut (now a subsidiary of Federated Department Stores) and SubmitOrder.com are examples of firms that have evolved for precisely this reason. SubmitOrder.com, a Dublin, Ohio–based e-commerce fulfillment specialist, defines e-fulfillment as the integration of people, processes, and technology to ensure customer satisfaction before, during, and after the online buying experience. Customers who partner with SubmitOrder contract to it everything related to logistics, including operating the call center and order entry. When customers place online orders with ZanyBrainy.com or Too, Inc. (formerly Limited Too) they may be buying products from these retailers, but they are also getting customer service, shipping, returns, and gift wrapping services from SubmitOrder.com. Because the company specializes in logistics functions that help get the right products to customers at the right time and in good condition, SubmitOrder helps its partners scale their businesses more quickly, satisfy their customers better, lower distribution costs, and build brand loyalty in the marketplace.

FINANCE AND RISK-TAKING

Some of the most important management decisions made in the area of finance revolve around pricing. Early e-tailers poisoned the minds, expectations, and behaviors of online shoppers by building e-tail models competing on low price. In this strategy's defense, supporters wave the white flag of "trial" as a sound reason to give away products and offer special sales discounts and free shipping. These lower online prices were possible because the waves of public capital and IPO-generated funds let dot-coms operate without the normal profit-monkey riding on their backs.

There's no way of escaping the conclusion that if you buy products online that are also sold in stores, the online prices should be higher than those offered in stores. The list price may be identical, but when shipping costs are added—as they must be if anyone expects to make money—prices will end up being higher, just as they typically are when buying from catalogs. The only alternative is for e-tailers to be willing to accept lower profits than traditional retailers or catalogs. As you can imagine, this is not a popular position to describe in the business plans of dot-com retailers.

Logistics realities are the reason for higher prices on the Internet because prices have to reflect costs for shipping, reverse logistics, returns (in addition to consequential lost sales), and distribution costs. One strategy to overcome the high price of Internet sales is to carry different products online than in stores, thereby preventing direct price comparisons. An alternative strategy is to sell only high-margin items online in order to cover the higher costs of online sales. That's why high-margin items are the only ones normally sold through catalogs.

In addition to pricing, risk-taking is a necessary function of all businesses; every business carries with it some risk. It can result from financial investments in new firms or new ventures. But it can also result from doing business with firms that have no proven track record or are part of a struggling industry. That's why banks are requiring personal guarantees from management or letters of credit before they allow start-up dot-coms to accept consumers' credit cards. Since many of the e-tail battles will be won based on the strengths and efficiencies within their supply chains, firms partnering with new dot-coms can expect to invest in the channel infrastructure. But these investments of time, staff, and budgets can be risky.

Finally, the greatest responsibility of an organization is to become and remain profitable. It is the only way to provide jobs to people in your community, reward shareholders for their investments, offer consumers your products and services, and ensure existence in the future. Figure 2.2 shows the profitability of some of the country's leading catalogers. Records indicate an uneven and generally low profitability throughout the industry, and that's what should be expected even for those e-tailers that survive in the future by virtue of their business models.

After five years of "success" and a billion dollars in sales, Amazon had yet to make a profit by the end of 2000, and even the most optimistic analysts publicly question its ability to ever reach profitability. Lesser-funded e-tailers didn't make profits either; they simply went away. The functions and business realities discussed in this chapter explain why. They ultimately affect the potential profitability and sustenance of all firms, not just the dot-com variety.

LOOKING INTO A CLOUDY CRYSTAL BALL

What's the future of e-tailing? Two fundamental factors determine the answer. The first factor is whether consumers will use the Internet extensively for shopping. There's no question they will use it for a lot of things, but there is no fundamental reason to believe they will use it for buying just because they use it for communications, entertainment, and information. We examine this fundamental factor in the next chapter.

The second factor is whether entrepreneurs large or small can ever make money selling consumer products on the Internet. The answer to

FIGURE 2.2 Catalog Profitability

	Net Profit Margin		Return on Assets	
	TTM (%)*	5 YR. AVG. (%)	TTM (%)	5 YR. AVG. (%)
Coldwater Creek	4.72	4.77	12.59	15.65
Delia's	−30.91	3.48	−36.37	7.31
J. Jill	5.21	7.67	11.49	12.32
Lands' End	2.38	3.70	6.58	11.54
Lilian Vernon	1.82	2.44	3.14	4.32
Sky Mall	−19.40	−3.35	−41.03	−1.54
Spiegel	3.35	0.98	5.32	1.53
Specialty Catalog Corp.	1.21	4.97	1.24	6.05
Catalog/Direct Mail				
Industry	1.26	3.47	10.62	15.05
Retail/Apparel Industry	6.16	6.69	15.89	16.57
S&P 500	12.15	11.05	8.95	8.36

*TTM: trailing twelve months
Source: Based on SEC data reported by *Market Guide Inc.*, Lake Success, NY (March 2001), www.marketguide.com.

that question lies mostly in their ability to perform the marketing functions we describe in this chapter and do them better than traditional retailers. After evaluating both the question of consumer acceptance of e-tailing and the costs of performing marketing functions, what's your opinion? What will e-tail sales be?

a. less than 1 percent

b. 1 to 5 percent

c. 5 to 15 percent

d. 15 to 30 percent

e. More than 30 percent

If you answered the question based on today's sales, the correct answer is "a"—0.64 percent to be precise, based on 1999 holiday sales, *the* peak selling period of the year. Answer "c" or "d" is consistent with forecasts of Web pioneers such as Jeff Bezos, who early in his career talked about Amazon.com being the "shopping mall of the Internet." Lofty estimates, made by the pioneers of online retailing, that Web retailing might take 30 percent of total retail sales have been downgraded substantially, just as the stocks whose inflated market caps depended on those predictions have been downgraded by analysts.

Having lived and breathed the realities of sourcing, transportation, and distribution, Bezos has settled on an overall online estimate of 15 percent of retail sales over the next ten-plus years. We believe that Web marketing may influence a majority of retail sales, with these activities housed primarily in the search, evaluation, and satisfaction stages of consumer behavior discussed in the next chapter. We also believe the percentage of retail sales transacted over the Internet is more likely to be in the 4 to 5 percent range in the next ten years—a hypothesis explained throughout the rest of this book.

But you have to develop your own conclusions. Your answer, however, should depend on the advantages of online buying over existing buying methods and its ability to perform marketing functions accurately, efficiently, and cost effectively.

At the end of the day, the correct answer is only important for individual firms. If you build an "e" strategy based on strengths that no brick-and-mortar retailer can offer consumers, as eBay has, massive growth in sales and profitability is possible. If you ignore how a business performs on various marketing functions, or how consumers make decisions, it is difficult to forecast taking much market share away from existing competitors.

DEAD DOT-COMS

History helps us understand and predict how existing institutions evolve into new forms based on principles that emerged from the old. The principles of commerce that provided a basis for success hundreds of years ago haven't been repealed, they have evolved. Successful retailers of the last decade have been looking for new avenues to connect with consumers and have succeeded in increasing their marketing and sales channels considerably.

They have developed new retail concepts, magalogs (a combination magazine and catalog that contains extra information and articles), upscale catalogs, direct sales and marketing techniques, and personal sales networks to satisfy consumers based on their buying preferences. Multichannel retailers boast a vast portfolio of operational advantages, and a strong presence on the Internet is yet another trick to add to their magic bag. Many will add e-tailing to their portfolio of ways to approach customers and relate to them. A vast majority of pure-play dot-coms will be squeezed out of the cybermarket as established retailers take their relationships with consumers to the Internet.

The results to date of a majority of pure-play Internet businesses have been dismal, but there is hope for some of the ideas, technologies, and models they have pioneered. Just as molecular biologists are sequencing the human genome in search of cures for cancer, Parkinson's, and many other diseases, e-tailers can find their own miracle cures in a laboratory they probably least expect—the traditional retailers, catalogers, and wholesalers. Business-to-consumer and business-to-business firms alike must master the basics of doing business, including knowing and attracting customers, sourcing products, building brands, establishing highly efficient logistics and distribution systems, and posting impressive growth rates and profits. It is these fundamentals that continue to evade even the most hotly hyped dot-com firms. And that is why most of them, in their purest forms, will die if they can't steal a page from the playbook of the firms that have successfully forged the business landscape as we know it today. Not all will die, however, and in the rest of this book we describe what firms must do to succeed.

CHAPTER 3

ANALYZING THE FUTURE OF SHOPPING: WHAT WILL CUSTOMERS BUY ONLINE?

THOUGH TECHNOLOGY continues to be a hot topic throughout the media, in boardrooms, and around watercoolers, never have we believed more strongly that *customers rule!* Wal-Mart founder Sam Walton championed this philosophy and so have all the most successful retailers, from Target to Kohl's Department Stores. This isn't just a service slogan, it guides strategies relating to product mix, operating hours, store layouts, and return policies. At the heart of the philosophy is the customer; therefore, how they make buying decisions and product choices—also known as consumer behavior—must guide customer-focused business organizations and their leaders in every avenue of commerce.

E-businesses take note. There is no place where understanding consumers is more paramount than in Internet business, an environment in which customers are asked to change their normal shopping behaviors and adopt new, computer-based solutions. By analyzing consumer behavior variables and consumers' decision-making processes—as successful retailers have been doing for decades—we can analyze how widespread acceptance of e-tailing as a major form of buying will be. With realistic projections about usage rates and applications, firms may decide to expand their sales on site or limit their online activities to marketing.

Contrary to conventional dot-com wisdom, neither business models, flashy graphics, high-end technologies, or cute domain names will equal success for e-tailers or B-to-B e-commerce players. That power belongs solely to consumers and customers who, with errant clicks and methodical trial-and-error, evaluate new versus existing solutions and "vote" with their dollars for the winners. Their final "yea" or "nay" depends on how each solution solves the same problems and addresses the same needs that they've always had.

For example, a consumer who has just run out of milk can either log-on and order it for delivery later or run down the street to the convenience store; a consumer who needs to order flowers can either call a florist or log-on and order online; and someone planning a trip can visit a travel agent, call the airline directly, or check out Expedia or Travelocity and make arrangements themselves. The bottom line: If consumers don't like to shop on the Internet and it doesn't address their buying needs better than in-store shopping, they simply won't buy online.

Businesses operating in today's economy can thrive only if they approach electronic commerce with the customer in mind. This means knowing or uncovering how the minds of their target audiences work. It means knowing how, when, and why they shop, and what their motivations, emotions, expectations, and fears are. Whether their transactions involve money, time, attention, votes, influence, affection, or some of each, the fact is that consumers spend their days obtaining, consuming, and disposing of things and ideas. And today, there are more entities interested in these consumers' behaviors than ever before—including e-based firms, which often wave the technology flag in hopes of attracting consumers.

But technology alone does not a winning endeavor make. The mother-of-all-goals of a new technology should be to solve people's perceived problems better than the solutions (or technologies) that are currently available. As such, the technology bridges what is technologically possible with what is consumer-desired. The best and ultimately most successful applications match technology with human behavior rather than try to alter the behavior to meet the technological possibilities.

WHEN TECHNOLOGY FORCES CHANGES
IN CONSUMERS' BEHAVIORS

American Greetings exploded onto the interactive-technology scene in 1992 with the introduction of Create-a-Card—a freestanding computer station placed in retail outlets selling American Greetings cards. Create-a-Card allowed consumers to create their own personalized greeting cards in the store—the machine printed the name of the recipient and sender on the inside of the card along with the message. Similar to the traditional buying process, once the Create-a-Card machine spat out the cards, the consumer paid for them, took them home, and sent them via snail mail to friends and family.

Technology may have fueled the buzz of Create-a-Card, but human behavior was the buzz-kill. People who were not accustomed to searching, typing, and making selections on a computer spent a long time creating a card, which ultimately, because of paper and print quality, wasn't as pretty as most ready-to-buy cards. What was technologically possible overshadowed the most basic consumer motivation for buying greeting cards—the need to communicate a sentiment for a particular occasion that may or may not be difficult for the card's sender to express. Creating their own messages or even matching pictures with preworded sentiments was a daunting task, and the rewards did not compensate for the added complication of the purchase. The bottom line was that consumers didn't want to pay to do something they were used to paying someone else to do—create cards.

Was the technology the reason Create-a-Card failed? Not exactly. The limited trial and acceptance of Create-a-Card can be pinned on the application of the technology. The technology itself was adequate—although today's faster computers and higher-quality printers would have improved execution greatly. The mass population (people who shopped in gift, card, and drug stores) rejected the idea of changing their "normal" card-buying behavior and thus doomed the project to failure. They may have tried it a time or two, but once the novelty wore off most consumers went back to the ready-made cards because the technology was not a better solution to their card-buying needs.

Fast forward to today. American Greetings has applied the same basic technological insight to its Internet e-card service, allowing consumers to click on, select, personalize, and send a colorful, musical virtual card. Consumers perform the same functions of greeting-card consumption as in the past—peruse, choose, and address. Computer-savvy consumer advantages abound—no stamps are required, e-mail is received instantaneously, and confirmation lets you know it arrived safely.

The application of the technology to the virtual world and to specific segments of consumers is the difference in success—*and* the fact that it is free. If American Greetings charged for this service, how would it fare? Blue Mountain, e-greetings, American Greetings, and Hallmark all count on advertising and transaction fees from "gifts" they hawk on their sites to pay for the service. If these revenues are not enough to keep these sites up-and-running, with updated and fresh ideas, how can these firms go from free to fee (a topic discussed in depth in Chapter 6)? Hallmark can certainly "write off" the venture as marketing and customer-retention management expenses to complement, and hopefully bolster, in-store sales. American Greetings can also use its online venture to promote its brand and physical cards sold through mass retailers. Bluemountain.com, e-greetings.com, and other pure-play dot-coms will have the most difficulty maintaining their presence. Collectively, these firms have created more than virtual cards; they've created consumer expectations about how much they should or shouldn't pay for them, and consumer expectations are even more difficult to change than they are to create.

"IT'S MY PARTY . . ."

The twenty-first century represents a shift of power in the supply chain— with the consumer acting as the ultimate master. Even manufacturers and wholesalers have joined retailers in paying homage to consumers by studying and understanding their behaviors and desires, recognizing that all industrial demand is derived from consumer demand. After years of developing consumer-driven marketing and product development strategies, e-tailers and retailers alike are left to survive in a world where consumers are, for the most part, pretty happy and satisfied with their current shopping solutions. Catering to most every whim, retailers such as Nordstrom, the Gap, and Target have increased shopping and checkout efficiencies, expanded available retail formats (from twenty-four-hour convenience stores and mass retailers, to traditional and discount department stores), and focused on customer service. In essence, this consumer focus has helped retailers collectively slam shut the door of opportunity for a new concept (or technology) to swoop in and take massive market share—with one exception. Anyone who can offer significantly better solutions and better lifestyles to consumers may be able to kick that door open. Look at the auction sites, from Amazon to eBay, and specialty product sites, such as Noggintops.com. These businesses give consumers access to items they would otherwise have difficulty finding. And online travel services that give consumers the flexibility to scan prices and routes and "build" packages at prices that meet their travel and financial needs best are the very definition of a better solution.

Peter Drucker, marketing professor and futurist extraordinaire, once said that the mission of every organization is to create satisfied customers—without exception. And what satisfies consumers today may not be enough to warrant a second glance from them tomorrow. It is definitely "their party," and they'll buy if they want to, buy what they want to, and buy when they want to. That is why all firms must closely examine the push-pull relationship between people and technology when deciding what their Internet strategies should be.

Ideas, from selling groceries online to inventing a consumer-friendly net-appliance, must pass the "adopt-adapt" test if they are to play significant roles in how people live and behave. Suffering from the chicken-and-egg dilemma, some inventors adapt their ideas to the conditions of the market to promote adoption by consumers. Examples would be Target's online store locator, which lets people search online and buy in the store as they are used to doing, and Albertsons.com online ordering system, which lets consumers place their orders then pick up their packages at the store. Others create radical or life-improving ideas they hope consumers will adopt and adapt their behaviors accordingly; this is what American Greetings hoped would happen with Create-a-Card.

Inventions (as radical as the Internet or as consumer behavior–oriented as the cellular phone) become part of human culture only when people adopt them into their lives; predicting how likely consumers are to adopt online shopping, for example, warrants a consumer behavior analysis. Because innovations without adoption are usually exiled to existence on paper only, firms integrating technology into their retail and marketing portfolios must understand how consumers will evaluate them based on their current lifestyles and behaviors. Such information guides how marketers position their websites and e-commerce divisions to target audiences and make their adoption more likely and quicker. When done thoroughly and in a forward-thinking environment, keeping an eye on the consumer can spark insights as to how to make e-tailing and websites more useful and attractive to customers rather than squelch the creativity of e-solutions developers.

Sometimes new offerings are so radical (but better for consumers than current solutions) that consumers adapt their behaviors when they adopt the innovations. Jeff Bezos hinted recently that his efforts in e-based technology creation are far from over, and that he hopes to unveil several "mind-boggling" applications in the coming years. As he and other inventors forge ahead, firms must closely monitor which technologies bridge the human-technology gap sufficiently to provoke change in human behavior. Even hospitals, governments, universities, religious organizations, political parties, physicians, and funeral service establishments must live with the digital reality of the role dot-com organizations will play in the life and lifestyles of the people who determine their future and fate—their customers. What some people reject today, they may reexamine in five or ten years if their lifestyles, behaviors, and preferences have changed enough to warrant a second look, providing a small group of adopters support the innovation or that the company monitors consumer behavior closely enough to know to reintroduce it to the market.

Every day there is an election to determine who the winners of e-commerce will be—and only consumers get to vote, with their eyeballs and their digital wallets. Organized on the Consumer Decision Process Model (first developed by James Engel, David Kollat, and Roger Blackwell and published in the book *Consumer Behavior*), this chapter provides a method to answer the questions:

- For what shopping activities are customers likely to migrate to the Internet?
- What are consumers likely to buy on the Internet and under what circumstances are they likely to buy from traditional shopping channels?
- How do customers compare and contrast their shopping options?
- Will e-tailing and Internet usage increase or decrease among different segments of consumers?

In order to predict when consumers will turn to e-tailing as their preferred method of buying, marketers must first examine *why people buy* and the *experiences* they want from their chosen methods of buying. This information can then be used to change store layouts, product mixes, and concepts to meet changing customer needs.

THE CONSUMER DECISION PROCESS

If you've just arrived at the airport in a strange city and have rented a car to get to an unfamiliar hotel, you have two choices: use a set of directions detailing the roads you need to take, or study and navigate with a road map. Though directions seem much easier at first glance, what happens when you hit a detour, need to go to a different destination, or simply get lost along the way? A list of streets is fairly useless in this scenario, but a road map can guide you to where you want to go. In the disruptive, discontinuous markets of contemporary and future business environments in which every successful operator has to understand the role of online buying, a "road map" of how consumers make purchase decisions is much more reliable than a set of "directions."

For many of the early movers of the Internet, there was no set of directions to follow; in fact, their final destinations were unclear. However, for firms eager to plot their customers' trips to "destination purchase," a road map does exist: the Consumer Decision Process (CDP) model—a simplified version of which is shown in Figure 3.1. The model captures in a schematic format the activities that occur during the decision-making process, allowing marketers to consider activities leading up to and occurring after the purchase of a product when they formulate strategies to increase customer satisfaction and loyalty. It shows how different internal and external forces interact and affect how consumers think, evaluate, and act—in other words, it helps explain why certain people do what they do and helps predict what they will do in the future. It also forces technology zealots and naysayers alike to think like consumers and face the realities they force on their enterprises.

Understanding the decision process of consumers is the foundation of marketing strategies for marketers as large as Procter & Gamble and General Motors, but is just as useful for firms as small as your local retail

FIGURE 3.1   How Consumers Make Decisions for Goods and Services

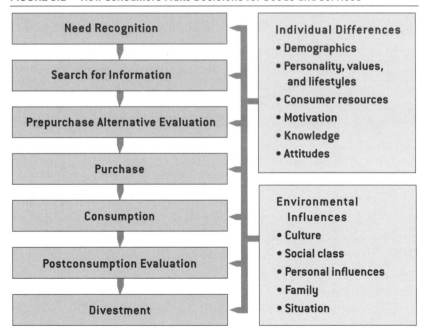

Most recently published in *Consumer Behavior,* 9th Edition, Roger Blackwell, Paul Miniard, and James Engel, Harcourt, 2001.

store. By combining research from marketing, sociology, psychology, and economics, consumer analysts can examine how individuals sort through facts and influences to make decisions that are logical and consistent for them.

Just look at how people buy food. Investors in such Web-based grocery firms as Peapod, Webvan, or HomeGrocer salivated over the fact that $450 billion is spent in grocery stores each year. Following the dot-com recipe—mix one part technology, two parts advertising, and ten parts outside capital; bake briefly; and serve to the public—these firms actually expected to carve out a significant slice of the grocery pie. But they forgot one important ingredient: consumer behavior.

When and how do people make food and grocery purchase decisions? The answer to "when" is when they begin to get hungry or when they run out of something. One study found that at 4:00 P.M., 70 percent of Americans have not yet decided what they want to eat for dinner. It makes sense that successful restaurants concentrate their radio advertising during late afternoon "drive time" because they know they have a good chance of stimulating need and getting consumers to decide that eating out is the easiest solution. It also makes sense for successful grocery chains, such as Kroger, to advertise (in some cities) their policy that "every checkout lane in the store is open and fully staffed at 6:00 P.M."

Now consider the online grocery model—log-on, choose food items (brands, sizes, and varieties), schedule delivery time, checkout, pay, and wait. For people who plan ahead, know what they want to eat and when, and have extra time and money to spend, it works fairly well, provided they are there when the delivery arrives. Time-impoverished, affluent consumers—the ones most likely to use the Internet—lack the time and perhaps the skill to do much food preparation at home. Instead, they opt for frozen, microwavable meals; HMR (home meal replacement) products sold by deli departments; takeout, or order in. Are there some families large enough to need to purchase food in quantities large enough to justify the high cost of delivery and the time cost of extensive home preparation? Probably, but unless their income is very high, you're likely to see many of them on Saturday morning at SAM's Club or Costco, where not only the prices but probably the selection beats any Web-based grocer hands down.

Preordering grocery items is nothing new. Since the popularization of the telephone, consumers have been able to phone in their orders and later fax them in as fax machines became mainstream. Some stores delivered while others asked consumers to pick up their orders during a specified window of time. Neither option ever really took off—consumers found it easier to assemble their purchases themselves, and retailers found it more profitable because they avoided extra costs (and also because consumers bought impulse items and "specials" when they visited the store).

What needs do online grocery shopping fulfill better than traditional shopping? What are the advantages? Desperate to boast advantages, some firms devised menu-planning calendars so people could plan their meals for several weeks at a time. Webvan offers preplanned menus for special occasions and for an entire week, as well as "important advice" on what to do with extra bananas, how to make a martini, and how to pack a lunch.

Although online grocery buying lacked a real convenience advantage, appealed to only a small segment of the population, and operated a high-cost business model in a low-margin industry, headlines proclaimed a revolution in the grocery industry and an explosion of online grocery shopping. Consumer behaviorists shook their heads and waited for the kaboom. It hit Peapod in April 2000 when the company's first-quarter net loss of $8.6 million on sales of $24.9 million caused investors to pull $120 million of financing. It couldn't recover on its own.

Although its venture capital supporters promised an additional round of financing of $110 million, that support evaporated when Peapod's CEO developed a serious medical problem and the stock dropped to a new all-time low of $2. Bob Tobin, CEO of the North American division of Royal Ahold, the Dutch-based grocery retailer, observed the rapidly deteriorating financial condition of Peapod and knew that without an infusion of capital, Peapod would have to close its doors.

Ahold had a window of opportunity. With support of a board that acted quickly, it bought a 51 percent interest in Peapod for a bargain-basement price of $73 million in May 2000. This purchase came on the heels of its $3.6 billion purchase of U.S. Foodservice, the second-largest U.S. distributor of food and related products, with annual sales of $7 billion. Though Ahold expects Peapod to have a negligible effect on earnings for at least three years, it committed to providing Peapod with goods, services, and fulfillment centers. In short, Ahold made a defensive investment in a well-established brand, which it will use across its six chains to serve the small but real segment of online grocery buyers.

In the wake of Peapod's escapade, Webvan perseveres, insisting its model is better because its warehouses (which the company expects to cost $1 billion to build) allow for more efficient, less costly order-picking. If Webvan passes savings on to consumers, time will tell if lower-priced deliveries will cause consumers to change their behavior often enough to sustain the company or if it will retreat to be primarily a distribution/transportation provider to other retailers, if it survives at all.

Peapod failed because it never completely understood who its customers were and their needs, missed the customer count and percentage of transactions they were likely to shift to the Internet, and was unable or unwilling to monitor what percentage they were actually moving. Businesses competing in the e-commerce arena can glean several lessons from Peapod. First, they must quantify how many consumers are likely to shop their e-tail location—and this number must be a realistic and conservative estimate. Then, they must identify what percentage of the transactions will likely shift to the Internet and monitor how that percentage is increasing or decreasing. It is also important to understand what their customers want to do online—do they want to compare prices, look for deals, find a store location, or make a purchase? Creating blended retail concepts based on what customers want is a critical success factor, but a firm can't do that unless it has analyzed the question "What do consumers want?" The CDP model allows firms to understand what purchase activities consumers are likely to migrate to the Internet for and adapt their e-tail strategies accordingly.

PREPURCHASE ACTIVITIES: UNDERSTANDING WHAT CONSUMERS DO BEFORE THEY BUY

For the most part, people are logical creatures who, more times than not, have reasons for what they do. Take buying, for example. Consumers don't just walk into stores and say "I happen to have some extra money that I'd like to get rid of. Just pick something out and charge it to my credit card." Nor do they surf the Web in search of opportunities to transfer digital bits from their credit card to e-tailers. And they usually don't just buy products without identifying and evaluating alternatives, unless the price is so low that making a wrong decision doesn't hold real consequences. Customers may fall victim to their own curiosity and buy something online "just to try it," but in the long run they will revert to the buying methods and the products whose abilities to solve problems or meet their needs are worth more than the prices they must pay.

Consumers Recognize a Need. Buying and eventually consuming start with recognition of a problem or a need—the first step toward a sale. Sound simple? At first glance perhaps, but recognize that what you think you know and what consumers tell you is often shrouded in hidden motivation. Ask busy parents why they bought Jimmy and Janie computers for their birthdays, and they may tell you "Because it helps them do their home-work." Granted, for some parents who restrict heavily the time their children spend on the computer, the primary reason may actually be to help with homework. In many cases, however, it's hogwash—a politically correct justification for buying a $1,000 baby-sitter. Kids want games and entertainment; parents want baby-sitters. Understanding the real needs of consumers, rather than the ones they may admit to on paper or in a focus group, leads to consumer insights that can explain motivation and why people really buy. These insights can also lead to better-positioned communication pieces and product add-ons, such as website blocking devices and games with educational value.

Hidden and transparent motivations aside, the fact remains that products and services that don't solve consumers' problems fail, no matter how dazzling the technology or how much is spent on advertising to convince consumers they have a problem. Yet problems and needs occur at different levels within the human psyche, a key factor in successful retailing. Needs are often hedonic rather than functional; they are fueled by consumers' desires for something beyond mere functionality. Hedonic needs involve the desire for beauty, esteem, status, comfort, and pleasure. A bar of soap from P & G gets a person clean, but a designer bottle of brightly colored, fruit-scented body gel from Bath & Body Works tantalizes the senses and makes consumers feel good while it cleanses the body. Apple accomplished a similar effect with its neon-colored computers, whose hedonic appeal converted some PC users into Apple buyers and users. Some online shoppers enjoy telling their friends about their online purchases more than they enjoy the actual experience—it helps them achieve status among their peers. The problem is that while some may go on to be loyal online shoppers, others may discontinue use as soon as Internet buying shifts from novelty to nuisance.

Most products and innovations don't fail because they can't perform the function they were designed to do. Products fail because the function designers set out to solve are not problems that consumers feel or recognize. Our personal favorite was brought to our attention in 1995 by a young e-entrepreneur hopeful. He had designed a program that allowed people to enter on their computers all of the "things" they have in their refrigerators (and how much of each), and then the software would spit out recipes for dishes they could make using these scrap ingredients. Who would use that? By the time you identified, let alone entered, the remains in your fridge, you could have bought new ingredients and cooked what you wanted—or better yet, you could've gone out to dinner. Sure, today's scanner systems make the task a bit easier, but time investment is a big factor.

For the purpose of starting a business ("e" or otherwise) or examining one to add to your investment portfolio, ask these questions:

- How major is the problem this product or application targets?
- How much better is this solution and how much more are consumers willing to pay for it?
- How large is the segment of people who recognize this problem?

If your answers are anything other than "large, a lot, and very," the potential is limited. But that doesn't necessarily mean doom and gloom for an Internet business that appeals to a small segment of the population. In fact, the beauty of Web businesses is that they can originate in a garage with inexpensive (or sometimes free) software, a low monthly cost ISP, and generate small but intense interest from a target segment. But those types of Web businesses don't require a lot of capital, and are probably not the path to a billion-dollar market cap for their shareholders.

Consumers Search for Alternatives. Once consumers recognize a problem or need, the search process begins, sending consumers on a quest to identify ways and products to satisfy their needs. The search may be internal, retrieving knowledge from human memory, or it may be external, collecting information from the marketplace. At times, consumers search passively, simply becoming more receptive to the information around them, perhaps noticing for the first time the ad about "male-pattern baldness." At other times, they engage in active search behavior, for example, buying *Car & Driver* magazine, visiting dealerships, test-driving cars, and, today, surfing the Net. Search is the Internet's big wow for consumer-based "retail" activity; it is the perfect application of the technology and spotlights its greatest advantage over location-based, bricks-and-mortar firms.

The degree to which people search depends on variables such as personality, social class, income, size of the purchase, prior brand perceptions, and type of purchase (with first-time and expensive items at one end of the spectrum and inexpensive, repeat purchases at the other). Some consumers conduct more extensive searches for products because, to them, search is fun; isn't that really what shopping—not to be confused with buying—is all about? Past experiences and customer satisfaction also influence search. If consumers are delighted with the products and buying methods they currently use, they may repurchase the brand in the same manner with little if any searching, making it difficult for competitive firms to catch their attention. Accordingly, firms place high priority on keeping customers satisfied and returning to the store or the website

because, if consumers deem products, brands, or online and in-store experiences as unsatisfactory, search expands to include other alternatives.

Existing knowledge also determines the amount of search consumers
undergo. When consumers think they have inadequate information to
make a decision, they become receptive to advertising messages, salespersons' efforts, and alternative forms of distribution. For example, retailers have lost sales to catalogs partly because consumers can quickly scan
a catalog page and get more information about styles, fashions, fabrics,
sizes, and color alternatives than they can from a trip to a typical retail
store. Put the catalog online, and consumers can discover even more alternatives. But unless consumers are actively searching, the Internet has few
ways of pushing information to consumers in the way that television,
newspapers, magazines, radio, or even direct mail does. In its embryonic
stage, Internet banner ads were the answer to overcoming the Net's pull-
relationship with consumers. Industry execs speculated that they might be
as effective as other advertising formats, but today, the techno-savvy dis-
able them and the rest of us just ignore them.

When Consumers Search the Net. Confusion about the role of the Internet
runs rampant throughout the retail industry, except among those who understand the search and other stages of the decision-making process. A
website may get thousands of hits per day or per week without a single online sale, causing marketers to question the value of the Internet and their
website. Yet these hits may not be complete misses for two reasons: first,
shopping (surfing) the Net may lead to eventual e-sales, and second, probably more important to the overall strategy of traditional retailers, Internet
search may result in in-store sales.

Every day consumers accumulate information about products from
skis and universities to art and vacations from the Internet simply because
they're playing on the Net. Much like consumers who enjoy browsing and
shopping stores and malls, some enjoy doing the same on the Internet. For
this consumer segment, search and information-gathering is a by-product
of a leisure activity, making this group likely to respond to contests, new
features, and information about new information they'll find on the site.

Recognizing that these consumers are often just "window shopping,"
attracting them is functionally equivalent to department stores filling their
windows with seasonal displays or fun holiday exhibits to attract attention
and build image. Though selling merchandise is not the first-and-foremost
goal, such marketing activities are designed with the hope that eventually
consumer interest will turn into sales. If you know some consumers surf
your site, give them a reason to come back—maybe they'll buy something.

Blue Martini introduced a collaborative shopping software application that allows several friends, regardless of location, to shop together. By appealing to the social experience of shopping, it hopes to help e-tailers increase their buying conversion rates.

Other searches are more deliberate—to fulfill a specific need for information about a product or service. If you know what you want, the Internet offers a host of possible solutions from famous and unknown firms around the world. Depending on how much time consumers invest in the search process, they can obtain more information about products, services, and companies in one hour than they ever could in the real world. Studies show, for example, that when consumers need to buy a new car, a majority now searches third-party websites (such as Consumerreports.com and Edmunds.com) for objective information as well as manufacturer and dealer sites. Searching for dealerships helps consumers find information about service policies and service center locations, test-driving opportunities, and who to call should a problem arise with the car.

Here's the catch: A vast majority of consumers armed with information they obtained online go to a local dealer to buy the car. Price negotiation still occurs; the difference is that today's consumer knows the manufacturer's list price and the dealer's invoice costs, making the negotiation process shorter and often less painful than in previous years. The website may be critically important to a majority of consumers in searching for information and choosing a dealer, but the dealer often remains the most important variable in the transaction stage.

Catalogs exceed online sites in one very important dimension: portability. Consumers can look through a catalog anywhere, at any time—while they're watching TV, lounging at the beach, traveling on airplanes, eating meals, talking on the phone, or even when they're in the bathroom. Well-designed, specifically targeted catalogs are not only useful, they are brief interludes to other activities. And for those of us who live by "polychronic" time expenditures (multitasking) catalogs beat-out Internet shopping, at least until we have computers in our cars and bathrooms. But will a Palm Pilot screen or a postage-stamp-size screen on a wireless phone be as effective graphically—or as much fun—as an L.L. Bean or Victoria's Secret catalog? While wireless technology is progressing rapidly, especially in the communication arena, there are some basic issues when using it for retailing and buying purposes.

Finding a Needle in a Haystack. If you wanted to buy a painting by Toller Cranston (a famous figure skater turned artist) or an autographed picture of Elton John, where would you go? The number of trips and phone calls to stores around the country necessary to find these special items is mind-boggling.

On the other hand, eBay built its business around similar search dilemmas that consumers face each day. It operates knowing that e-tailing works particularly well when searching for rare, old, out-of-circulation, and used items, all of which are specialties of eBay. Other types of products that lend themselves to online retailing are products with limited distribution or limited appeal, products that are too large to house cost-effectively in a store, and specialized products (of which most retailers can carry only limited assortments).

Take shoes, for example. As soon as the starting gun went off, nearly fifteen hundred shoe retailers raced to get online and open their virtual stores. Why? Because individual stores don't have the space and cannot afford to carry anything but the most popular sizes, colors, and styles. From a consumer behavior standpoint, when people find brands or styles they really like, they often buy them repeatedly and in additional colors, and since shoe size doesn't change much as we age or change weight, consumers know what sizes they need. An e-tailer operated by a manufacturer or a centralized retail distribution center can stock a wide range of sizes and colors in many styles, making it easier for consumers to search and find precisely the shoe that fits them.

Hunting for that special toy at the holidays can be as challenging as finding a size 13 AA aqua pump. If your child or grandchild had his heart set on a Sony Play Station, you had several options available to you this season to ensure holiday joy. You could travel from store to store, battle crowds and traffic, and, if the planets aligned just right, emerge triumphantly from the store with the last one in hand. Or you might persistently call these same stores, enduring endless busy signals, only to get a salesperson who has to "check inventory" to know if the toy is in stock. After enduring a lengthy "hold" (otherwise known as retail purgatory), the salesperson tells you there is one item left in stock, but it cannot be placed on hold due to store policy. The best solution seems to be sitting in front of a computer long after the stores have closed, sipping eggnog, and clicking through your shopping list. Receiving an e-mail a few minutes later confirming that the gift is on its way is the icing on the cake. Of course, it goes without saying that if the computer says an item is in stock and will be delivered in a few days, it better be true. KBkids.com, eToys.com, and ToysRUs.com found out the hard way that delivering Christmas gifts on December 28 doesn't build customer loyalty. In fact, some consumers vowed "never to trust e-tailers again," but whether they carry through with their threats in the long run remains to be seen.

This toy example is anything but child's play; it reveals an economic problem inherent to this specific business model. Assume that consumers flock to a website during the holidays, avoiding the hassles of holiday shopping, but return to their "normal" shopping and buying methods during the year. The Internet-based retailer is left with significant overhead built to serve peak demand (such as warehousing, staff, site maintenance, and server costs) even though it sits mostly idle the rest of the year. Even Disney, the master of creativity and efficiency, finally closed its Web-based toy store, concluding that in today's environment the basic economics of supply and demand just don't work on the Net.

How Consumers Evaluate and Compare Alternatives

Consumers identify various alternatives during the search process and then evaluate them, ultimately narrowing down the field of options and selecting one to purchase. Although alternative evaluation is intertwined with both the search and choice processes, understanding it separately helps identify the most influential attributes for product choice, which often vary substantially by consumer segment.

So how do consumers evaluate alternatives and choose one manufacturer, retailer, or brand over another? Different consumers employ different evaluative criteria—the standards and specifications used to compare different products and brands. How they evaluate their choices depends in part on their individuality and on environmental influences, making evaluative criteria a product-specific manifestation of an individual's needs, values, lifestyles, and so on. Some attributes are *salient,* or the most important—like does the car drive well, does the parka keep me warm, and does the store sell what I need. But if all the alternatives perform well on the salient attributes, consumers make their choices on the basis of *determinant* attributes—how many cup holders the car has, how many zipper pockets the parka has, and how clean the store's rest rooms are. Though they might seem minor in nature, these attributes differentiate one product or one supplier from another. You might also think that the most important attributes would always be the ones that determine purchase, but actually consumers often choose products and retailers based on attributes lower in salience, making them the real determinant attributes.

Word-of-mouth influences how consumers consider and evaluate products. Take the e-book business, for example. Several industry attempts at e-books, published for SoftBook Reader, Rocket eBook, Microsoft Reader, and Palm Pilot, led to disappointing sales of only a thousand or so of each title. But e-book publishing turned the corner of legitimacy and popularity when Stephen King, master mystery writer, put *Riding the Bullet*, a sixty-six-page short story, on the Internet. King fans, hungry for his latest tale of the bizarre, couldn't rush to their local bookstore to pick up a copy; they had to log-on for their e-copy. This first major attempt by a popular author to involve fans in his book via the Internet was a great story in and of itself, and TV programs and newspaper headlines hyped its release. Publicity created word-of-mouth around the world, and 500,000 people downloaded it within the first two days of its release—a blistering pace even for Stephen King. Yet, it is rumored that King has decided to drop publishing online, as the electronic format struggles to live up to the hype created around it.

E-tailers must examine alternative evaluation from two angles:

- How do consumers evaluate and compare traditional retail buying methods with online buying?
- How does electronic buying facilitate customer evaluation of alternative goods?

How Consumers Evaluate Buying Methods. How do consumers compare buying online with other forms of buying? And which evaluative criteria are most important to them when they makes these evaluations—price, convenience, time-savings, or something else. To date, most e-tailers have focused on appealing to the ever-popular attribute of price. On this variable, the Internet excels; in fact, offering lower-than-retail prices has been the hallmark positioning of e-tailers, one that will be difficult to change in the minds of consumers. Other e-tailers have touted convenience as their relative advantage, yet more stores have moved to extended and even 24/7 operating hours. And catalogs are even more convenient in that they can be read anywhere and have a real-live person available to answer questions consumers may have. E-tailers also "sell" the attribute of time-savings when convincing consumers to shop online versus in stores, but people have found that in certain instances, it is quicker and easier to go to the store, buy what you need, and have it in-hand than it is to order it and wait for its arrival. Then there's the "now factor"—the antithesis of convenience, when time is of the essence. If a consumer wants or needs a product immediately, ordering online or from a catalog won't cut it. For an added shipping charge, the item might get there overnight if it's in stock, the order is placed before the last shipment goes out, and all the planets are aligned just right.

Understanding how customers evaluate shopping methods in this manner helps firms avoid the trap that caught many early online retailers by surprise—failing to understand the real and desired benefits of shopping online. Hedonic attributes refer to those variables that give pleasure, evoke emotion, or in other ways go beyond strictly functional or performance values. Much of the thrill of "surfing the Web" is hedonic with consumers enjoying their leisure time by navigating between websites and looking for something to buy. Yet by the time most people have spent a few years surfing the Net, the thrill is gone. Just as the masses bought CB radios decades ago only to abandon them later, we believe the levels of online shopping will settle back to include those users who find the functional advantages of shopping online—such as not leaving home to shop or not having to send gifts to out-of-town relatives—greater than the advantages of other shopping alternatives.

How Consumers Evaluate Alternatives on the Web. Another key area to examine is how readily consumers can compare alternative products and brands on the Internet. For specific products identified during search, such as specific book titles or CDs, the Internet makes it easy for consumers to compare prices across e-tailers. A few clicks quickly show consumers whether Amazon.com or bn.com has the lowest price for that title, and technology now permits a lesser-known competitor to invade major sites with a spider to offer an even-lower price offer. Shopping "bots," born of the price evaluation and comparison function, extract data from several competitors and display the prices of each, in descending order of lowest price (or sometimes in the order of which competitors paid the most to be listed first). Auction sites take it one step farther and broker deals for consumers based on the prices they think are reasonable for products.

Beyond price, e-tailers can provide information that lets consumers evaluate alternatives based on other attributes. The airline industry, in an uncharacteristically forward-thinking marketing move, developed sites that not only provide their own flight schedules but offer those of other airlines. United Airlines, one of the first to offer competitive information, allowed consumers to evaluate flights based on the attribute of time without exiting and entering several different airline sites, each one requiring a password and reentered data. Although United, U.S. Airways, and now others risk losing sales to competitive lines, they may keep customers from shopping Expedia or Travelocity and ultimately build loyalty to their sites. Some airline sites provide information about other attributes, such as on-time performance of specific flights, in-flight entertainment, the availability of AC outlets for PCs, and seat configuration.

Attributes that are objective (price, time requirements, location, and weight) and can be written and interpreted accurately can be compared fairly well through e-tail channels. Comparison and evaluation of subjective attributes, on the other hand, are more accurate in the physical rather than the virtual world. How something feels, tastes, or smells and how a skirt or suit fits are better evaluated in a store than online. Trust and past experience do play a role in how consumers evaluate these types of attributes. If a customer has purchased a brand of clothing or line of beauty products before, he or she may feel more comfortable about interpreting written descriptions and pictures of products. Still, color, look, and feel are difficult to translate digitally as well as they can be experienced in stores.

Customers' ability to evaluate alternatives gives insight into the question "How much market share will online selling gain from traditional selling methods?" You can begin to decipher quickly which product categories lend themselves better than others to online selling, yet we've talked with e-tailing entrepreneurs and their investors who barely thought about these influences on their business plans. For airline tickets, consumers weigh heavily attributes such as price and schedules, information the Internet provides well. For product categories such as food, apparel, and others in which hedonic attributes are generally more determinant than functional attributes, the Internet faces a formidable challenge in taking market share from traditional retailers.

How Gateway Addressed Consumer Search and Evaluation. Gateway shocked the e-tailing world when it first opened Gateway Country Stores, strategically placed where consumers could go to see, operate, touch, and understand the right computer for their needs and then buy online. Beyond virtual stores, Gateway Country Stores offer a real place to return products when there is a problem, compared to the classic online service problem faced by its competitors who expect consumers to fix a broken computer online. How do you fix a computer online when it's broken?

Taking an online business off-line can be prohibitively costly if a firm tries to build a network of stores. Rather than build, pay for, and manage a lot of bricks-and-mortar real estate, Gateway found a partner. OfficeMax, a nationwide chain of office supply stores, manages stores well but needed a stronger computer offering for its many business customers. Out of the desire to serve their customers better and thereby grow revenue, Gateway mini-stores were born. Visit your local OfficeMax and you'll probably find a Gateway store inside, staffed by Gateway sales associates who recognize that most customers still want to talk to someone and see or try the product before they buy it. Once their decision is made, associates place the order online, remaining true to Gateway's strategy of increasing sales by selling off-line and ordering online. Gateway also captures a truth about winning technologies in its advertising slogan, "People Rule."

What can a retailer like OfficeMax expect to get out of such a union besides rent or sales commissions? After consumers buy a computer in the OfficeMax store, where are they likely to buy the cables, disks, software, printer paper, and miscellaneous computer paraphernalia? Bingo—a win-win partnership.

And Then There Was One. Evaluating alternatives lead to the identification of the best solution and to the most important and pivotal stage in the decision process—purchase. It is the stage in which e-tailers continue to focus their attention, hoping to entice consumers to change their buying behaviors, wooing them away from traditional, shopping cart–based buying to fun, click-and-order shopping.

PURCHASE: WHERE I.T. HITS THE FAN

Purchase is the moment of truth for all businesses, including Internet companies. After consumers identify what they want to buy, it's time to put the product in the cart, check out, and pay. E-tailers hold their breath and cross their fingers that more and more potential online customers will consummate their visits with a final click to submit payment rather than abandon the shopping process prior to sale. Studies indicate that 50 to 70 percent of consumers who do decide to buy on a website and move to the checkout portion of the purchase process terminate without buying. The number of consumers who actually purchase online will determine not only company revenues but future funding and growth opportunities as well.

After deciding to make a purchase, consumers move through several phases before they actually buy a product—choosing a retail format and choosing a specific retailer. Though evaluation of the various available forms of retailing occurs during evaluation, the final choice of a preferred format takes place here. Then the specific retailer or e-tailer is chosen—Pets.com or PETsMART? Finally, consumers make product and brand choices.

But even the best-intentioned plans can change unexpectedly. For example, a consumer may intend to buy premium dog food from Pets.com, for example, but instead buys a doggy raincoat (much to the chagrin of the dog) because of a special sale. The same consumer might not buy at all because of a confusing checkout system or because he or she doesn't have all the needed information handy and becomes overly frustrated. There are hundreds of ways to influence consumer decisions at the point of sale, including salespersons, product displays, kiosks, and point-of-purchase (POP) advertising. For online retailers, these choices might include finding sites (search engine registration), Web navigation, the influence of banners and other ads, payment systems (usually credit cards), security issues, and checkout procedures. Consumer expectations of and satisfaction with these specific activities greatly affect choices made in the first two phases.

POSTPURCHASE: WHAT HAPPENS AFTER THE SALE

After the purchase is made and the consumer takes possession of the product, consumption usually occurs—either immediately or sometime in the future. For example, a consumer may stock up on frozen entrées because of a special offer, buying more than can be consumed in a normal time frame. If this is a common pattern among some market segments, they may be receptive to e-tail buying because delivery costs to homes are very high for small orders, but leveraged against a large "stock up" order, they become a smaller portion of the total amount.

How people use products gives insight into how, when, and why they buy them. That's why consumer research increasingly focuses on usage or consumption in the home and in daily life. Consumption studies conducted via shadowing research, which audio- and videotapes consumers buying products and using them at home, provide insights useful in product and retail strategy. They investigate, for example, how consumers prepare and store food, how they spend their time, how products are used in connection with those activities, and how wearing one garment (a dress) affects the usage and therefore purchase of other products (lingerie or shoes). Consumption studies, conducted with newer shadowing techniques or tried-and-true focus groups and surveys, help manufacturers design products more satisfying than those of other firms. They also help retailers decide which products to sell, how they should be displayed in association with other products in the stores, and which services aide in customer retention and loyalty.

For an e-tailer, understanding how people "consume" the Internet is an important key to gaining competitive advantage. Consumption studies disclose which market segments use the Web for buying and which use it for shopping, who uses it at work or at home, and which related interests (sports, finance, news, etc.) can be used for interlinks and advertising.

Understanding the consumption process often reveals the attributes consumers use in the alternative evaluation and purchase stages. In the design of a website, for example, e-tailers may develop a good navigation plan and spend valuable funds to develop good graphics, easy checkout procedures, reliability, and speed, all of which are probably salient attributes for most consumers. An important determinant attribute of why some sites get more traffic than others, however, might be password procedures. Sites that let consumers use any combination of letters and numbers make it easier for consumers to log on than sites that confine consumers only to digits or only letters (or sometimes a few of either). A minor operating issue can act as an unnecessary obstacle to developing consumer loyalty because consumers can't possibly remember a different password for every site that wants them as regular customers. No matter how much money is spent on the "salient" attributes of a website, it is likely to fail if the developers don't spend enough money to investigate how real people really use websites.

Consumption research is vital in developing Internet tools and technology applications for B-to-B markets as well. Zefer, a technology incubation firm based in Cambridge, Massachusetts, sets itself apart from other similar firms by focusing on the human behavior side of technology consumption. In addition to surveys and questionnaires, designers and marketers work with customers' employees who will be using the technology day-in and day-out to understand firsthand how they currently do their jobs. That may mean spending days watching people place orders, procure equipment, or make follow-up sales calls, but in return, Zefer gains insight into how best to develop and introduce new Internet or software systems. Zefer's goal is to create customer solutions that their customers will use because they are better solutions than what they now use. The premise is that if new systems force customers to vary their behaviors greatly, they will avoid using the new technology.

The Web is a marvelous tool for improving the consumption process, even for manufacturers and retailers whose sales haven't yet hit cyberspace. For example, consumers who have questions about product use can log-on to the manufacturer's website and consult its FAQ (frequently asked questions) section. For consumers who lose product instructions and operations manuals, manufacturers or retailers can make those items available online—a solution that costs less than an 800 number and provides better service than traditional customer service centers that typically are only open from 9:00 A.M. to 5:00 P.M. The possibilities are numerous. Look for the most consumer-friendly manufacturers and wholesalers to make these types of services available. Best-practice sites allow consumers to e-mail comments and questions and receive quick responses. Sears.com now sends e-mails to its customers telling them about items they previously ordered but were out of stock at the time and are now back in stock. This is a nice postpurchase service for customers who haven't been able to find the item elsewhere or have been too busy to look.

Determining Satisfaction: The Goldilocks Principle

After all of the effort exerted by manufacturers, retailers, and marketers to create a sale, it all comes down to whether the consumer liked the product or not—satisfaction or dissatisfaction. Similar to Goldilocks, who tried several bowls of porridge (and later chairs and beds) before she found the one that was "just right," consumers spend time, energy, and money finding the brand or retailer that satisfies them best. Their evaluations are stored in memory and referenced in future decisions. Satisfaction increases a consumer's propensity to buy the same brand and makes subsequent decision processes much shorter, sometimes translating into habitual buying behavior. Under these circumstances, competitors, for the most part, have a hard time getting consumers' attention, let alone getting their sales. Dissatisfied consumers, on the other hand, are ripe for the picking by competitors who promise something better.

How big is the market for online retailing? It is directly proportional to the dissatisfaction with current retailing. If most people are satisfied with current products and retailers, the future of e-tailing is limited. On the other hand, when dissatisfaction runs rampant through consumer segments, the sky's the limit.

Divestment: Trash or Treasure?

Once consumers have used a product, they have several options to get rid of its remains—outright disposal, recycling, or remarketing. The latter has meant traffic and revenues for e-auctions that understand that "one person's trash is another person's treasure." Connecting these individuals, who might otherwise have relied on selling their wares at a garage sale, has created second, third, and fourth lives for some products and a community of people who enjoy browsing for hard-to-find or out-of-production items.

A host of B-to-B firms flourish in cyberspace thanks to companies' divestment needs. Visit the sites of Redemtech and techDisposal.com, and you'll find two firms that resemble high-tech versions of Sanford & Son. Both are similar in services and scope. For example, techDisposal.com works with clients to develop technology retirement plans; transports, audits, and tests equipment; erases data stored on hard-drives; remarkets products to buyers or manages donations to charitable organizations; and disposes of older, nonfunctional equipment. These firms have carved out a profitable niche of the market by bridging the needs of consumers and small businesses (access to and good deals on older-but-functional technology equipment) with the divestment needs of companies and consumers.

Strategies for Addressing Online Buying Characteristics

As you analyze how your customers proceed through the various stages of decision making, you can begin to see when e-tailing falls short of the traditional retail model and where it exceeds it. Blended retailers can capitalize on the strengths inherent to each model throughout the various stages to create a variety of strategies to satisfy customers better, including:

- Using in-store signage, personnel, and information to promote online sales

- Making your website easy for consumers to search for products and information, including bridal and general gift registry information

- Using your website to provide product information that might otherwise take up too much room in a store (where made, interesting features, etc.) and make suggestions on complementary products

- Giving consumers the option to select products online and pick them up at a store

- Reassuring consumers that your site is secure and private and update them with security information

- Tracking consumers who fill their shopping basket but abandon it before purchase—they have obviously shown interest and intent—and offer them assistance

- Making returns as easy as possible—include preprinted return labels—and accept them in any store location

In general, marketers need to evaluate the advantages and disadvantages of e-tailing over traditional sales methods in each of the consumer decision-making stages. Other members of the supply channel should also evaluate these types of trends to anticipate better the changing nature of their partners' sales opportunities and challenges. What do you think? Will e-tailing diffuse to the masses or will it be a great application for a small segment of consumers? Whether you are a retailer or a manufacturer, your marketing and strategic plans will have to be adapted accordingly.

CONSUMERS HAVE THE FINAL WORD

Understanding how consumers make purchase decisions can help real businesses earn real profits. It can also explain why some early websites, though deemed successes, were actually doomed from the beginning. Often focused on the "e" portion of e-commerce, few had a thorough understanding of the key ingredient in developing successful commerce ventures—namely the consumer. Figure 3.2 contains a matrix to help firms analyze future opportunities for various forms of retailing and how they can best compete against the inherent strengths of each model and specific competitor.

Consumer behavior analyses show that consumers are more likely to use the Internet to gain information about competitive products and retailers than they are to buy the product online. Most of the online activities today occur during the search stage of the shopping process rather than the purchase stage, which is often completed in the store. And while many firms are focusing on capitalizing on the "transaction" function of e-tailing, the CDP model provides a consumer-based paradigm to analyze other ways to profit from e-tailing technology. These profit opportunities may be in providing information during the search process, creating ordering and operating efficiencies, cutting costs, reaching new markets, improving cus-

FIGURE 3.2   Analyzing Sale Channels' Strengths and Opportunities

	Strength of Current Retail and Buying Strategies	Strength of E-Competitors	Opportunities for E-Tail Strategy	Strategies for Improving Current Retail and Sales Models
Need Recognition				
Search for Information				
Alternative Evaluation				
Purchase				
Consumption				
Satisfaction/ Dissatisfaction				
Divestment				

tomer service, and providing instruction manuals or FAQs to ensure that consumers actually receive the desired utility from the products they buy. Some of the best companies will find that many of the rewards of having an online presence will not necessarily come from online transactions; rather, they may come from making off-line purchases more satisfying.

The Internet is a marketing tool that must be placed in its proper context to facilitate the creation of profitable business transactions. In the end, none of this is really about technology; it is about customers. They will decide which retail formats will win and which ones will lose. The fact of the matter is that consumers demand convenience, ease of buying and returning, selection, and service, but most of the early dot-com firms based their strategies on the assumption that people want new technology and are driven mostly by low prices. Nothing could be more wrong as a basis for designing successful e-strategies. The history of commerce shows that consumers resist technology more often than they embrace it and effective marketing is not just low prices. The establishment of a physical presence, through strategic alliances, will facilitate success in e-commerce in addition to providing greater opportunities for face-to-face feedback and relationships.

CHAPTER 4

SEGMENTING CYBERSPACE: WHO'S ONLINE AND HOW TO REACH THEM

FROM THE TIME we begin school, we are taught about the differences between people—some people smoke, others don't; some laugh when they're happy, some cry; some roll their tubes of toothpaste from the end, others squeeze it from the middle (the latter being the "right" way, of course). At first glance, segmenting the marketplace may seem to be an old-economy task of defining people based on differences in their ages, incomes, and ethnicity. But at the heart of the exercise lies recognizing behaviors that distinguish some people from others—being able to put your finger on why certain people roll rather than squeeze and how to sell them a new, improved tube of toothpaste.

Never has a tried-and-true concept fit the realities of a new economy better than market segmentation, which helps predict the future of e-tailing by classifying who is online and what they are doing on the Internet and understanding why. Before building websites or blended retail strategies, marketers must formulate a realistic picture of the future scope and scalability of online sales. Only then can they begin to determine what portion of their budget to spend on their e-ventures.

During any time of perceived upheaval, people want succinct answers about the future; at the front of their minds today is the question "How big will global e-tailing be?" Yet it is next to impossible to look at the six plus billion people in the world and predict what their online activities might be in the next ten years. Still, by examining groups of individuals who have similar behaviors (and activities, interests, and lifestyles), the task becomes easier and much more accurate.

Enter the world of cybersegmentation.

Here's a snapshot of the cyberworld today. In the year 2000, there were 304 million people linked to the Internet via 80 million stationary computers (with 100 million portable computers projected by the year 2005). Of those users, 110 million live in the United States—the first time that over half of the people online live outside the United States. Those 194 million users represent more than 160 other nations around the world. Points of interest include Japan, which today has the second largest number of Internet users at nearly 19 million, and Iceland, which has the highest proportion of wired consumers—over 70 percent with Internet access. Whereas 41 percent of U.S. consumers are wired, Finland, Canada, and Sweden flaunt higher proportions of their populations online. By the time you read this book, these numbers will undoubtedly increase.

What this means to marketers is that at this moment, there are 304 million different "stories" on the Web, each one of which is unique. They represent the lives and usage patterns of people who, at any moment and for any reason, may click onto your site. Now, how can you anticipate who will come to visit and what they will want and expect when they arrive? The key lies in identifying categories of individuals that can help firms define these 304 million people and anticipate the products and services they might want, and then design messages and solutions as close as possible to their individual needs.

Ask Sherwin-Williams

Sherwin-Williams, paint-giant around the globe, helps industry professionals and paint laypersons make the world a little brighter and a lot more pleasing to the eye. The company has grown by dispensing paint, décor, and other related solutions through its 2,650 stores and 25,500 employees. Now, men with "paint the house" on their "honey, do-lists" and the professionals they often hire to complete the job, can click on its website and get answers and products galore.

At Sherwinwilliams.com, customers choose which descriptor best matches their situations and behaviors—painting contractors, builders, property managers, facility managers, architects, designers, engineers, OEM production finishers, automotive finishing, industrial and marine finishers, aerospace coatings, and the ever-popular do-it-yourselfer (DIY). From there on, the experience is specifically designed based on the interests and activities of that segment.

Before reorganizing its site to its current form, Sherwin-Williams looked like many others—housing and hustling a confusing array of products, assuming different people could figure out which products were for them. Now, however, its site, developed by DigitalDay, is tailored to types of users instead of types of products, a segmentation strategy based on individuals' painting, coating, and sealing behavior. Although the site contains over twelve thousand pages, this user-based orientation lets the company identify those pages relevant to a specific segment of buyer, who then is just three clicks away from easy-to-use information relevant to his or her specific activities and interests.

What type of information can a nervous first-time DIYer expect from the Sherwin-Williams answer center? A common question is "How much paint do I need to paint my bathroom?" Knowing consumers don't want to store gallons of unused paint in their basements, Sherwin-Williams helps them calculate exactly how many gallons of a specific type of paint are needed for a given square footage. It also details a list of everything needed to complete the job, from brushes and solvents to masking tape and a drop cloth. In about three Java-scripted clicks, browsers select the shape of the room, determine the right materials and quantities, delete paint not needed for windows and doors, and conquer special problems (such as getting rid of mildew around the shower tiles). In other words, "honey" is ready to start doing.

If you've ever planned to paint the exterior of your house, the one question you need answered is: "What's tomorrow's weather?" Sherwinwilliams .com offers a swift answer for your particular zip code. Web weather in and of itself is nothing new, but this forecast (a service of Underground Weather, Inc.) provides an impressively accurate hour-by-hour forecast. The information is so specific and includes so many other helpful features that in-the-know families and caterers alike check it any time they are planning an activity or traveling outside their area.

As it turns out, weather is a pretty important behavior-oriented variable for segmenting the paint market. Exterior paint for a house in blistering Birmingham, Alabama, can be different from the paint needed in frigid Fargo, North Dakota, making customers' zip codes important in satisfying their specific needs.

Sherwinwilliams.com excels in providing special services to its customers via the Web, and that is its primary goal—not selling paint online but letting customers browse, narrow their choices, organize their projects, and answer their questions outside of the store. Selling paint online poses problems. Sure, even the most pigmentally challenged can learn about color options, wallpaper patterns, and paint type online, but actual color selection needs to occur in the store. To date, nothing replaces the good old-fashioned color chip to select a specific hue.

The other online challenge is distribution. For the small quantities of paint and supplies involved in residential sales, picking up paint at the store is most efficient. For that reason, Sherwinwilliams.com locates the store closest to the buyer and provides a map as well.

Sherwin-Williams, well known among consumer circles, sells even more products to its professional and industrial customers through its network of stores. The pros rely on the store managers and staff to answer technical questions, schedule deliveries, and solve the myriad situational problems they encounter working on different jobs. Instead of solving these problems on the phone, during specific business hours, professionals can access technical spec sheets for all products at Sherwinwilliams.com. After evaluating their alternatives, they can choose to contact the store for additional advice or just call to place an order, freeing up time for both the customer and store personnel. The relationship between professional customer and the store is an important one that Sherwinwilliams.com doesn't want to weaken or bypass. Customers are used to buying from their local stores, calling or visiting them, and scheduling deliveries, and the company doesn't want to disrupt the preferred buying behaviors of their customers.

Shermanwilliams.com and Sherwin-Williams stores complement each other and create a harmony found only in the best of marriages. The beauty lies in the execution of the information function simplified by how it is disseminated—segment by segment. Instead of visiting a store, asking time-consuming questions, and shopping for what they need, consumers enter the store armed with a list detailing paint type and quantity, brushes, and other materials they need for their project. As a retailer, saving even twenty to thirty minutes of difficult-to-hire and expensive-to-train employees' time far outweighs the costs of an extensive website.

Ultimately, Sherwinwilliams.com borrows a page from its longtime retail practice: devise strategies to satisfy consumers better to retain loyal customers. Professional segments that are used to dealing with store personnel on a face-to-face basis still do so; they just have the online option of making the shopping process quicker. Consumers, who want to experiment with new colors and different types of paint, can explore the website, knowing that there are people in the store to make sure they get the colors and textures they want. By tailoring strategies to different segments, Sherwin-Williams hopes to increase customer satisfaction and focus on customer retention, not just new sales.

SEGMENTING THE CYBERWORLD

Segmentation is based on identifying and appealing to customers with similar behavior, not necessarily similar characteristics. Sherwin-Williams paints a clear picture of how behavioral segmentation can be applied to online retailing. It shows how two customers with very different incomes, zip code, gender, or experiences might buy the same specialized paint for a specific application. Marketers fall back on customer characteristics, such as demographics, for segmentation because they are correlates, or "proxies," for behavior and not because the characteristics are determinants of why people buy.

The need for segmentation results from the differences between people. If all humans were identical in their preferences and behaviors, market segmentation would not be needed, because every product and every marketing communication piece could be the same. In other words, Nordstrom and Dollar General, bargain retailer superstar, could position their products and stores similarly. Because people differ so much in their motivations, needs, decision processes, and buying behavior, products and ads ideally would be custom-tailored to each user to give maximum satisfaction to consumers. Drugstore.com sent out e-mails offering current customers discounts on online purchases, thereby reaching a group it had targeted for additional sales.

The goal in measuring market segments is to allocate consumers into categories that minimize variance *within* groups and maximize variance *between* groups—the Mini-Max rule. By identifying market segments that are similar in their behavior, products and communication strategies can be developed that are exactly matched to the preferences of that group. By maximizing variance between that segment and other segments, a differential advantage is obtained that, hopefully, will be so appealing that it will command a premium price greater than the cost of catering to specialized preferences of that segment. But the more individualized the product and the smaller the segment for which it is designed, the greater the likelihood that the costs to the marketer will increase. Adaptation to the need of a specific segment may require a higher price than consumers in that segment are willing to pay.

The Mini-Max rule requires marketers to learn a lot about current and potential customers in order to narrow segments substantially. But just because segments can be identified doesn't mean they are the right target for your company or specific marketing programs. Successful implementation of market segmentation strategies involves matching market opportunities with the firm's capability for developing marketing programs. Viable market segments should be scrutinized according to the following criteria:

- *Measurability.* How easy is it to obtain information about the size, nature, and behavior of the segment?

- *Accessibility* (or reachability). How easy is it to reach the segment, either through various advertising and communication programs or through various methods of retailing?

- *Substantiality.* Is the market size large enough to generate enough volume to support the development, production, and distribution costs needed to satisfy these segments?

- *Congruity.* How similar are the behaviors and other defining characteristics of members within the segment?

The more congruous, substantial, accessible, and measurable a segment is, the more likely targeted consumers are to respond to product offerings, promotions, and distribution channels.

WHO'S ONLINE?

Because the Internet is still a relatively new medium (product), marketers must rely on general consumer information to predict the future—how many people will be wired by when and who is most likely to do what on the Internet. Demographic trends, changing consumer needs and wants, consumption patterns, and consumer lifestyles provide insight into why certain online applications are successful today, which ones might catch on soon, and which ones are likely to fail. Such information can lead to new product ideas, product adaptations, improved architecture of a website, or even new services to help consumers in varied segments meet their changing needs.

Today's world is getting larger (in terms of population) and smaller (because of connectivity) simultaneously. With a majority of the population growth coming from third-world countries, one of the most important changes in the consumer marketplace in recent years has been the widening of the gap between the haves and the have-nots. The erosion of the

middle class has given way to more people who are able to purchase computers today than ten years ago and more people who are not. In the
United States, a similar chasm exists, which continues to widen along
ethnic and income fault lines.

Ironically, those who have the most dollars to spend live in time
poverty. On average, consumers work more hours per day than in the past,
making it difficult for individuals to shop or buy services during normal
business hours. That's why online travel agents and stock brokerages have
been one of the more successful applications of Internet retailing. Feeling
the stress of time constraints and deadlines in their lifestyles, consumers
want flexibility, and e-commerce may have a superior ability to deliver this
benefit. To save time, consumers have decreased the amount of time they
spend evaluating alternative products, relying instead on past experience
and brand names.

Another key word that will pop up more and more in discussions on
lifestyles and technology is portability. Recognizing that consumers sometimes can't or don't want to work only in their offices, don't want to shop
strapped to a desk, and want to communicate from anywhere they happen
to be, portability of computers and other technology items is vital to the
adoption of specific applications. Cellular phones are the perfect example,
leading the way to wireless technology for some Internet applications. The
Wireless Internet Newsletter forecasts 830 million mobile devices worldwide by 2005, and many researchers predict that more people will be connected to the Internet by alternative devices, many wireless, than by PCs.
Internet portability, however, doesn't have be a feature limited only to
alternative devices such as Palm Pilots. In fact, Dell is actively developing
laptop PCs with wireless capability.

So who is on the Net? Consider Figure 4.1. We assume that most
everyone reading this book is actively connected to the Internet, but the
reality is that if you are online, you are not "normal." It is estimated that
59 percent of all Americans are not connected—meaning they don't have
access to or use the Internet. Of the 111 million that are, most (67 percent) use the Internet for information or leisure but not to buy products.
Of those who do buy online, based on research by Jupiter Communications for the year 2000, average sales per person are estimated to be $589
per year. Within this "Net segment," most *buyers* are men between the
ages of thirty-five and fifty. If Internet shopping does increase substantially
as some predict, women could overtake the men in the near future, just
as they already have in many sectors of retail. Women already account for
about 50 percent of Internet *users*.

FIGURE 4.1   Who's Online

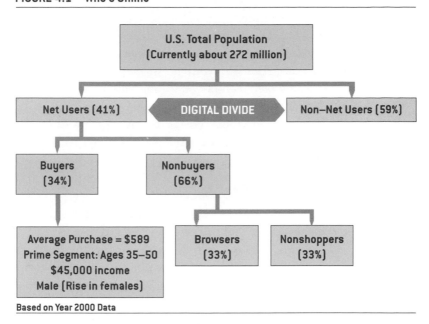

Based on Year 2000 Data

Looking to the future, we expect the greatest growth segments for online usage to be among the young (kids who today are between two and eighteen years) and adults over age sixty. Buying by kids is constrained because of the limited availability of credit, although CyberCash, RocketCash.com, and similar Web currency may increase transaction capability. RocketCash, a private firm that grew from a casual conversation with a baby-sitter about teen online shopping, targets Generation Y teens and enables them to shop and buy on the Internet in a free, parent-approved environment. But CyberCash, the largest of these service providers, was still operating with big losses by the end of 2000 even though it had signed 26,700 merchants to use its Internet currency and expanded into B-to-B markets. Keep in mind also, that although children are online communicating with their friends and learning in school, they are also going with their parents and friends to the mall and to retail stores. They will not completely abandon these activities to which they have been acculturated. If for some reason e-tailing were to become the primary method of consumer buying, it still wouldn't happen until the children of today's teens become family or household buyers.

Older adults—what we call the "young again" segment—represent one of the prime and growing market segments. They not only have money,

but they have the time to spend it on the Net. In addition to e-mailing pho-
tographs of grandchildren to unsuspecting friends and relatives, many in
this segment seek information on prescription drugs, travel and vacation
sites, financial services, and retirement communities, just to name a few.
Just because the Net started out with younger market segments and draws
heavy usage from kids and teens, don't count older adults out.

Online market segments can also be identified on the basis of their
lifestyles and behaviors. Three categories of prime importance are
described as "Net nerds," "daily dependents," and "Average J and Js."

Net Nerds

The original Net users were mostly "techies"—young adults who as kids
ran the computer labs at school and tinkered with electronics in their parents' garage every moment they weren't studying. Among the first to use
computers at their job, they were also the first to buy computers for personal use. Racing home from Radio Shack with their Commodore 64 or
Tandy computer under their arm, they were among the first to get connected—and the first to redefine a sense of "coolness." As early as the
1980s they could buy Brooks Brothers shirts, Hammacher Schlemmer
wares, flowers, and a wide array of other merchandise on CompuServe or
Prodigy Shopping Malls, but mostly they bought computer software and
related materials. What they buy today has not changed much, except now
they are more likely to buy from online expert marketers like Dell,
Gateway, or MicroCenter—e-tailers that sell what Net nerds buy. This
group spends eleven or more—sometimes many more—hours on the
Internet each week, but other than computer-related products (and
pornography, which continues to be the most profitable category of Web
sales), their most likely purchases are music CDs, videotapes, and other
consumer electronics.

Daily Dependents

Another prime segment of Internet users is what we call "daily dependents"—people for whom the Internet is a must-have tool to do their jobs.
You've seen them—online at the office, in airports, on commuter trains,
and often logging on when they get home. Although they are heavy users,
they are not necessarily online shopping enthusiasts. In fact, over time,
many develop a sort of love-hate relationship with the Internet—they can't
live without it, but increasingly are questioning whether they enjoy living
with it. Symptoms include e-mail rage, similar to the road variety but usu-

ally not fatal, and Internet-avoidance in which they refuse to spend another minute looking at a computer screen.

For typical consumers, the first two years of Internet usage are novel. Visiting websites, clicking on banner ads (yes, some actually want to see what happens), sending and receiving messages from friends, and placing that virginal e-tail order. Similar to Pong (the first computer game whose simplicity would cause even the youngest of the computer-literate to roll with laughter) and CB radios (do you remember your handle?), consumers can't get enough. But soon the novelty wears off as delivery, returns, and other problems inherent in online shopping continue to be an issue. After a few years, buying online is the last thing on the daily dependent's mind. That doesn't mean they may not buy some items where clearly there is an advantage, but the advantage must be clear—they must have a reason to go to your site and spend their precious leisure time online.

Business buyers fall into the same category. There are those who, because they order online all day and know how to purchase efficiently and which sites are best, actually might order more personal items online than other buyers especially if they can bundle some personal items with business orders. But since their B-to-B purchasing activities dominate their days, they yearn for a different way to buy for themselves. For most daily dependents, Internet and other computer-related activities at home are too similar to "work," end up losing social and leisure appeal, and become just another chore.

Average J and Js

Another significant Net segment is the average Janes and Joes who use the Internet sometimes during work and occasionally at home. They usually want their children to have ample access to computers and the Internet for schoolwork and future career development. If online retailing is expected to jump beyond its current 0.89 percent of retail sales, growth will have to come from this segment. Net nerds probably won't expand much beyond their present proportion because the number of new Net nerds is realistically limited to the number of youngsters turning age twelve each year. And since most businesses today are already connected, don't expect a surge in the number of daily dependents, unless there are new technology applications that increase Internet dependence in more jobs.

That said, you can see that the growth in the number of e-tail buyers is concentrated mainly among people who are not currently connected and average J and Js. Keep this in mind when market analysts talk about increasing the numbers of new buyers for the e-tail industry.

The fact that significant e-tail growth lies in their hands warrants a closer look at this segment. Average J and Js watch TV most evenings (perhaps catching-up on *Oprah* while assembling dinner) and divvy up chores that need to be done that day. What they buy in stores is influenced to some extent by TV advertising, and some occasionally buy from the Home Shopping Network. They may have WebTV—providing increasing opportunities to respond to Web retailing sites. They browse catalogs and pick up a phone to dial 800 numbers. Still, a vast majority of their purchases occur in grocery and department stores and mass retailers. To date, there exists no evidence that average J and Js will buy on the Internet more than they do from catalogs or TV shopping channels. Some will, and will buy quite a bit, but most will buy only on those occasions they find an offer more attractive than their favorite nearby stores.

Nevertheless, this group represents the best segments and greatest growth areas for B-to-C e-commerce. To the degree that e-tailers understand the minds of these ordinary consumers, offer specialized products that are viable online, and can perform business functions efficiently, consumer-based e-commerce will grow. Failure to perform on any of these dimensions, however, darkens growth forecasts from sustainable double-digit growth throughout the decade to slight growth that will occur at a decreasing rate before settling back to levels experienced by other competitive mediums.

Using Segmentation Information

Many data are collected by research firms highlighting who is online and tracking their online activities. E-tailers and retailers should keep a close eye on Internet users and should:

- Monitor and understand how the makeup of users is changing—categorize them according to their online behaviors not just characteristics

- Monitor what types of consumers are spending time and money online and which ones are abandoning online e-tailing

- Give the segments you identify human characteristics; don't just look at the numbers and statistics, but understand the psychology behind their actions

- Understand what is important to various consumer segments—are they looking for online "deals" or value-added services

- Take general market data and compare it to individual research on your customers—begin to profile what makes your customers unique.

WHAT WILL SELL ONLINE?

People buy different products in different ways. Suffice it to say that you spend a little more thought and time purchasing a car than a mop. When consumers share similar buying patterns for specific products, it is useful to analyze product categories as segments, identifying marketing opportunities for manufacturers, distributors, and retailers alike.

Highly segmented products offer the most potential for online retailing because the World Wide Web offers the ability to appeal to small segments of the population across wide geographic areas. There may be segments of only a few hundred or a few thousand potential customers in any particular geographic area or nation, but the Internet has the potential of reaching the people in those same segments around the globe.

Manufacturers of clothing, music, food, cars, computers, or even paint contemplating the opportunities and threats from e-commerce should analyze each product line by product category—convenience goods, shopping goods, specialty goods, or services. Figure 4.2 summarizes the characteristics of product types and indicates why some categories are better matches for the e-tail environment than others are.

Buying Convenience Goods Online

Convenience goods are generally inexpensive, frequently purchased items for which buyers exert only a minimal purchasing effort. Examples abound in personal-care items (toothpaste, shaving cream, deodorants, cold remedies, soft drinks, most food items, gasoline, newspapers, and batteries). Buyers may be extremely brand loyal to particular items—hairspray and hair color—but will often accept substitutes, perhaps under the influence of a coupon, even with strong brand preferences. Since consumers generally spend little time planning these purchases or comparing available brands and sellers, manufacturers peddle their products in whatever retail outlets will have them. Even though margins are low, these items are still profitable because of purchase frequency, rapid inventory turnover, and highly efficient distribution methods.

Catalog and online retailers generally find that selling convenience goods doesn't work—there is not enough margin to sustain the inefficient distribution system of individual delivery or picking costs. Unfortunately for them, convenience goods command a large share of consumers' wallets, which to naïve e-tailers may seem like a world of opportunity. Don't look for many convenience goods to be good buys on the Internet unless you live

FIGURE 4.2   Evaluating Which Products Are Best Suited for Online Selling

Charactistics	Convenience Goods	Shopping Goods	Specialty Products
Margins	Low Margins	Medium Margins	High Margins
Inventory Turns	High Turns	Medium to Low Turns	Low Turns
Price	Low Price	Low to Medium Price	High Price
Ease of finding Product	Easy to Find	Easy to Find	Difficult to Find
Now Factor	Need Product Soon	Often Need Product Soon	Will Wait to Receive
Price Sensitivity	Price Sensitive	Moderately Price Sensitive	Low Price Sensitive
Brand Substitution	Will Substitute	Compare before Substitute	Will not Readily Substitute
Degree of Search and Planning	Limited Search and Planning	Medium Search and Planning	Extensive Search and Planning
Ease of Current Shopping Method	Easy and Convenient to Buy Products	Easy and Convenient to Buy Products	Difficult and Inconvenient to Buy Products
Product Evaluation	Don't Need to Touch	Need to Touch and See Product	Need to See, Receive Information and Assurance
FIT FOR ONLINE SELLING	LOW	LOW TO MEDIUM	HIGH

in a geographically remote area where essential items are not readily available in local stores, making quantity buying practical. Drugstore.com, DrugEmporium.com, and Peapod all tried to sell convenience goods online, but languished at the hands of low volumes and low margins.

Buying Shopping Goods Online

Shopping goods, from clothing and furniture to cameras and bicycles, are items for which buyers expend considerable effort in planning, comparing, and purchasing, often because the products are expected to last a fairly long time. Consumers are willing to spend time comparing brands and stores and perhaps visit multiple stores if at first they don't find exactly what they want. They evaluate product features, quality of items in comparison to competitive models and brands, the ability to obtain service (for example, clothing alterations), warranties and return policies, and compatibility of color and size with other products with which the products will be used or worn. Price is likely to be an important variable, but it is usually evaluated in relationship to the other variables. To make the best decision, consumers often rely on salespeople to help in the evaluation of many of these attributes.

Department stores, mass merchants, and a vast array of specialty stores found in shopping malls sell shopping goods efficiently. Even though they have lower inventory turns, require higher margins than convenience goods, and generally appear in fewer outlets, they still comprise a significant portion of consumers' budgets.

E-tailers, as well as catalog retailers, offer a mixed bag of advantages to consumers in their search for shopping goods. Except for Crate & Barrel and Restoration Hardware, which provide detailed product information throughout their stores, catalogs and websites often serve up more information about the products than bricks-and-mortar retailers, especially those that have all but eliminated salespeople from the retail floor. They also make it easier for consumers to evaluate and compare product prices. Furniture.com suffered devastating losses from lower than expected sales and high infrastructure and operating costs. It had to close its doors in August 2000—consumers didn't want to buy furniture over the Internet without touching, feeling, and measuring it. The involvement with the physical product was too high to migrate it easily to the impersonal online sales method.

Although price is important when consumers evaluate shopping goods, it is normally compared with a lot of other attributes including fit, texture, color, compatibility with other products (in size, style, or connectivity), and so forth. When shopping the Web, a browser or a personal "bot" (software that compares a number of online alternatives) is reasonably capable of comparing the prices of different retailers. But it is not very good at looking at two different shirts or blouses, and deciding if the lighter weight of fabric or slight color discrepancy is worth a lower price.

Buying Hard-to-Find Items Online

The third category of consumer goods is specialty products—those unique things on which most of us like to splurge. Consumers usually spend considerable effort, attention, and time to obtain them, often because they can't be found at your local discount and convenience stores. Highly specialized home items and appliances, collectibles, or perhaps unusual foods fall into this category, as do specialty brands such as Versace (apparel), Mont Blanc (writing instruments), and Loewe (television). Consumers are willing to search far and wide for a store that carries these products and labels. Although most consumers don't buy these products with feverish frequency, they are willing to pay substantial dollars for them. Retailers need to get high margins on these items because sometimes they sit in the stores, taking away space from fast-turn items. They sometimes require special assistance from sales personnel as well.

Specialty items are what catalog and Web retailing dreams are made of. These methods reduce search time and effort for consumers. They also provide the perfect environment to "house" a world of product possibilities that would be economically impossible for most physical retailers to carry. If size is an issue for you, catalogs and websites probably fit your needs better than a local retailer that can't afford (economically and spatially) to stock the inventory. The same is true for a wide array of colors, brands, and styles. With margins around 50 to 80 percent, e-tailers can avoid getting killed in the delivery and distribution game (even if they are still less than efficient) and still make some money.

A rosy picture, right? Think, however, of two questions: How much of your total budget as a consumer is spent on specialty items compared to shopping and convenience goods? And, when was the last time you bought something from a catalog because it was cheaper than the same item purchased in a local store? The picture of potential total retail sales online is a little less rosy, isn't it? Catalog retailers know their costs; and it takes high prices to make profits. They also know that their customers are buying because they've found something special—buying in spite of the price, not because of it. The perfect example of attracting consumers looking for unique items—from autographed pictures to collectible figurines—who are willing to pay whatever it takes to get them is eBay's auction site.

Securing Services Online

The economies of industrialized nations are not about cars and computers anymore. The U.S. service sector now generates 74 percent of gross domestic product and 79 percent of all jobs—and more than 50 cents out of every dollar consumers spend goes to services. Producing approximately a $58 billion balance-of-trade surplus (versus a deficit of $132 billion for goods), it is the fastest growing part of the economy.

Services are products that come into existence at the same time they are consumed. Their intangibility (though they may involve physical products, such as airplanes, banks, or surgical scalpels) makes it difficult to judge the level of quality among alternatives, which forces first-time buyers to rely on the reputation of the seller or third-party endorsements (such as the Federal Deposit Insurance Corporation). When consumers are satisfied with the quality of a service provider, such as their physician, banker, barber, or funeral director, they are loyal and reluctant to switch to a different service provider, even for a lower price.

Services tend to be inseparable from the person or organization providing them (such as a physician or hospital or food preparation in a restaurant). They are also highly perishable (such as vacant airline or movie seats, unused telephone or electric service in off-peak times, or unsold meals in restaurants).

Although the service sector is growing rapidly, it provides e-commerce's biggest challenges as well as its biggest opportunities. The challenges arise from the simple fact that most services cannot be delivered online. A restaurant can't ship food over the Internet nor can the Internet beam a person from New York to Los Angeles despite the best efforts of Nicholas Negroponte and the MIT Media Lab to transmit human personages online with holograms.

Selling services, rather than performing them, is a major opportunity if it is done right. And there are emerging models of how to do it right. They include Charles Schwab, which now performs 80 percent of its trades online, up from 10 percent just two years earlier. But here's the reality check: Two years ago, 70 percent of new assets were brought to the company through its branches; today that number is still 70 percent! That's disconcerting for e-brokerages strong on Internet access but short on physical offices staffed by associates of the human kind. The bottom line is that consumers feel more comfortable handing over their money inside comfortably outfitted bricks-and-mortar offices. It's not good news either for "e-banks" with limited access to low-cost money selling low-cost loans on the Internet. They lack the physical branches that serve older consumers who put money in banks to be loaned to other customers.

The hard part about succeeding in the service segment is hiring people to provide quality service, training and motivating them, and building a reputation for standing behind the service when something goes wrong. ServiceMaster, one of the world's premier service organizations, has already done that with its legendary human resources and management methods and well-established brands such as ChemLawn, TruGreen, Merry Maids, and its own corporate brand, ServiceMaster. Who do you think consumers

are most likely to choose when they want to buy home cleaning or maintenance services, Servicemaster.com or TheUnknownCleaningGuy.com?

Flowers are another great example of the importance of trust in an
increasingly impersonal world. Finding someone you can trust to create a
tasteful arrangement, use only fresh flowers, and deliver them before or
on a birthday (rather than the day after) has been simplified by 1-800-
Flowers and its website. Consumers are accustomed to placing an order
over the phone, and selling on the Web doesn't change that behavior
much. Still, with the website, consumers can log-on to see a picture of
what they're ordering. They can also order online, but many choose to call
and talk to a person who can assure them that the order has been received
and that the flowers will be delivered. Orchestrating the whole process is
challenging to say the least; not only does the company have to search for
partners (local floral shops), it has to track orders and partners' performance ratings and maintain a workforce that can communicate to customers well.

Where will services find their greatest success with e-commerce? We
believe it will be solving the perishability problem. When an airplane takes
off with empty seats, that revenue is lost forever. Since the marginal cost
difference between an empty seat and a filled one is not much more than
a bag of peanuts, the airline makes more money if it can sell the seat for
almost any price above the cost of the nuts. This works, however, only if
it can "discriminate" or keep time-sensitive customers willing to pay the
full price from waiting to get the seat at a low price. That's what the airlines have done by listing those seats on Priceline.com or, in some cases,
on their own websites. If you are willing to take any carrier, fly anytime
during the day or night, and be flexible about departure dates and airports,
you may be able to buy that otherwise vacant seat for mere peanuts.
Potential for great profits lie in the business models that dispose of services that otherwise would spoil—and that potential is not limited to airlines.

Selling services, we believe, represents an opportunity for firms of all
sizes, especially when consumers are selecting a provider for the first time
or in a distant city. For the "connected" segments of a market, an effective website can be as useful and even more informative than the Yellow
Pages. Though e-commerce may be most useful to Net nerds and daily
dependents, even average J and Js occasionally will use it to find and hire
Pete the Plumber or Rheva the Realtor. But they'll probably use it only
once for each of those service providers, unless the firm performs poorly,
causing the search for a new plumber to arise. If the service firm has the

physical tools and facilities as well as the skills, it will probably have a customer for years. If, however, the quality of service doesn't measure up to the expectations of the customer, that person may be reluctant to use the Internet to find and buy from other online service sellers. In short, trust with the service provider and the Internet has been broken.

Looking at the Gift Horse

Gifts are a unique category of product—not so much defined by the item but by the fact that the buyer will not be its future owner. People will often go to great lengths to find the right gift for a friend or relative, knowing that even more important than the gift's monetary value is the thought that went into buying it. Consumers search and evaluate several options more extensively than normal, mimicking specialty product purchase behavior.

Online shopping works well in this instance, not just because of the search process but because of logistics. The problem consumers face when buying gifts for out-of-town relatives is getting them there. Consumers lug the gifts home, wrap them, address them, load them back in the car, and mail them via post or parcel service. With catalog and online retailing, the products need to be shipped anyway—just elect to ship them to Uncle Al directly and a hassle-laden function has been shifted from consumer to retailer without additional cost. The deal is sweetened further with some of the fantastic gift registry programs, offered by many sites (discussed in Chapter 6), that take the guesswork out of gift selection.

Strategies for Selling Online

E-tailers must develop segmentation strategies not just for the consumers to whom they market but for the products they hope to sell. E-tailers will likely find greater success online if they:

- Focus online sales on specialty products—unique, hard-to-find items not readily available in stores
- Sell items that consumers are not able to access easily locally (national real estate)
- Offer a limited selection of products online—don't sell everything in your store online; give consumers a reason to go to the store
- Use the Internet to sell off-season items or clearance items that never made it to the retail floor

- Sell items that retailers don't want to carry in stores because of low inventory turns or because of physical limitations

- Concentrate sales efforts on digital products, repeat orders, parts and instruction booklets, and low-touch, consistently sized items

THE INTERNET DOES SEGMENTATION

If segmentation theorists had a god to worship, it would be the Internet. (Don't laugh, just as some people are passionate about hats and paint, others are passionate about segmentation.) It makes segmentation goals that were mere dreams yesterday possible today. Why? Because no medium is so well equipped as the Internet to treat every consumer as a unique individual with specific needs.

Personalization is perfectly possible with today's software. It recognizes every unique consumer (or at least their computer address) when they hit a website, making it possible to identify their behavior patterns and special interests based on their activity on your site as well as their journeys throughout the World Wide Web. But personalization is just the first step in the thousand-mile journey of building a successful e-commerce business. Delivering individual solutions is a more difficult problem, forcing firms to fall back on the basic-but-critically-important concept of segmentation.

In short, the Internet does for segmentation what the telephone did for communication—creating a new supersonic improvement of a long-lived function. No one knows your age, ethnicity, or educational background when you first log on to a website, but after tracking your clicks they know what interests you. In marketing, this represents a paradigm shift away from using demographics to predict behavior and toward reporting actual behaviors. E-businesses sit poised to soak up reservoirs of information on their current and potential customers.

Think back to Sherwin-Williams for a moment. The company provided Internet solutions for various behavior-oriented customer segments that were classified based on their behaviors off the Web. Now what happens when a firm segments customers based on their behaviors *on* the Web? A new Internet-fortified segmentation process is born—combining consumers' online behaviors with specific interests. Again, a paradigm shift for the prophets of traditional market segmentation.

As marketers begin to understand better how consumers make purchase decisions, they will quickly come to realize that just because a person buys at Wal-Mart doesn't mean that person should necessarily be included in the Wal-Mart.com potential-buyer segment. Focusing on what your customers are doing online creates a more realistic vision of what the future will hold in terms of potential new sales and sales extensions.

The Internet can aid marketing planning and execution in the cyber-marketspace, as illustrated in Figure 4.3, which depicts the following steps:

1. **Identifying people who behave in the same way.** For the first time, with the exception of the limited application of scanner data, marketers can measure consumers' behaviors that are most relevant to their businesses—namely, which consumers visited a site and bought (buyers) *and* which consumers visited but left empty-handed (nonbuyers). This phenomenon resulted not necessarily from intentional design but more as a result of the nature of the beast—behavior is

FIGURE 4.3   Tracking and Profiling Online Customer Segments

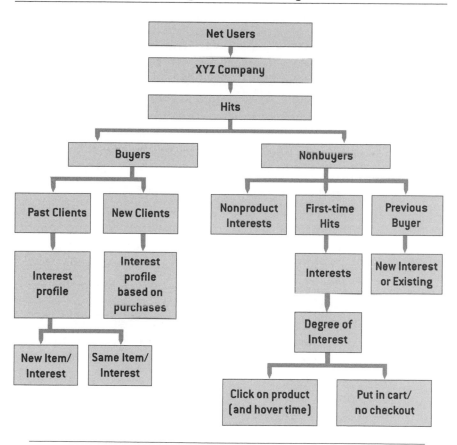

the only variable available to describe and identify Internet browsers. Heads above marketing research that asks consumers about their intentions or about past behaviors (neither of which are always accurate reflections of fact), the Internet identifies immediately which consumers bought and what they bought.

That's only the beginning. Although an e-tailer might not know who didn't enter its cyberstore, it does know who surfed in and what they found interesting. Even if the interest didn't result in a sale, nonbuyers can be segmented based on the items in which they showed interest and their degree of interest (clicked-on but didn't buy, or click-on, put in cart, but didn't buy). These areas of interest become good descriptors for that person and identify potential product-specific marketing opportunities to reach him or her. Then there are those browsers who hit a site yet never look at a single product—perhaps this is a potential investor conducting his or her own due-diligence or someone looking for a store location (in the case of a blended retailer). Either way, just knowing someone showed interest makes that person a viable potential customer.

2. **Identify what other items customers may be interested in buying online or in stores.** Once the segmentation process has been adopted, an e-tailer can create a profile for every person who has visited its website, identifying both products that have been purchased and products that were not purchased but created interest (measured by clicks and hover time). Examining which items were of interest gives marketers an opportunity to target that person with offers regarding that particular item or products in related categories.

3. **Expand the size of the segment.** The more you know about people with similar behaviors, the more likely you are to expand the size of the market—with the ultimate goal of creating more buyers. Marketers can use information about buyers' and nonbuyers' interests and activities to help explain their behaviors and determine how to target them best—getting current buyers to buy more and nonbuyers to purchase for the first time.

4. **Individualize offers based on behaviors and create more tailored communication and marketing approaches.** Based on the categories of buyers and nonbuyers identified in Figure 4.2, there exist a variety of offers appealing to each group. For example, current clients who buy a new item online could be targeted with an offer for a product in a related category. An e-tailer might want to notify a customer when a new suit or accessory item from a designer of interest becomes available for sale. The goal is to increase the amount of

spending and frequency of buying for this active buyer segment. A current customer who buys the same product repeatedly might be targeted with a till-forbid offer (sending them the item X times per year until the customer forbids you to do so) or a reorder reminder offer. With new buyers, the goal is to move them from the trial to repeat purchase stage as quickly as possible. A special discount based on quantity orders might make sense here.

Nonbuyers should also be targeted with special offers tailored to their expressed interests. Price promotions for items viewed but not purchased during the last visit might create trial. It might also make sense for a blended retailer to promote in-store services or specials to nonbuyers. In some instances, firms might get valuable information from online surveys sent to nonbuyers asking why they didn't buy online. Finally, e-tailers must monitor closely the nonbuying activities of previous buyers—keeping an eye on the possibility of discontinuance.

SWITCHING EMPHASIS FROM ATTRACTING CUSTOMERS TO RETAINING CUSTOMERS

Retailers have found over the years that it is much more effective to sell more to their current customers than to attract a constant barrage of new customers with specials only to lose their patronage when the promotion is over. The same holds true in the world of e-tailing. Unless dot-coms can convert first-time buyers into loyal customers, the drain on profits caused by the costs of acquiring new customers will put many of them out of business. In 1999, e-tailers (or e-tail divisions) spent about $40 for each new customer attracted, while pure-play dot-coms (companies that market only on the Web) spent about $100 per customer.

Mass Advertising Sometimes Misses the Target

You undoubtedly saw all the mass advertising campaigns for no-name dot-coms that hit the airwaves in 1999 and 2000. Sure, this creative free-for-all was a much-needed shot in the arm for the advertising industry, but most consumers were left staring blankly at their television screens wondering if they were the only ones who "didn't get it." With an "I don't care who's watching, I just want someone to notice me" attitude, dot-com ads were all about image—good or bad—and clutter breakthrough. Well, some may have broken through for a brief moment, but most alienated more people than they attracted.

The dot-coms were advertising to hoards of people who didn't use the Internet and frankly didn't intend on using it. And often it wasn't clear what message they were trying to convey. Still, one signal came across loud and clear: They didn't know who their customer was and from where their new customers would likely come. It was a blatant selling approach rather than an innovative marketing segmentation approach to cultivate buyers rather than mere browsers.

Does that mean traditional advertising is worthless? No. What would television be without those slick, almost movielike car commercials? Most of us need cars at some point or another and will buy about five during our lifetimes. Sure, this is still a hit-or-miss approach, but updating what consumers know and perceive to be true about a specific model warrants such an approach, even though there might be a more effective, targeted method of switching buyers of competitive brands or keeping current customers. When e-commerce matures, however, advertising will become more strategic in nature as it has in autos, detergents, food, banking, and most all mature industries.

Evaluation of the dot-coms' collective early advertising blitz can only be fair if results are compared to their objectives. If attracting long-term paying customers to their sites was the primary objective, a vast majority failed miserably. What of the notion that the hype may have been created not to promote products but to promote the stock of these companies instead? At a time when a new brave breed of individual investor was looking for the next Cisco or Yahoo!, blasting a dot-com name on the screen with a glitzy, revolutionary image was similar to throwing raw meat to hungry dogs. Perhaps the real segment reached by these ads was amateur day-traders. In that case, perhaps a resounding bravo is in order.

Keep Them Coming Back

With the number of new Internet shoppers expected to peak sometime in 2001, dot-coms are focusing on retaining their customers and increasing the sales and profitability of each. The typical marketer spent about $315,000 on online promotions, a number that can be decreased if fewer, more targeted promotions are developed. And Forrester, a leading independent technology-focused research firm, expects online promotion budgets spent on retention programs to jump from 15 to 35 percent by 2005. Why? Because online retailers are able to target effectively their current customers using the information supplied to them by customers—such as e-mail and home addresses, product preferences, buying behaviors, and interests. Traditional retailers, however, have the advantage of promoting online shopping in their stores, printing information on receipts, store signs, and on shopping bags.

A host of dot-coms have developed programs to reward loyalty. Gap.com offers a gift reminder service to customers who want to be notified in advance of birthdays, anniversaries, or other gift-giving occasions. Gap.com allows customers to list up to ten customers and their addresses to which gifts should be sent; the company also stores billing information to expedite checkout services.

"Getting to Know You"

First sung on the Broadway stage, the song "Getting to Know You" might better serve as the theme song of consumer marketing in the new economy. In traditional retailing or manufacturing, it is difficult to measure behavior for the purpose of developing a targeted marketing mix, but with e-tailing the situation is reversed. Generally, little is known about the age, gender, or traditional segmentation variables, but a great deal is known about their behavior.

Advertising.com helps its clients find and get to know their customers better. A recent ad headline for the company reads, "You sell sombreros for lizards? We can find your customers." A seemingly impossible task for anyone, Advertising.com's message is poignant. With AdLearn, its revolutionary, real-time targeting and optimization technology, Advertising.com scientifically and automatically directs clients' ads to reach their most likely prospects through several Internet-enabled channels, such as Web, e-mail, desktop, and wireless devises. AdLearn correlates terabits of empirical data while tracking, profiling, and evaluating anonymous consumers' Internet behavior and preferences. It then processes and matches this information with site performance and client criteria data, and within twenty milliseconds, selects and sends the ads with the highest probability of response to these specific targets.

If you've ever logged on to search engines, such as Google, Alta Vista, or Hotbot, you know that you can punch in someone's name and find pages of information on them. You also know it's possible to pull up your "surfing" profile and get a day-by-day itemized list of all the websites you've visited in recent months. Frankly, it's a little scary—a customer's interests and activities are an open book on the Internet, free to be read by any hacker but also collected for analysis and promotional use by many Web marketers with today's sophisticated tracking software. With "spider" software, it's even possible to insert a special ad for one marketer when the customer is buying on a competitor's website. We're not recommending that you do this; however, it is possible unless the customer has taken steps to prevent it.

Customer relationship management (CRM) software, on the other hand, provides a legitimate approach to capturing consumers' behaviors on the Web and a variety of information about them. It has become an essential tool for tailoring a firm's marketing mix to individual segments, even "segments of one." Used correctly, CRM programs enable everyone in an organization—including sales staff in stores, employees in call centers, and self-service Web applications—to have access to the same information and can therefore present the customer with a single view of the company. In short, it allows companies to link customer interactions across all channels to improve the ability to tailor special products or deals to the needs of specific segments or individual customers.

In an industry that is growing at the rate of 60 percent a year, more than fifty CRM vendors sell sophisticated programs linking the "front door" or sales function of a firm with the "back room" or operations, increasingly linked to enterprise resource planning (ERP) software. Front-end CRM solutions can be as basic as sales force automation (SFA) using programs such as ACT, SalesLogic (both owned by Symantec), or Leadscape, solutions software from an innovative Detroit firm that links "leads" to lines of operations.

An example of CRM firms is SPSS, Inc., a firm that, since 1968, has been specializing in getting information on what consumers want and predicting what they will do. It analyzes and interprets consumer and operational data to provide strategies that will help clients better anticipate their customers' needs. Figure 4.4 highlights how it takes this information to minimize costs through better customer attraction, maximize profits through better cross-selling and up-selling (through vertical markets), and extend profits through better retention.

Among leading CRM providers in the banking industry is NCR, which has been serving up innovative technology solutions at least since the dawning of the cash register. CRM software for banks alerts them to significant changes in an individual customer's behavior, making it possible to segment customers and gear marketing programs based on these behaviors rather than direct it to a demographically based segment. For example, the software may monitor accumulation of large cash balances in a customer's account, which can be interpreted to mean the account holder may be contemplating a major purchase, say a house. This in turn signals the opportunity to present the customer with a special offer on a home mortgage. For Web visits, the NCR software measures things like "hover time," the amount of time people wait with their mouse poised over

**FIGURE 4.4 How SPSS Uses Customer Relationship Managenment (CRM)
and Data Mining to Address Customers' Needs**

CRM analytical solutions empower you to:	By mining your data to:
Gain a deeper understanding of your customers and maximize your marketing ROI	Identify customers who exhibit similar behaviors and identify who is most and least likely to purchase within specific affinity groups and model best customers in terms of purchase behaviors to identify events, attributes, and behaviors that occur together
Develop targeted marketing programs and offers that match customers' natural buying patterns and increase response	Predict who is the most likely to respond to different marketing programs
Recommend the mix of products, services, and offers that customers are most likely to buy, at the optimal time and increase sales	Model "market baskets"—which products and services are purchased together, or in sequence
Spend resources wisely by matching spending relative to expected lifetime value and maximize customer profitability	Model your customers in terms of lifetime value and profitability to your organization; identify risky and non-profitable customer groups
Develop targeted customer retention and loyalty programs and reduce customer defection	Model churn behaviors—look at customers who have left the organization and profile when an why they leave
Respect Web visitors' time and privacy by limiting the questions you ask them to those that are necessary to improve the relationship	Refine surveys and forms with knowledge of the factors that are important and asking the right questions at the right time
Develop new product and service features based on what your customers value, increase satisfaction, and extend your customer lifetime	Conduct customer satisfaction surveys and evaluate changes over time; combine with customer profiles to identify programs and specific actions to take

SOURCE: SPSS

a certain box or link on a Web page. Banks implementing CRM-based strategies report high response rates (often 25 to 30 percent) because they are usually more relevant to customers' needs. Some banks that have implemented the CRM approach report that as much as 80 percent of their new business is generated from these segments, even though the programs may represent only 20 percent of the bank's marketing efforts.

Can We Talk?

Once marketers know their customers, the next obvious step in creating a relationship is talking—or dating, as Seth Godin, author of *Permission Marketing,* likes to call it. Getting people's permission to contact them via e-mail to let them know about specials, extend tailored offers to them, or solicit their feedback (research) is about as "one to one" as you can get, especially if firms really use all available information about consumers. Then, targeting offers to specific consumers with specific behaviors is possible.

If targeting individuals with tailored offers via e-mail sounds too good to be true, it just might be—not because there are inherent faults in the delivery system but because of basic human behavior. E-mail rage graphically describes how some people respond to the barrage of e-mail messages that find them in the office, at home, and on the road. What started as a fun and efficient way to communicate is cascading into an avalanche of information overload, which has hit corporate America in epidemic proportions. American office workers send and receive over two hundred communications a day, the big culprit being e-mail. A report from *eMarketer* indicates Americans sent 3.4 trillion e-mails last year, more than 9.4 billion per day. That means everywhere in the world, people were receiving 9.4 billion e-mails per day. Wow! In an attempt to increase e-mail productivity and decrease e-mail rage, firms are examining policies to limit items not related to work and individuals are setting filters to prevent unwanted e-mail.

None of this is good news for e-mail marketers. What seems the perfect personalized solution for reaching wired consumers on an extremely personal level, e-mail marketing's rise in the ranks of advertising will be hindered by people's skepticism about the content and uneasiness about an unknown sender. But there are other shortcomings that can reduce the number of consumers who hit the delete key automatically. Opt-in programs are on the rise—getting consumers' permission to send them offers and notices increases the likelihood that they will actually open and respond to the offer. And as important as opt-in is the offer itself. Consumers are savvy—they know that their actions and preferences are being tracked and they expect to get offers that they find interesting and useful. CoolSavings. com and others have consumers visit their websites and pull the offers they find most useful. While this is one way to make sure consumers get only what they want, the company relies on the consumer to initiate contact—a big risk in a time-starved world. Other firms are beginning to market to organizations who want to offer their employees a "perk"—for example, a buy-one-get-one-free offer at a local restaurant. Selling to an organization, rather than e-mailing individual consumers, decreases the likelihood of offering consumers exactly what they want, but it does increase the possibility that the e-mail will be delivered, rather than filtered, and read by the individual.

IT'S A SEGMENTED WORLD

People are not all alike; they are different in many ways. Knowing consumers' age, income, likes, and dislikes is valuable information but represents just a snippet of the information about consumers that firms need to know if they want to get the attention and sales of increasingly elusive customers. While identifying the most profitable segments for a firm is one step, determining whether they can be reached online is the next. In spite of the value of the Sherwin-Williams approach and similar ones, it can never be the firm's primary communications strategy for the simple reason that the Internet itself is highly segmented. It's a medium that reaches only a portion of the total market.

One company that "gets it" is eBay. It put all of these segmentation, marketing, and communication concepts together and designed segment-based strategies. And it executes beautifully in cyberspace. It initially identified a large core market segment—consumers with similar needs and behaviors (wanting to buy, trade, or outright sell items in an informal format) that differ from those of the entire mass market. These are the people who can be found hosting and hunting garage sales and antiquing on weekends. This core segment is further honed based on specific activities they perform online—buy, sell, browse—and interests they have—collectibles, porcelain dolls, autographs. It also gets consumers' e-mail addresses and permission to talk to them about new auction items in their area of interest and the status of bids they may have submitted.

Computer programs run on the binary system, where by means of a 0 or 1 (on or off) networking path, computers carry out the functions we instruct them to perform. But in e-commerce, not all is black or white—there's still a lot of gray.

E-tailing works very well for a few segments for specific products and special situations. Find those customers and deliver the product well online and off-line, and you can expect substantial profits and enhanced shareholder value. Fail to understand the concept of market segmentation and what it takes to deliver a marketing mix that delights that segment, and e-commerce fails as surely, and probably more rapidly, than any other form of commerce.

CHAPTER 5

CREATING ONLINE AND OFF-LINE BRANDING STRATEGIES

THE MOST IMPORTANT asset on a firm's balance sheet is something that is not actually on the balance sheet—the firm's brand. It is the difference between a car and a Mercedes; a cup of coffee and a grande of Starbuck's house blend.

A brand creates an image and an identity for a product or a company that distinguishes it from a competitor; it makes a promise to consumers, telling them what they can expect and that they can trust the company. Thus, as traditional retailers and product manufacturers have learned, a product with a great ad or promotion will not evolve into a good brand unless the company has the systems to deliver (on time and in the right quality and quantity) and the discipline to follow up on ad claims. If you say a consumer can get a holiday gift delivered by December 23, you better deliver on the promise or risk the long-term reputation of your brand, not just with the one disappointed customer but with the dozens of others he or she tells. Several e-tailers, notably eToys.com and ToysRUs.com, learned this lesson the hard way, suffering the negative word-of-mouth backlash of angry, giftless consumers interviewed on December 26 by national television and print media.

The importance of brand was recognized in the early days of the Internet. It is not enough, however, to create a string of commercials and a flurry of random activity and expect to create a meaningful brand in the eyes of consumers. Branding involves strategy—creating a unified, coordinated, integrated set of promotion and marketing activities to send consumers messages about what makes the product unique and why they should try and trust it.

One reason we believe most bricks-and-mortar firms that successfully migrate to online commerce will eat the lunches of most pure-play dot-coms is the power of the existing, successful firms' brands. Established retailers can leverage their existing brands in an e-tail environment. For e-tailers, building a brand is the second-most important thing they can do—after getting the commerce side of the business functioning smoothly (which ultimately becomes an extremely important brand attribute).

As crucial as branding is to all businesses these days, it is even more important for e-tailers than it is for bricks-and-mortar retailers. Why? Because in the physical world, consumers can drive by storefronts and see retailers waiting with open doors, inviting them to come look at, hold, taste, feel, and compare products. On the Internet, consumers can cruise through cyberspace without distraction, and e-tailers can only hope these potential customers remember the name of their brand. With a glut of new, unknown, and for the most part untested dot-coms, brand is all that consumers can rely on to guide their purchasing decisions.

Mark Brier, former vice president of marketing at Amazon.com, agrees that competing on the Internet revolves around branding. "It [branding] is more important here than it is off-line," Brier says. "People have to remember your name and type it in. There are no Coke cans or Golden Arches to remind them." When neither you nor any of your friends have tried a brand, and there's no store that you can go to if something goes wrong, something has to earn your trust for you to make the purchase—brand is that trust-builder. How firms execute the promises of their brands determines whether they become trust-keepers.

The necessity for creating a "brand" on the Internet did not escape early e-commerce entrepreneurs. In a perverse and ironic twist of e-commerce history, it was in fact the need to establish a brand that caused many online firms to go broke. Desperate for hits to keep funds flowing, and often at the behest of financial advisers, dot-coms spent whatever it took to create brand awareness among large numbers of Internet consumers. Expenditures of $10 to $100 million on TV, newspaper, magazine, and other forms of advertising were commonplace in firms with minuscule revenues and nonexistent profits. The problem was lack of coordinated effort to extend the presence of the brand in people's minds beyond the thirty-second run-time of the commercial. Often there was even a lack of a coherent sense or strategy of what the brand really was. Additional forms of off-line activities, such as publicity, word-of-mouth, or promotions rarely accompanied the ads. Also, those consumers who did visit the site were disappointed with the experience once they arrived.

Priceline.com created a name-your-own-price service for tickets, hotels, and groceries, a service desired by many consumers. Though its advertising campaign was suspect to many, it did generate a great deal of awareness, publicity, word-of-mouth, and trial. To promote its brand, Priceline.com turned to William Shatner, the eternal Captain Kirk of the starship *Enterprise*.

Soon after the beginning of the new millennium, Shatner embarked on his new journey as Priceline.com's TV spokesperson. In a series of TV spots, he sang (if you can call it that) songs ranging from "We Gotta Get Out of This Place" and "Convoy" to the theme song from *Mahogany*. Shatner proved that sometimes things are so bad they're good—at least at creating awareness.

Priceline.com used star power to get people's attention and banked on word-of-mouth and free publicity (which ranged from *USA Today* to parodies on *Saturday Night Live*) to create awareness of its brand. While competitors spent millions on flashy, in-your-face ads that appealed primarily to Mountain Dew–guzzling twentysomethings, Priceline.com went after baby boomers. Shatner's fame among this target group and his appeal among former "Trekkies"-turned-"techies" ensured publicity and word-of-mouth. These people would more than likely relate to Shatner, appreciate his humor, have money to spend, and benefit from the product's features and services—savings on airline tickets, groceries, and a host of other products. After stints on *SNL*, even young people, some of whom knew him from his blockbuster movies, actually thought his self-deprecatory attempts at music were "kinda cool."

Did the branding strategy of Priceline.com actually work? From January 2000, when Shatner began the campaign, to June 2000, the number of unique customers at Priceline.com jumped from 3.8 to 5.3 million and the number of airline tickets sold jumped from 707,000 to 1.25 million. The company was ecstatic that the campaign brought Priceline's brand awareness among e-commerce companies to second place, surpassed only by Amazon.com. Similar to Mr. Whipple's "Don't squeeze the Charmin" ads, Priceline.com demonstrated that an ad doesn't have to be liked to be effective—it does, however, need to be remembered. It also exemplifies the need for a great product to satisfy customers once they visit the site. Advertising and brand may attract consumers, but great products and experiences turn them into loyal customers.

Few dot-coms have had the ability to get attention, publicity, and word-of-mouth and turn them into profitable sales as Priceline.com did because of the enormous edge that traditional retailers with reputable established brands have over online retailers. Advertising costs for promoting online ventures for the Targets of the world are minimal, consisting primarily of "stuffers" in mailings to existing consumers, in-store signs and handouts displaying their e-addresses, registering on search engines, and perhaps some online advertising purchased at bargain prices from AdOutlet.com or similar services. These retailers can ride on the coattails of their current brand and image, yet they find themselves in a sticky predicament because they have just as much to lose as they have to gain by going online. Just as Target can leverage the trust and image of its current brand to boost online recognition and initial sales, it can quickly destroy the trust it has taken years to establish with poor e-tail performance. True dot-coms face an uphill battle in creating brands in a few months that are equivalent to those it took retailers decades to mold. However, an even steeper hill awaits well-known brands that disappoint customers they've worked for years to cultivate.

But even this initial success may not guarantee survival. Whether the Priceline.com model will work in the long run remains to be seen. Skeptics point to its stock tumble (from $160 in March 1999 to around $1 by December 2000) and the demise of WebHouse Club, a major licensee that offered groceries and gasoline on the Priceline.com website. Believers point to the strength of the brand, Priceline's commitment to its core areas of travel, financial services, telecommunications, and auto businesses; its global initiatives; the company's "intensified focus on customer and supplier satisfaction"; and the company's new spokesperson, Sarah Jessica Parker. It is clear that Priceline.com, as well as any other e-based company that serves as a middleman to the consumer, will only survive as long as it is able to perform its business functions better than the company selling products through Priceline can perform them itself. Priceline's strong brand makes it a more valuable supply chain partner than many other firms that might otherwise be able to perform the same e-services functions, but if the airlines cut off its supply (unfilled seats), even a strong brand is not sufficient for survival.

USING MULTIPLE CHANNELS TO CREATE AN OCTOPUS BRAND

One of the most effective methods of catapulting a brand from fledgling to frequent favorite is with an octopus approach, whereby each tentacle represents a different method of reaching consumers. Yet all tentacles extend from the same creature (in this case the brand) and relay the same message. As is true for the beast of the sea, it is much easier for a brand to capture a consumer with several tentacles than it is with one—thus the theory behind multichannel branding strategy.

Multichannel branding strategy uses multiple media to communicate the promises and personality of the brand and multiple channels of distribution to deliver the promise. Borrowing a page from the Integrated Marketing Communication (IMC) strategy handbook, the goal is to provide a consistent brand promise to defined segments through a variety of communication channels. This strategy has helped retailers, manufacturers, and distributors alike, selling a range of products from bras to bearings, build customer loyalty and grow profits in the old economy.

Blended retailers can form consumers' perceptions of their brands with a combination of in-store experiences, advertising, websites, and word-of-mouth. When formulating brand strategies, dot-coms should remember: Activities off-line are just as important in creating awareness and extending brand personality as online activities—in fact, they are often more important. That's why www.AskJeeves.com sent ten to twenty gentlemen dressed as butlers to high-visibility areas of major cities to help people hail cabs and carry packages. It was all in the name of creating awareness, memorability, and a personality closely tied to the name and services of AskJeeves so that consumers wouldn't think of it as just another search engine.

The ability to evoke an emotional response—"Wow, that's the brand for me"—is critically important for online and off-line marketers. It provides a basis and a desire for a relationship between product and consumer. Good relationships produce brands that overcome price competition and build brand loyalty over time. Marketers must inject emotion to create effective brands. Emotion is usually more important than price—just ask Victoria's Secret and Manco.

Touched by Angels

Victoria's Secret is the world's worst-kept secret. The most recognized brand of lingerie around the globe, the brand is everywhere—popping up in the dialog of television sit-coms, in millions of mailboxes each year, and in fashion and business magazines. With humble beginnings as a small San Francisco chain, it was purchased by Limited Inc. and grew under its corporate umbrella in the company of The Limited, Express, Structure, Abercrombie & Fitch (which was later spun off), and Lane Bryant. It left

The Limited nest along with Bath & Body Works in October 1995 to form Intimate Brands, Inc. (IBI)—a parent company that creates and nurtures firms whose business is intimacy. Today, Victoria's Secret products are available through more than nine hundred lingerie and beauty stores, its glamorous catalog, and VictoriasSecret.com.

If anyone still questions whether or not sex sells, check out IBI's financial results—clearly, intimacy is "in." In 1999, IBI reached sales of $4.5 billion (and took 10.2 percent to the bottom line); it surged beyond $5 billion in 2000 and projected modest profit growth for 2001. Responsible in part for IBI's growth is its commitment to three major initiatives:

1. Maintaining brand dominance through constant innovation in products with integrated brand marketing

2. Increasing presence of brands via stores, catalog, e-commerce, and international distribution channels

3. Developing new business opportunities to maximize the strength to create new markets

Victoria's Secret's focus on dominating the sexy, glamorous bra category while building modern, "everyday" offerings is core to its brand development strategies. To support its branding zeal, the company spends about 6 percent of store sales on marketing, which in 1999 included forty-seven weeks of national television and over a hundred pages of national magazine advertising. Then throw in that "little marketing tool" called the catalog, of which 365 million are distributed annually, and the brand competes for a top spot among those most exposed.

IBI took a big step into the spotlight when it launched its famous Angels line of lingerie. Marketing executives fashioned an extensive campaign of TV advertising, appearances on late-night talk shows, and dramatic in-store signage and catalog layouts. At the center of it all were the Angels—supermodels clad in barely there underwear and feathered wings floating in clouds of intimacy. A barrage of media coverage closely followed the launch of the campaign. It was a breakthrough moment for marketing and branding at Victoria's Secret and everyone knew it.

Since its introduction, the Angels campaign has attracted consumer attention and the product line has kept customers coming back. Each year, the envelope of creativity and "wow" that is required to keep the brand abuzz gets bigger and harder to push. Who can forget the holiday catalog featuring Claudia Schiffer clad in a million-dollar, diamond-studded bra? (Believe it or not, the company actually received legitimate inquiries for buying the wearable gem.) Or the guest appearance of the same bra, with escort Tyra Banks, on *Late Night with David Letterman?* The superpowers of the supermodels to capture consumer interest and media coverage didn't go unnoticed by the company's marketing executives. They would go on to create their own slice of branding heaven that would reign supreme in the physical and virtual worlds of retailing.

Victoria's Secret is *the* prototypical example of how a blended retail model can operate profitably on the Web. The strategies behind it show what's required for dominance in the cutthroat world of new economy retailing.

Strategy number one: build the logistics and operations side of the business before you launch branding campaigns and attempt world-brand dominance. On an e-commerce ground-zero level, Victoria's Secret lays claim to a recognized and trusted brand, a loyal customer base, and existing retail and catalog operations, complete with a fulfillment and customer call center. Logistics, the Achilles' heel of most e-tailers, is the sword and shield that leads VictoriasSecret.com's charge to victory over lesser rivals on the e-tail battlefield.

Strategy number two: get the site right. In addition to mastering logistics, Victoria's Secret shines in the creative arenas. Thanks to significant partnerships and substantial investments, the Victoria's Secret website is unique as well as efficient. The goal, according to Jon Ricker, president and chief information officer of Limited Technology services, was to build a strong technology infrastructure to provide online customers with the best possible experience. Limited Technology developed proprietary technology and partnered with industry leaders such as Akamai Technologies, Inc. (content distribution), IBM Global Services (Web hosting and website traffic management), Microsoft Corp. (transactional shopping feature), RADWARE Inc. (website traffic management via global load balancing), Yahoo! Inc. (live Internet broadcasting/streaming video), and Resource (website evaluation and creative services) to construct the infrastructure required to carry out its integrated marketing communication program.

Strategy number three: create "an event" and involve your customers. The world's most glamorous, most widely followed fashion show made Internet history in Cannes, France, on May 18, 2000. Among those strutting their stuff were supermodels Tyra Banks, Heidi Klum, Stephanie Seymour, Daniela Pestova, Karen Mulder, Laetitia Casta, and others. Two million consumers, all seated around their computers, watched the single-largest live Web event in the history of the Internet. Of the millions who logged-on, 100,000 were international viewers scattered across more than

140 countries, extending the brand penetration to countries in which the only sales channel available for Victoria's Secret products is e-tailing. Millions more accessed the stored version of the fashion show in the ensuing weeks and months, bringing not only viewers but also sales to the site. In the days following the Web-cast, online sales reached peaks previously associated only with holiday shopping periods and topped only by the peak day of the Christmas shopping period.

Ed Razek, president of brand and creative services for Intimate Brands, explains, "The heightened awareness of Victoria's Secret through the fashion show and Webcast brought exposure of the brand to over 1.5 billion people worldwide. One in three people will have seen or heard of the event. That is worth hundreds of millions of dollars in brand exposure. The return is tremendous."

Strategy number four: give consumers a reason to visit your site. Give consumers worthwhile content and let them participate in something bigger than they can create on their own, and you'll begin to see what the Internet can be. Victoria's Secret does it with events, but they're not alone. We would argue that eBay does the same thing—every day. By nature of its business, eBay constantly changes its content, giving consumers an endless stream of new reasons to browse its site. It also gives consumers a sense of community, letting them connect with buyers, sellers, and treasures they would otherwise not be able to find, especially on their own. Though the Victoria's Secret strategy may be beyond your budget or outside the world of your product category, the theory holds true regardless of your firm's size or industry. What costs fledgling e-commerce firms tens to hundreds of millions of dollars to accomplish, costs Victoria's Secret approximately $10 million—and that's leveraged across nine hundred stores, millions of catalogs, and the website.

The true beauty of Victoria's Secret is its masterful integration of all business functions to create a supermodel among new economy business models. Generating profits since its inception, Victoria's Secret relies on its brand's established consumer appeal and current customer base, in addition to its catalog fulfillment operations, to follow through on the promises the brand makes to consumers.

At the heart of the model is brand. Leslie H. Wexner, chairman and CEO, says it best: "We've worked diligently to integrate every aspect of the brand, ensuring the sum of the whole is greater than its parts. Today, across every channel, stores, catalog, and e-commerce, there are tight brand standards with no shortcuts, no compromise. Products are launched at the same time, in the same way, with the same quality, at the same price. Same, same, same."

It's Just Ducky

Walk though most mass retailers throughout the United States and in select countries in South America, Canada, and Europe, and chances are you will see Manco products bearing the Duck or Henkel brand. Best known for its flagship product, Duck Tape (so named because of the way most people say duct), Manco also sells home insulation products; mailing and shipping supplies; office, school, and art supplies; shelf liners; and mats. The Avon, Ohio–based wholesaler and several formidable foes, including 3M and Rubbermaid, duke it out on retailers' shelves every day, vying for consumers' precious attention and loyalty. Though some competitors fight these product category wars one price-slashing battle at a time, Manco has taken another approach—branding.

Manco's branding strategy involves branding activities directed up and down the channel. What does that mean? In short, Manco recognizes that not only is it vital to build brand awareness and loyalty with consumers, it is imperative to build brand image and reputation with other current and potential supply chain members. Why? Because brand, in turn, builds trust—the cornerstone of any long-term strategic partnership. On a business-to-business basis, Manco's brand reflects its performance in the market. The company stands as one of America's exemplars in demand-oriented management and marketing. It breaks the mold of the traditional wholesaler by taking over functions often performed by the manufacturer or the retailer. It develops products that fit consumers' lifestyles and solves their consumption problems, employs first-rate logistics systems, and builds, promotes, and preserves brands that consumers want to buy.

Manco embarked on its branding journey in 1984 when it designed and adopted Manco T. Duck, a bright yellow, Disneyesque caricature that is as huggable as the Pillsbury Dough Boy is pokable. The goal was to create a caricature with character that embodied the heart and soul of the company. What they got was a whole lot more. Among consumers, the duck symbolizes a fun, imaginative, upbeat, down-to-earth personality and attitude. The duck appears on all product packaging, thereby uniting the Manco family of product names under its strong, protective wing. He also appears on special in-store displays, stars in a series of television and radio commercials, and makes guest appearances at store openings and community events.

Leave it to a company whose headquarters is located on a street named Just Imagine Drive to one-up most other brand-building efforts. Manco's Duck Tape Club reaches a core group of people who can't live without Duck Tape. Just click on www.ducktapeclub.com and you'll be connected to a world in which people make art, write stories, tell jokes, and sing songs about this wunderkind of tapes. You'll even learn a Duck Tape fact of the day—by the way, did you know a duck's quack has no echo? (Use this information as you need.) If this world appeals to you, register with the site and you'll be issued a passport that will make you privy to parts of Duck Tape World that only members can visit.

Sound a little quacky? Sure, but it works.

Think about the nature of Manco's products. Falling into the "last-mile delivery" trap discussed in Chapter 2, Manco knows it can't possibly deliver its products to individual homes cost effectively; no one can use enough Duck Tape or EasyLiner to justify the shipping costs. Consumers can pick these items up conveniently, inexpensively, and immediately at their local Wal-Mart or Ace Hardware store. That is why the "Where to Buy" button on the Manco site takes you to Web pages for Ace Hardware, Albertson's, Canadian Tire, Costco, CVS, The Home Depot, Kmart, Lowe's, Menards, OfficeMax, Rite Aid, SAM'S Club, Sears, Staples, Target, TruServ, Walgreens, Wal-Mart, Winn-Dixie, and Zellers. If the site has piqued your interest so much that you want a roll of Duck Tape *now*, you can type in "Duck Tape," as we did on the Wal-Mart link, and immediately order a roll. If you do the same, consider yourself warned: The shipping charges are actually greater than the cost of the tape!

In addition to all of its product-related information, Manco.com allows consumers and customers alike to learn more about the company. A click on Jack Kahl—whose fanaticism for the brand fueled its growth and dominance—imparts reading suggestions and thoughts for the day. Consumers can also learn about the community and charitable activities Manco supports, with S.I.F.E. (Students Interested in Free Enterprise) holding a spot near and dear to its corporate heart.

It's clear that Manco's intent is not to sell its products online; its intent is to sell products (lots of products) off-line. It wants to make sure that it has done whatever it could to guide your brand choice toward the Duck.

Therein lies the goal of Manco.com: to promote the Duck and the Henkel brand. But Manco is more than just Duck Tape. Although it would be difficult to generate that much fervor for each of its products, Manco effectively transfers the personality of the Duck from the tape to the entire array of products, helping customers learn they can trust products with the Duck on the package.

Another important brand strategy becomes apparent when you review the names of Manco's products. Each name communicates, as best it can, the benefit of the product. Examples include DraftBusters (a product to reduce drafts that enter through windows and under doors), CareMail (mailing and packing supplies to help consumers send parcels carefully and with care), and Correct-It (a correction tape designed to replace correction fluid).

Manco's story on how a distributor can use the Web to build brand equity and grow off-line sales is so rich with strategies and applications, it could become a book on its own. In fact, the brand and corporate culture are so heads and shoulders above most of its competitors that The Henkel Group, the world's number one consumer adhesives company, literally bought the book. Today, Manco is part of the Henkel Group. The union gives the $13 billion German-based juggernaut branding knowledge, marketing strategies, and business relationships and makes it possible for Manco T. Duck to go global.

THE ARCHITECTURE OF A BRAND

Building brands is a many-splendored process, as seen in the cases of Victoria's Secret and Manco. It involves the selection and promotion of a name, term, design, symbol, and other features that distinguish one seller's products from others. Careful detail goes into choosing a brand name (the part of the brand that can be spoken), a brand mark (not words, but rather a symbol or distinctive design), and a logo that becomes associated with the brand (Mickey Mouse and the Microsoft window come to mind). In an e-commerce age, selecting a logo that is readily visible on a computer desktop is a special consideration, as is the URL (domain name) describing where users can find the website of an organization.

These essential elements are the building blocks of a good brand, for both online and off-line organizations. Like any structure, however, it is not the materials used as building blocks that determine the strength of the brand so much as the skill of the architect and the builder to integrate the blocks to create strength, longevity, and presence. The primary process involved in developing a brand can be reduced to three basic steps:

1. Define precisely the core segments for whom the product is designed.
2. Understand exactly the attributes those segments expect from the product (including the priority or weights they attach to each attribute).
3. Deliver those attributes (benefits) consistently and reliably throughout all points of contact with consumers.

Regardless of whether you are an e-only firm, a manufacturer, distributor, or retailer, these steps guide the brand-building and brand-preservation process. When beginning the process, the first essential question to be answered by all members of the marketing team is "What should the brand look like in the eyes and minds of consumers?" Further, marketers must know "What activities does the company need to undertake once the brand is established?" For answers, we turn to the letter *P* for inspiration; all elements of brand begin with that letter. Promise, personality, and protection are the attributes that radiate from the brand to the consumer. The other side of brand is the activities firms undertake to create a successful brand in the marketplace—promote, protect, peddle, and preserve the brand. When branding is done well on all of these levels, yet another *P* results—profits.

Promise

A brand is a promise. It tells consumers what you promise to do for them. That's why every organization, whether online or off-line, should start its brand development process by answering the question "We promise to deliver *what* to you?" Victoria's Secret promises consumers that they will get quality fashions that make them (or recipients) feel and look good. It goes on to promise that they will receive what they order in a reasonable time, and if for some reason they are not satisfied, consumers can return items and receive refunds (both in stores and through catalog and online outlets).

For the brand to connect with consumers, it needs to promise people in core market segments that the attributes (or benefits) they want most will be delivered by the product they buy—not just the first time but every time. And if for any reason customers don't get what they expect, the brand assures them that the seller will try to correct the situation and deliver the desired benefit in the future. When customers perceive this to be true for a brand, customer loyalty and willingness to pay a price premium generates profits and long-term brand equity.

Brands are shorthand for the promises a company makes to consumers when it sells its products. If there were a pledge companies made to consumers through their brands, it would contain the following promises:

- A promise that you will like the product and you will like the brand
- A promise that we will live up to the "hype"
- A promise that you will be satisfied with your choice

- A promise that we will be there if something goes wrong
- A promise that we will fix what goes wrong
- A promise that you can trust us to keep the promises that we make

On the Internet, customers deal with unknown organizations in distant and unknown locations, which to most consumers don't feel real. That makes it difficult for consumers to know whether sellers will keep their promises or even be there in the future. Migrating consumers to online sites for bricks-and-mortar firms such as Charles Schwab, BankOne, and Wal-Mart is easier than getting them to trust e-only dot-coms. When there's a physical location, consumers who don't get their orders, receive the wrong orders, or are just plain unhappy can visit the store of a traditional retailer and pound on the manager's desk until they get some satisfaction! But why buy from Wingspan.com (Banc One's online banking entity) when you can buy from BankOne.com? When customers buy from retailers such as Bank One, Target, Sears, or a local firm that has served the community for years, consumers conclude—and rightfully so—that the firm has a proven track record and will most likely keep the brand's promise. Only experience (which takes time) and significant marketing dollars can overcome the natural advantages that bricks-and-mortar firms carry to the clicks-and-order environment.

Promise-keeping by a brand builder should occur with the fervor of a religious movement, making sure every feature, package, communication, price point, and policy consistently "keeps the promise" of the brand. Look at many of the failed dot-com firms and you'll see more fervor for technology, for being "first mover," or for launching the IPO than for understanding the benefits desired by core segment customers and how to deliver them profitably under the umbrella of a brand. Often, they totally confuse awareness of the brand name with its image or reputation for consistent delivery of desired attributes to key market targets.

In its purest form, a brand is a promise from companies to consumers. To ensure long-term success of the brand, that promise must be communicated and fulfilled with costs low enough to be profitable. Then, and only then, does a firm have brand equity.

Personality

In addition to a promise, a brand embodies the personality of a firm or a product. To analyze a brand, imagine it has human characteristics that allow it to talk to you. When it speaks, is it serious and status-oriented or is it fun and unpretentious? Ditzy or dignified? Considerate or profane?

Cautious or irreverent? The Victoria's Secret brand emotes a sexy, feminine, sophisticated, and romantic personality that invites consumers to feel glamorous by wearing its lingerie and clothes.

Customers use these terms every day to describe the products, brands, firms, and websites they evaluate and eventually choose. Regardless of what marketers intend the personality of a brand to be, what counts is what consumers perceive the personality to be—a case of "perception is reality."

Pets.com relied on a suite of off-line activities to developing brand personality by introducing the world to a cast-off sock, outfitted with dog ears, a puppy face, and a microphone. When you think of the Pets.com sock puppet, what do you feel? Some people smile, some laugh, others shake their heads wondering how a sock with an attitude could become so popular so quickly. Regardless of whether you like the brash little guy or not, consumers responded to the brand with online fan mail and website hits, and the media responded with blasts of publicity. The sassy sock puppet gained so much attention that he appeared on television shows, did interviews on *Good Morning America,* and eventually sold his soul to the licensing-devil so that fans, of the human or canine type, could own their own sock-puppet toys.

The sock puppet became an icon of the e-tail heyday. As such, he did his best—people talked about him, sang his praises, and recognized him on numerous brand recognition research questionnaires. But in the world of commerce, that is not enough. Pets.com created an icon but failed to communicate the core strengths of the company as a one-stop, online source for pet products and pet-related questions. Ultimately, he was failed by the inherent flaws of the Pets.com business model and operating system—inefficient distribution systems, low margins, limited consumer orders—flaws too damaging for even the mightiest of sock puppets to overcome. With its stock falling from $8 per share in January 2000 to $.60 by August, its fate was sealed when PETsMART bought the Pets.com URL and made the original company a piece of e-tail history.

Protection

In addition to promise and personality, a brand provides protection for consumers and companies alike. For consumers, a brand assures that the product they are buying was made or marketed by the firm representing the brand. If another firm uses a name, design, or trade dress that is likely to confuse consumers or cause degradation of a firm's brand, legal remedies exist.

Internet law is evolving rapidly on many subjects, including the use of URLs or domain names that would cause confusion with existing brand names. Even if "Koke" were available and you registered it, you could expect a letter from Coke's attorneys if you tried to use it. Hence, the barrage of meaningless names that Internet start-ups invented and around which they tried to create a promise and personality.

The real protection a good brand provides is insularity from direct price and product comparison with competitors. A consumer who wants to buy an SUV has many choices from all the major auto manufacturers. An Isuzu Trooper and Subaru Outback will both fulfill the promise of getting people to their destination just as well as a Mercedes, BMW, or Lincoln Navigator, and consumers can easily discover which costs more or less than the others. Brand protects each from direct price comparison, even when the price is identical. When the functional attributes are nearly identical, a brand protects against direct comparison, as in the case of the Ford Expedition and the Lincoln Navigator.

Position the Brand

When consumers are asked to describe your brand, what do you want them to say and which adjectives should roll from their tongues? Low price or fair value? Cutting-edge or with-the-times? The Victoria's Secret brand is aspirational but attainable—positioned as affordable luxuries on which women can splurge without overwhelming economic guilt.

Consumers position brands in their minds by comparing them to products that are "similar," creating a mental podium upon which various brands stand on the gold, silver, or bronze platform. To increase the likelihood that a brand will take the gold in its category, marketers must first define the attributes that are most important to consumers (as described in the alternative evaluation stage of the consumer decision-making process) for that particular product. Whether it is reliability, dependability, convenience, status, entertainment, return policies, or price that sways brand choice, marketers have to determine how their brand should be positioned in each attribute. A brand's position highlights for consumers those attributes that perform better than its competitors. If you don't know which attributes are the most important, invest in the marketing research to identify them.

Promote the Brand

Another crucial step in creating a brand is promoting it. Regardless of what the promotional mix includes, each element must reach consumers with a consistent look, feel, and message, so consumers don't get confused and marketers get greater return on their individual promotion activities. Victoria's Secret has done this by creating consistency among its stores, catalog, website, advertising, fashion show, and in-store displays.

Beyond simple awareness of a brand, it's even more difficult to communicate the specific attributes on which the brand excels. Communicating specific benefits—making them stand out and say "this is why you should buy me"—is critically important in influencing customers to choose one brand over others. Building the consistency of a brand's attributes to ensure that the promise is communicated effectively is part of what we describe as the brand's personality.

Preserve the Brand

Once a brand is created, it must be preserved. Never take for granted that consumers will remember you and never assume that just because they've been loyal in the past they won't stray in the future. As a marketer you need to decide: Do you want to be a Cracker Jack or a Mickey Mouse? Victoria's Secret chooses to go the Mickey route by investing in promotions, creating excitement and new events for the brand, enhancing customer service, and improving its logistics and fulfillment systems. Not only does keeping up with the Mickeys involve continuous marketing and promotional support, it involves operating the company in a way that is consistent with the brand of the product and firm.

For example, many first mover dot-coms promoted price as their primary advantage over traditional retailing channels, and thus, their brands (and eventually e-tailing in general) became positioned as the "low price" alternative—a bargain bonanza, if you will. Premium brands and retailers often work years and spend hundreds of millions of dollars to create top-quality positioning in the minds of consumers, but what happens when they begin selling in the price-slashing world of e-tail?

MarthaStewart.com and Nordstrom.com might find it challenging to change consumers' expectations and convince them to pay the same premium prices online that they would at other retail channels. But one of the most damaging things these firms could do to their brands would be to sell their merchandise Amazon-style—everything at discounted prices so it "moves" through the system. If a brand's positioning doesn't match the realities of Internet selling, and marketers have to sacrifice brand position to get e-sales, maybe that brand shouldn't be selling on the Web. Online promotion might be the strategy most consistent with that particular brand.

Preservation of the brand is key.

If you've ever been to a big city, chances are you've been approached by a guy willing to make you a great deal on a Rolex—for $35 you can walk away with the style of your choice and the status of the brand. After three such encounters on a recent trip to New York, we figured out how to stop this sales tactic quickly; just ask the guy if he's an authorized Rolex distributor. Guaranteed, he won't stay around long. With the arrival of the Internet, however, it is possible to put one of those "unauthorized distributors" into the home of every person who has a computer, making it difficult to preserve the brand it took years to create.

Manufacturers of branded products, especially those in luxury categories, depend on authorized distributors and dealers to provide the services necessary to command a premium price. Those services include maintaining a staff knowledgeable about the products, displaying the products in approved ways, and owning a substantial (and expensive) inventory, sometimes including parts needed for repairs. Customers expect the dealer and the manufacturer to accept returns if there is a problem, and that requires longevity of relationship built on trust and reliability. It also usually involves pricing agreements between manufacturers and distributors that prevent the price of the branded product from falling to a commodity price.

Peddle the Brand

Closely related to preservation of the brand is selection of the best distribution channel, one that fits the brand's promises and personality best. Search far and wide and you'd be hard-pressed to find a firm that thinks it shouldn't be selling online. But for some firms, it is not the best strategy. In fact, selling well-known brands on the Internet today is at a standoff.

Let's return for a moment to the luxury brands market. Rolex is not alone in its online practice of promoting the brand but forgoing online sales. Go to similar sites and chances are you'll find an active market in used products (such as "estate" jewelry), but a pretty limited selection of new branded products for sale. These websites are designed to show off products and refer buyers to a local retailer to make the purchase. On the Rolex manufacturer's site, for example, we found the firm's "legal notice" that states that "Genuine Rolex products are sold through Official Rolex jewelers and are not available on the Internet."

Direct-to-consumer sales would let manufacturers keep prices at the list level, but you can imagine the reactions of major retailers to manufacturers' requests to bypass them. If manufacturers want to bite the bullet and sell online exclusively, they risk losing, on average, 95 percent of their current sales (the proportion that comes from retail stores). How does that uphold the direct-to-consumer model that has been held up as the e-commerce poster child?

Strong brands of other consumer goods also face significant risks if their manufacturers attempt direct sales on the Internet. Manufacturers run the very real risk of losing their core distribution—reputable, high-volume retailers, from Tiffany's to Home Depot, that account for most of their sales today and in the foreseeable future. Retailers also run a high risk of eroding margins and deteriorating brand image if the manufacturer sells to e-tailers likely to discount merchandise on websites. The result is that power brands, especially those that depend upon selective distribution outlets, are not readily available online, except perhaps for specific items the retailer doesn't want to carry. Even retailers who carry top-quality brands don't make their top sellers available on the Internet; that outlet is better for overruns, merchandise that didn't sell last year, and noncore merchandise that retailers don't want to stock. In short, it's the kind of stuff manufacturers previously sold through "factory outlets" or, historically, sent to tourist-laden Duty Free ports in the Caribbean Islands.

So who will make the next move in the online sales game? Manufacturers could but won't if it means they risk losing their core retailers. Retailers might like to sell prestige brands online, but not at the risk of the substantial price erosion, common to online selling today, that would jeopardize store margins. In some cases, trade associations representing retailers, manufacturers, or wholesalers will cooperate and develop an e-commerce site for an industry, but in other cases it will be organizations that profit by protecting the brands of all members of the demand chain.

Imagine a consumer portal that links sites between manufacturers and retailers. A trip to a consumer market portal would be similar to a trip to an expansive shopping mall. The shopping process can begin with the desire to shop for a specific brand or the desire to shop a specific retailer. Consumers would search and browse a particular brand, most likely on that brand's own site. But when consumers click on the magic "buy button," they are routed to the site of a local retailer to complete the purchase. Consumers have the combined advantages of ordering online and buying from a physical retailer, such as local service, local reputation in case of a problem, and the ability to go somewhere to talk to a real person. It also allows smaller retailers to set up shop on the Internet's Main Street.

We believe these sites will be developed cooperatively by various demand-chain partners to allow manufacturers to build and protect their brands globally while maintaining and building the strength of local retailers. Cutting out retailers or distributors, unless they believe the Web will become the majority of their sales, is too risky. Referring Web customers to existing bricks-and-mortar dealers leverages the advantages of the existing market as well as builds sales to consumers who buy on the Web. In turn, the process builds brand equity for all demand-chain partners.

If You Can't Build a Brand, Buy One

If developing an octopus brand is likely to take longer than you can wait to penetrate the market, perhaps buying a brand would be more efficient. That's what Proffitt's, the profitable Birmingham, Alabama–based bricks-and-mortar retailer did as it began developing a long-term strategy for its online brand.

The company and its visionary CEO, R. Brad Martin, recognized the potential of e-commerce, but also recognized that it would take time to gain widespread acceptance. "We were not willing to slap something together just to meet the timing of the Internet," he says. "That could have potentially negative effects on our brand. We approached this as an extension of our brand and a real, live business, not some Internet craze."

He also recognized that the Proffitt's brand, although well known and respected in southeastern states, was relatively unknown in the rest of the nation. What it needed was a well-known brand, one that already delivered on the promised attributes of quality and service for luxury goods, and one that had the margins needed to make online retailing successful. The brand would ideally enter consumers' minds in multiple ways, including stores in fashion centers, a successful catalog, and a favorable image in glamour magazines and newspapers required to develop a "fashion" personality. The brand should also have global recognition, since the Internet would increasingly attract global consumers.

Proffitt's found the answer to its branding prayers in 1998 when it bought Saks Fifth Avenue. The department store chain had a brand respected worldwide, a healthy dose of "Saks" appeal, and declining profits. Why would a profitable Southern department store chain buy a troubled New York–based chain and take the name for its own? Brad Martin explained in an interview for *Corporate Board Director*: "Implicit in the 1998 acquisition was the idea that we could begin the development of an online retail strategy with a huge competitive advantage—that is a great national brand with enormous international potential." Today, the online business operates as Saks Direct, which includes the catalog business (helpful in e-fulfillment) as well as saksfifthavenue.com.

In June 2001, shareholders will be asked to vote to spin off Saks

Direct, including the Saks stores, to realize more value for shareholders. Martin will go with the Saks spinoff, indicating apparently that he believes his strategy made the brand-rich acquiree more attractive than the acquirer.

BRANDING STRATEGIES THAT CREATE VALUE FOR CUSTOMERS

Branding strategies are not exclusive to the retail world; in fact, they are increasing in importance in the B-to-B world. Brands are also not the exclusive responsibility of the manufacturer or the retailer; wholesalers can increase their value in the supply channel by taking on branding activities. Well-positioned brands lead to higher profits because they take a product out of the commodity category (where buyers make decisions mostly on price) and position them in a preferred category (where decisions are made more on quality, aesthetics, and other attributes as subjective as image). Without a brand, price rises or falls, as everyone who survived Economics 101 knows, to a level that matches supply with demand. At that price level, the only firms that make above-average profits are those with below-average costs.

From Selling Parts to Imparting Knowledge

What's more glamorous than lingerie and bras? How about ball bearings and power transmission belts? OK, maybe not, but don't tell the management team of Applied Industrial Technologies (AIT); they are pretty passionate about bearings, drive systems, industrial rubber, fluid power, linear technologies, and the other 2 million related items they offer for sale. An industrial distributor with sales over $1.5 billion, AIT serves thousands of customers, ranging in size from local machine and "job" shops and agribusinesses (don't call them "farmers" anymore) to global enterprises of the Procter & Gamble and Weyerhauser size. Applied's customers operate manufacturing plants, warehouses, mines, fleets of trucks and construction equipment, paper mills, and just about any other type of business you can imagine.

You might think Applied sells parts, and that's not incorrect, but the folks at AIT see their business differently. They see their mission and brand promise as "selling uptime." The difference results in brand equity rather than commodity status.

By virtue of AIT's business definition, brand plays an important role in the company's performance in the B-to-B arena. Most competitors focus their brand attributes on the physical products and parts they sell. Conversely, AIT built its brand around the promises of customer care, product information, and vendor knowledge. Usually that knowledge involves far more than the parts and materials (commodities) side of the business; it involves knowing customers' industries, understanding which AIT services and products each customer values the most, and knowing how these parts solve buyer's problems. These pieces of knowledge make up the brand's ultimate promise: to apply industrial technology and knowledge of the customer's operations to find solutions that produce documented value added (DVA). Further, AIT promises that if something goes wrong, it will minimize a client's downtime and maximize its uptime.

Applied has evolved its brand over the company's seventy-five-year lifespan, emerging from a sea of competitors as one of the two largest distributors of its kind in North America. The company changed its name from Bearings, Inc. (which reflected its origins and largest product line) to AIT as the company expanded its scope and brand. It envisioned becoming more than a "parts" company, recognizing that knowledge often meant the difference between profit and loss and between success and failure for industrial manufacturing and distribution firms. Thus, it developed certain services and capitalized on others. A new service focuses on customers who want to expand their businesses but aren't sure what equipment they need; AIT will provide consulting services to make equipment recommendations and configure and design the operation. It also works with customers to identify exactly which parts they need in order to get their equipment up and running; so, AIT doesn't just take orders for part numbers, it helps customers ask for the right parts. With its extensive knowledge, AIT also protects and preserves the brands of its world-famous vendors, including Timken, SKF, Goodyear, Emerson, and Martin Sprockets. In essence, Applied delivers "technology and parts" solutions for U.S. paper plants, automotive factories, and mobile power and transmission units (such as trucks and railroads) as well as Canadian potash and uranium mines.

Applied employs numerous "normal techniques" to promote and preserve its brand—trade advertising, a distinctive and modern corporate logo, literature that both provides information and develops image, and plenty of logo apparel for both customers and staff. The company supplements these branding activities with highly regarded training programs for its employees and customers. Key to the relationship between customers and the brand are Applied's four hundred local service centers, where customers connect with the AIT brand. It is through these "stores" and their managers that customers usually place orders, pick up or schedule deliveries for supplies, and communicate with the company. Requested items that are not in stock can be quickly delivered from one of the nine regional distribution centers to the service center or directly to the customer.

So what does a firm like this do with the Internet?

The company studied potential applications of the Internet: Would it reach a significant number of new customers? Would current customers be served more efficiently online? It also carefully examined what it would take to migrate its current offerings onto a website, keep the same part numbers and extensive product information customers need to have available, and utilize its current database and information technology system.

If its mission had been to deliver online the same high level of customer service it delivered off-line and maintain its brand equity, then Applied-Access.com's mission is accomplished. The online system integrates with its extensive bricks-and-mortar distribution and branch facilities to ensure quick deliveries to customers. Consumers can have items shipped to their local service centers if they want to maintain these relationships, or they can be shipped via UPS direct to their offices. Customers can also obtain online the information about supplies and parts they previously obtained off-line. Applied knew its greatest assets were product knowledge and great service personnel; it was determined not to sacrifice brand promises in its move to the Internet.

Initially, Applied-Access.com was modestly successful. The strength of the model at the time was its "back end"—all the activities that occurred after the consumer hit the send button. The order processing, distribution, and delivery functions operated status quo. The difference between the traditional AIT model and its Internet cousin was the "front end," giving its customers an additional, convenient way to access product knowledge and opening the door for new customers.

The success of Applied-Access.com increased dramatically when it added a sales force dedicated to e-commerce. Using this team of "E-commerce Champions" to visit customers and show them how to find and order the parts they needed online boosted e-transactions. The one-on-one, human-touch sales approach, common in the world of B-to-B sales, could not be replaced. It puts a human face on a large company, gives customers someone to call, and provides assurance that someone on the "inside" is on their side.

This genre of sales approach works for selling e-commerce services to B-to-B organizations as well. Applied was pleasantly surprised by the loyalty of its customers to their local service centers. Even those who migrated ordering to the Internet wanted to pick up their items at the center; furthermore, they wanted to make sure the local center got "credit" for the sale. Customers made it clear that they didn't want anything to jeopardize the support services they received from the centers.

As reports from service center staff and the E-commerce Champions team filtered back to the company, it became apparent that while many of the customers liked being able to order from a comprehensive, single-source product guide, they didn't have computers in the plants where problems usually occur. So Applied developed a catalog business. This decision was supported by a basic segmentation analysis of Applied's customers and vast array of products. In addition to the technically complex and knowledge-intensive products it offers, AIT sells many general supply items and maintenance tools that can be used by any business (or do-it-yourselfer, for that matter). For these products, Applied created Maintenance America—a Victoria's Secret equivalent for guys who love tools, hardware, and maintenance supplies. The new, consumer-friendly Maintenance America brand lets Applied reach a consumer audience without jeopardizing the AIT B-to-B name. It also allows firms to order products any way they like—via phone, service center, fax, or computer.

Applied forged ahead further and identified another segment of customers to target with an AIT brand extension. Consequently, it developed Farmwarehouse.com for agricultural segments that have difficulty finding locally the heavy-duty drive shafts, bearings, and other products needed to maintain the massive agricultural equipment found on five-thousand-acre farms. This Web-based business supplies products to agricultural buyers in a wide geographic area, shipped from its strategically located distribution center in Kansas City or picked up, perhaps, from any one of Applied's nationwide system of branches and service centers.

One final overriding branding issue remains. When a firm develops new brands to reach new segments of customers, which brand attributes and promises will transfer from the existing brand to the new ones? In other words, which core attributes expressed in the AIT brand will extend to Applied-Access.com, Maintenance America, and Farmwarehouse.com? And conversely, which brand attributes, promises, or benefits will be unique to each of these? For AIT, the brand attributes are product knowledge and immediate solutions to solve customers' problems. The brand promise is that if the customer can describe the problem, AIT can probably solve it.

AIT provides several lessons regarding e-commerce strategy. First, knowledge can help build a brand and differentiate a brand from a commodity. This involves using knowledge about customers to create tailored solutions and services and providing information to customers to help them make better purchase decisions. Second, brand promises made off-line should also be made online in order to build brand equity and maintain brand identity. Third, the development of an online business may lead to additional channel strategies, reaching new customers, or offering new benefits to existing customers.

James T. Hopper, Applied's CIO, summarizes the role of a distributor in an online world: "Distributors like Applied are built on a foundation of highly efficient logistics. We can deliver more than 1.5 million times to tens of thousands of customer locations every day. Local service, product knowledge, and up-close familiarity with a customer's unique operations support those transactions. E-commerce doesn't change that." He adds, "It builds a stronger bond between Applied and the customer by linking our systems electronically. This technology adds a whole new dimension to the distributor/customer relationship."

GUIDELINES FOR BUILDING STRONG BRANDS

The Internet is a fascinating tool that is only effective if it is used properly. Some firms will find that selling online works for them; others won't. Regardless, branding online works for nearly everyone, but it is not a one-size-fits-all approach. Individual firms will have to determine which strategies work best for them, picking and choosing from some of the strategies discussed in this chapter. Among the lessons learned are:

- Brand promises made off-line should be met online as well—consumers expect consistency.
- Brand personality must carry over between channels so consumers hear one voice.
- Expanding into new sales and information channels can extend the brand to new customers and offer new brand benefits to existing customers.
- Channels must be consistent with the brand position and promises.
- Do not promote the brand until the operations systems work well—breaking a promise is the quickest way to lose a customer.
- If personal interaction is an important part of off-line branding and selling, formulate strategies to incorporate a human touch in other ways.

- Leverage off- and online knowledge and information capabilities to move from commodity position to brand.

- Forgo any activity or sales channel if it is not consistent with your brand strategy—*don't sacrifice the brand.*

We think Mr. Wexner, Intimate Brand's branding mastermind, says it best: "Today we think of ourselves as a 360-degree brand. One position. One voice. Anytime. Anyplace. Worldwide. Period. The end."

CHAPTER 6

STICKY EYEBALLS AND HAPPY FEET: STRATEGIES FOR CREATING CUSTOMER SATISFACTION

BUILD A WEBSITE and they will come" seemed to be the philosophy of many online retail pioneers. While this field-of-dreams approach might have worked for a select few first movers, it doesn't fly today. For every eBay, there are millions of rookie e-tailers and entrepreneurs around the world building cool sites and hoping to attract customers. But before their cool sites become centers for commerce, they have to attract customers. E-tailers classify these consumer-connections as "eyeballs"—how many eyes see their site—while traditional retailers talk about traffic—how many feet walk through their stores. The acid test for both sorts of retailers is wallets—how many customers actually plunk down hard-earned money and buy something.

Longevity in the overcrowded retail sector depends on how good a particular company is at turning consumers into customers—people who become accustomed to coming into your store or space and making their purchases. How often they patronize one retailer over another (not because they have to but because they want to) is the definition of customer loyalty. Converting shoppers into loyal customers in e-commerce means turning eyeballs into sticky eyeballs; in traditional retail it means turning foot-traffic into happy feet. For the almighty blended retailer it means both.

How can retailers work their own magic in creating sites and stores in which consumers will want to spend time and money? After years of spending precious time and marketing dollars on attracting new shoppers to their stores, retailers championed the notion of focusing on satisfying customers and creating a reason for them to come back. Many of the principles of old-fashioned customer service hold true today, and many can be applied to the Web. Few retailers who thought customer satisfaction was important then could have predicted its magnitude today.

Why the resurgence? What else is there? Brand, price, shopping experience, individual human characteristics, and distribution ultimately blend together to create customer satisfaction and the increased likelihood of repeat purchases. In today's competitive marketplace, consumers have umpteen retailers and shopping methods to choose from, but few give reasons substantial enough to keep them coming back. Sure, inertia may cause consumers to go to one store more often than another, perhaps because it's convenient. But any suitor who captures their attention can easily woo them, including Internet alternatives that break the geographic proximity barrier and make it easier to find and buy unique or other specialty items. Retailers have the advantage of being able to offer consumers services—such as easy returns, order pickup, face-to-face personal assistance, and social interaction—that e-tailers can't.

Understanding what satisfies customers requires analysis of what causes customers to defect. First-mover advantage, all the rage in e-circles, can capture consumers' attention and eyeballs, but who cares who gets consumers first if they're unhappy with the experience. Flawed and complicated systems, bad delivery experiences, and overall poor customer service will devastate any customer-retailer relationship and wipe out any first-mover advantage.

In these competitive times, some retailers are cruising on easy street, others sit bumper-to-bumper on the information superhighway, and some are sweating it out on the highway to e-tail hell. Customer satisfaction, from sticky eyeballs to happy feet, will determine your road to the future.

COLD FEET

Leon loved to hunt, but he grew tired of coming home with wet, sore feet from the heavy woodsman's boots of his day. So tired, in fact, that he invented a new kind of boot, combining lightweight leather tops with waterproof rubber bottoms. The practical advantages of his quirky new footgear appealed to his fellow sportsmen so much that he soon sold a hundred pairs through the mail. Unfortunately, ninety pairs were sent back when the stitching gave way, but Leon had guaranteed satisfaction or their money back. True to his word, he refunded his customers' money and started over with an improved boot. The year was 1912.

Today, you'll find Leon's company on the Web selling the very boots he created ninety years ago. In 2000, his company was selected by independent evaluators as one of the best in e-commerce and awarded gold stars for its visual presentation, customer responsiveness, and customer satisfaction. Reminiscent of the guarantee he made his fellow sportsmen, his website devotes an entire Web page to its satisfaction policy, which states: "Our products are guaranteed to give 100% satisfaction in every way. Return anything purchased from us at any time if it proves otherwise. We will replace it, refund your purchase price or credit your credit card. We do not want you to have anything from us that is not completely satisfactory."

Leon couldn't have said it better himself. By the way, have you guessed Leon Leonwood's last name yet? It's Bean. Most people called him L.L. for short, and today everyone knows Leon's company as L.L. Bean.

L.L. Bean is a great example of how a historical, traditional retailer can successfully evolve from the old economy to the new economy without abandoning the strategies that made it great in the past. There are many morals to the L.L. Bean story, but none so poignant as the company's visionary, driving force: delivering customer satisfaction.

Recognizing the importance of delivering on brand promises and avoiding customer disappointment, the company developed business processes and technologies to prevent things from going wrong. When consumers place an order they know instantly whether merchandise is in stock and when it's coming because e-mail confirmations assure them that their orders have gone through. But if something does go wrong, it's not enough to just return customers' money. Leon's firm has been rated "exceptional" in customer interaction. Its toll-free call center is open twenty-four hours a day, every day of the year, and is staffed by real people with real knowledge who listen to your problems and answer your questions. Who would you trust most to stand behind a 100 percent guarantee, a firm in business nearly a year or one in business for nearly a century?

Like many of the evolving success stories in e-commerce, L.L. Bean is a multichannel retailer, effectively combining clicks and bricks. Known originally as a catalog retailer and more recently for its online excellence, it also operates lots of bricks-and-mortar, from stores in the United States and Japan to warehouses, a call center, and logistics facilities that allow it to sell and ship around the world.

The Bean Boot that originated on a cobbler's bench in Freeport, Maine, is now produced, along with 300 other items, from a 130,000-square-foot state-of-the-art manufacturing facility housed in nearby Brunswick. Known for its modern, safe, and efficient methods of producing handcrafted products, the factory and its 450 employees win quality awards and still maintain a "doing more with less" motto.

An important part of its physical presence—and a major contributor to its "brand"—is its flagship store in Freeport. Consumers hike through the store to see, touch, and try merchandise, learn to fish in an indoor trout pond, traverse an in-store climbing rock, and hunt for special sales on catalog overstocks. Children visiting the Kids Learning Center will discover an indoor waterfall, a trout pond, and a kid-sized climbing wall. No doubt the experience ensures that they're on the road to becoming satisfied customers of the future. This adventure-in-a-store is open twenty-four hours a day, every day of the year—the front doors don't even have locks! It attracts 3.5 million visitors each year; many often incorporate a store visit into their vacation plans, some with the help of the L.L. Bean website, which offers a 288-page guide of area attractions from the Maine Tourism Agency. When these customers go home and want to order L.L. Bean, it is important that some of the brand personality transfer over to the website, which now lets customers around the world partake in the L.L. Bean experience without leaving home.

Many of L.L. Bean's products lend themselves well to online sales, since consumers can't readily find unique products that make outdoor living more bearable and comfortable. For years, they've turned to L.L. Bean for everything from warm flannel shirts with ample pockets and tightly woven, cold-resistant long johns to water- and weatherproof boots and tents that are easy to carry and assemble. And some customers have favorite items that they buy over and over. If someone needs to buy a man's shirt, blue, button-down, 16 neck and 34 sleeve, inventory replenishment is made easy. The standard L.L. Bean shirt will always fit the same way, with no style or dimension changes made to a particular size.

The company understands the passions of its customers and translates them into its own passions for merchandising, information technology, and logistics. And passion also filters into the image of the brand. You'd have to agree, L.L. Bean is more than a brand; it's a lifestyle. Let's face it, not all of us need the survival qualities built into these famous products, but we feel good about buying and wearing the clothing and fitting into that "outdoorsy," New England lifestyle.

And 4.5 million customers would agree. Each year L.L. Bean's call center, which is staffed by 3,300 people during peak times, handles 180,000 orders a day from more than 15 million calls a year. Because it's a privately owned company, we cannot report its financial results, but frankly, there's no reason to believe it is exceptionally profitable because even the best catalog firms or online retailers rarely make much money. The company, however, has done a masterful job of transferring its existing retail excellence to its website. But with all of that online acclaim, what was the big news at L.L. Bean during the summer of 2000? It opened its first retail store outside Maine in July 2000—in Tysons Corner, Virginia.

L.L. Bean has evolved and survived almost a hundred years, managed today by L.L.'s grandson Leon A. Gorman, who has led the company from sales of $5 million three decades ago to its current level well in excess of $1 billion. During this evolution, L.L. Bean's development and application of Internet technology is just as important and innovative as Leon's waterproof boots a hundred years ago. Its evolution is not driven by a desire for the latest servers, software, or systems, although it has all of those. The evolution is driven by the desire for ever greater customer satisfaction.

GETTING EYES TO FOCUS ON YOUR SITE

As evidenced by L.L. Bean, it's not passion for technology that defines an e-commerce firm's ability to satisfy its customers. Rather, it's a paramount passion for satisfied customers built on a foundation of quality products and services that lend themselves to the new technology application. Those are essential ingredients of retail success online or off-, regardless of whether the products are those of Sharper Image, Gateway Computers, Victoria's Secret, or Hallmark.

So what does it take to attract people to websites? And once they visit, how can retailers get them to keep coming back? The concepts are similar in nature to what retailers have worked on at the store level for years, but the applications to an electronic world in which consumers really do run the show warrant review.

Getting things right is more important than ever. When consumers visit stores, fill their carts with goods, and wait in line to check out, basically you've got them. They may be unhappy waiting in line, but rarely will they just leave a full cart sitting at the front of the store. First of all, they don't want to sacrifice their investment of time and effort, and second, they don't want to embarrass themselves in front of other customers. In cyberspace, however, consumers litter the aisles of virtual stores with half-filled carts about 60 percent of the time (down from the massive 88 percent rate of early e-tail days). There's no one watching—no embarrassment, no real sacrifice.

So e-tailers must accomplish several tasks: attract customers, make it easy for them to buy, and fulfill on their promises so their customers will return. Winning firms combine mass and personal communication tactics to reach their target customers as efficiently and effectively as possible.

Staking Claim to Cyberspace Real Estate

You've undoubtedly heard about location, location, location being the three most important factors in everything from selling a house to attracting customers. Though simplistic, it's proven true in both instances. While word-of-mouth, the Yellow Pages, and radio or TV advertising may help attract customers, they are not primary for most retailers and service firms. Day in and day out, it is a retailer's location that is paramount in attracting customers.

A good location does not guarantee success; it's simply the initial force in attracting shoppers. What happens inside the store determines whether people come back again and again, becoming loyal customers and telling friends about their satisfaction. What happens inside a website and the e-fulfillment process has the same effect in e-commerce.

Retail firms sometimes try to overcome a poor location by spending lots of money on advertising. Sound familiar? The history of retailing, however, shows that it is more profitable to bite the bullet and spend the extra money to build a highly visible, easily accessible location than spend it on advertising.

In fact, the race for prime cyberspace is really a race for customers' mindspace. Unfortunately, dot-com firms without high visibility in the physical world are like retail stores with really bad locations. Successful retailers known for their delivery satisfaction already have the best location available in cyberspace—the minds and memories of consumers. In order to carve out their own tiny sliver of recognition in the minds of consumers, most dot-coms have relied heavily on traditional advertising. Despite a lot of funny ads, the ability to get people to remember the ad and visit the website was limited to a very few. Those that were successful, such as E*Trade (Money Out the Wazoo campaign), spent millions on media advertising, at a level not sustainable in a profit-driven e-commerce environment.

Paid advertising is just one tactic. Is it possible to pick up a magazine or business journal without reading some article on e-commerce or websites that consumers will find interesting or useful? In the same way auto manufacturers provide cars for test drives to editors and reporters of auto magazines, so must e-commerce firms provide information about their site, software, or products to writers who might describe the business in their columns.

Publicity is a cost-effective off-line strategy to attract customers to online sites. But publicity doesn't just happen—it is a carefully orchestrated strategy of planned marketing efforts. Perhaps someone in your organization can develop and coordinate the events and maintain regular contact with writers in the media, or perhaps an agency is a better solution.

For B-to-B firms, attracting online customers off-line may mean standing in booths at trade shows, enticing the tired feet of attendees to your booth with the hope of attracting their eyeballs to your site. It may mean becoming active in trade associations as an officer, or sponsoring keynote sessions and educational workshops. It often means working closely with the trade publications that generally are influential in disseminating information in your industry.

Start Your Engines

Is there an online method to promote your site that doesn't cost an arm and a leg? If you are a blended retailer, the obvious answer is with signs and information inside the store—similar to what Kmart is doing with BlueLight .com. But without stores to house such promotional activities, search engines are a relatively inexpensive way to attract eyeballs. Registering with Yahoo!, Excite, Google, or one of the many others lets your site pop up on every Internet user's screen, sending their eyeballs to your cyberspace location. But be prepared to wait up to six months to get on the most powerful of browsers—and then, they only accept 10 to 20 percent of those who apply. However, for a $199 fee, your request can be expedited somewhat.

The problem, of course, is that even the best search engine reaches only 20 percent of Web pages, but since simply cruising the Web eventually loses its appeal, this is the place to get into the race. Still, this may not be enough to win, since Internet-savvy consumers usually settle into a routine collection of sites related to their interests or their work and check those and few others. For these Net veterans, the standard browser is pretty tedious. Some are turning to meta-browsers, such as Quickbrowse .com and Onepage.com, both of which combine pages from their most frequently visited sites into a quick search without needing to type addresses or visit millions of unnecessary pages. However, a majority of the uses of these meta-browsers are probably work-related, giving little opportunity for most retailers who are not included on them to attract the eyeballs of "Net nerds" and "daily dependents."

Fly Your Banner

After you've started the search engines, what can be done to "lap" your competitors in the race for consumers? In the early days of e-commerce, the answer was banner advertising, those pesky but colorful logos, slogans, and special offers that pop up at the top, bottom, and sides of Web pages. Unlike television, radio, and magazine ads, banner ads provide the advantage of measuring the number of consumers who click on and click through to the advertiser's site. Furthermore, it is easy to track the consumers who actually make a purchase on that site, and from there, it doesn't take long to calculate the actual cost of attracting a new customer.

But even the best formulated plans can go awry when consumers don't always behave as marketers hope they will. Rather than read, click, and take part in the special offers flying across the screen, most consumers ignored them. In addition, as consumers become more familiar with the Net, they go where they want and when they want and are not easily drawn away from their primary reason for visiting a site. These behavior characteristics made the cost of attracting new, "spending" customers via banner ads very inefficient. Once marketers realized this, the price of banner advertising dropped precipitously in a desperate attempt to continue to attract advertisers, fill unsold perishable pages, and keep some advertising revenue. Dot-coms all but dropped advertising as a source of revenue from their business plans (except for a few dominant players, such as AOL and Yahoo!). Consequently, share prices and venture capitalist funding plummeted as investors realized that "information for free" should be "information for a fee" on commercially viable websites. As the advertising paradigm falters, e-tailers are turning to a variety of other methods of attracting customers, from special one-to-one offers to affiliate marketing.

Special Offers

E-tailers increasingly rely on special offers to attract consumers to their sites. These can be very effective because of the speed and reach of the Internet. Unfortunately, there are a lot of general and unnecessary offers out there offering consumers the same "rewards" for visiting a site or making a purchase. Many of these are communicated through banner ads, which hit current customers and noncustomers with the same message. The most effective are targeted to past customers, buyers of related products, and people with related interests. Most often they are transmitted by e-mail, but some e-tailers use TV, magazines, catalogs, newsletters, and, yes, even snail mail to advertise offers designed to entice viewers to a site. Some of these are coupons for online purchases, pioneered by Amazon and today used by Barnes and Noble and many others. Just as effective as discounts, and usually less costly, is airline mileage, a "currency" used not only by airlines but by car rental firms, hotels, and others. Entries for lotteries are also reasonably effective, especially when tailored to the interests of viewers. AutoWeb, for example, placed banner ads around cyberspace, enticing people to its site with a lottery in which the grand prize was a Mercedes SLK convertible. Despite our repeated efforts, we did not win the car.

When done correctly, tailored special offers can be quite effective in grabbing and keeping consumers' attention. Once a marketer knows its customers, the next obvious step in creating a relationship is talking. Getting people's permission to contact them via e-mail to let them know about special sales, extend other special offers, or solicit their feedback (research) is about as one-to-one as you can get, especially if firms really use all available information about consumers. Then, targeting offers to specific consumers with specific behaviors is possible.

Chat rooms and interest groups extend the effects of special offers, which is good and bad. On the weekend of July 4, 2000, a Buy.com coupon meant to be worth $50 off any order of $500 or more made its way onto the Web and actually gave people $50 off any purchase over $50. Executives at Buy.com thought the coupon was still in development, but someone using a "crawler" to monitor the site electronically found the coupon and immediately posted it on his website (designed for everyone with an interest in special offers). Before the computers stopped spinning, Buy.com logged in 4,500 buyers, emptying its virtual shelves before executives discovered the computer glitch.

The same Fourth of July weekend, business giant Staples.com mistakenly sold $59.95 briefcases for a penny. The penny-offer was supposed to be for customers spending a minimum amount, but the computer program forgot that little caveat. One Web-savvy consumer signed up for five briefcases at a penny each, using various user names. Paying 5 cents for the five briefcases, plus 33 cents in tax and $3.95 shipping charges, his total was $4.33 for the five briefcases. Talk about customer satisfaction!

Special offers such as these travel around the Net at supersonic speed—they are popular topics in chat rooms. Infomedia Inc.'s Deal of the Day, FatWallet.com, and Ezboard.com are in the business of posting these special offers. Word-of-mouth has always been powerful. Now throw in the speed and depth of the Internet, and word-of-mouth is more powerful than ever. Even eBay encourages word-of-mouth. When we recently made a purchase from eBay, for example, our confirmation ended with the simple request, "Thank you for using eBay! If you have already not done so today, it would not hurt to mention eBay to your friends!" Consider this a mention.

Affiliate Marketing

Currently, one of the most popular ways to attract eyeballs is with affiliate marketing, developed partly because of the decline in effectiveness of banner ads. Affiliate marketing programs are alliances or partnerships in which a firm pays partners a percentage of the sale price, usually between 5 and 20 percent, when a partner's viewer buys on the affiliate's site. Affiliations are more than "hotlinks," which simply allow people to jump between sites. In true affiliate relationships, a website becomes a virtual storefront for the company with which it has a relationship—in return for the commission it receives.

Affiliations give consumers access to a firm's products, but they may also build positive associations for the retailer because consumers probably are doing something they enjoy on the affiliate site. That's why the affiliates that are most successful are those related to market segments with common interests and activities—such as gardening, fishing, music, and movie stars—or topics such as parenting or divorce. The good news for the retailer is that if the purchase experience is good, consumers often bypass the affiliate and buy direct from the retailer's site in subsequent transactions.

Good affiliate programs replicate online what off-line businesses have done for decades—obtaining referrals from related but noncompeting businesses, just like the funeral firm that recommends a local florist. It's the same old process with new Internet technology. Nonprofit organizations and websites that provide information for free can add their own line of revenue-producing product sales with software and assistance with Aelogis, a Ft. Lauderdale, Florida–based firm that uses its experience in retailing and merchandising to provide guidance on products and retailers likely to succeed with a site's users. Doing this well may provide a source of revenue to cover the cost of providing free information. You'll find an example of how this works at unodostres.com, a site that offers shopping-, entertainment-, and information-based content of interest to the Latino segment.

Getting Consumers Where They Shop

Bricks-and-mortar retailers have the most effective method of all for attracting eyeballs to their websites: promote it in existing stores at a fraction of the cost of advertising that e-tailers must undertake. Think about the inherent promotion advantages of Barnes & Noble over Amazon. With stores full of customers buying books (the market segment most likely to buy more books), Barnes & Noble has "free access" to consumers who may purchase online. Everyone receives a bookmark inside each book they buy directing consumers to bn.com, perhaps with a special offer on their first purchase. Signs throughout the store, domain names on every page of the firm's catalog or direct-mail pieces, and a URL listing on every charge card invoice—these are the ways bricks-and-mortar firms attract eyeballs to their cyberspace location.

And then there are the "billboards." Drive down Highway 1 in California and you'll see dozens of billboards standing alongside the Silicon Valley stretch telling passersby to "click on us" and "check out our website." For a few thousand dollars a month, these drive-by advertisements do a fair job of getting attention. For retailers, their stores are their billboards.

The current potential for signing up e-customers from retail stores has been limited because of the low usage rate of Web-based retailing among consumers. But if Web sales were to increase substantially, retail chains sit poised to use in-store programs to register customers for the site or for special e-mail promotions in much the same way they now sign customers up for credit cards—complete with employee spiffs. Perhaps customers could use an in-store kiosk to order items currently out of stock or items the store normally doesn't carry. Either way, think of the added supply-chain efficiency, exposure, and customer contact that TruServ's nationwide chain of hardware stores, for example, could have if it signed up customers in the store and delivered orders from its warehouses to the store (or, for an extra charge, to customers' doors). The more contact that a True Value store or any other retailer can have with customers, the more likely there will be an increase in the amount consumers spend with that retailer compared to its competitors. According to Eddie Bauer, which works three channels—stores, catalogs, and website—shoppers who use all three methods spend five times more than those who shop only by catalog.

Lifetime Value of a Customer

The value of attracting eyeballs to a site occurs when customers keep coming back, making them more valuable to a firm than fickle, infrequent visitors. For example, if customers buy an average of $100 per visit, the profit margin is $10 and they return an average of five times before changing their allegiance to another site, the lifetime value of that customer is $50.

Here's the problem. The average e-tailer spends over $100 to acquire a new customer, but some of the most desperate are spending upward of $500. That is a monstrous price for any car dealer, department store, or food chain to pay, even for a customer who spends thousands of dollars per year in the store. For e-tailers the cost is even steeper, because the average amount a customer annually spends per online retailer is minuscule. Amazon, the most successful retail brand in e-commerce, has average annual sales of only $121 per customer. Multiply the average annual sale by the profit margin (which for Amazon is negative) and acquisition costs loom eternally.

The economics of e-commerce work only if the lifetime profitability of most customers exceeds their acquisition costs.

ARE YOU SATISFIED, REALLY SATISFIED?

When customers log-on to your website, what will they find? An easy to navigate site built around how your customers are likely to search for information or look for products? Or a mystic Internet jungle plagued with difficult transaction procedures and poor customer service? Though progress has been made in creating customer-friendly sites, customer disloyalty and Internet discontinuance indicate that many sites fall short of satisfying their customers. One of the top priorities of marketers should be developing more than what is seen on the screen, namely the service that surrounds the online offering. When you operate in a world in which customers rule, the best businesses set their goals at least a notch above satisfaction. Today, customers must be delighted. That's critically important in developing the kind of loyalty that turns sticky eyeballs into sales and creates a valuable customer for life.

So the obvious question is "What delights online customers?" (The answers can be applied to traditional as well as online businesses trying to serve customers better.)

For answers we turn to our good friends at Resource, Inc., a leading technology marketing and communication firm specializing in integrated marketing solutions for high-tech clients based in San Francisco and Columbus, Ohio. If you've watched CNN or read *Fortune* magazine, you may have seen references to "E-commerce Watch"—an analysis of what consumers want from e-commerce and which e-tailers perform best. Under the direction of Kelly Mooney, CXO (Chief eXperience Officer responsible for analyzing how experiences need to be defined and developed on the Web and other retail channels to meet demanding consumer needs), the company Resource evaluates leading e-tailers on 500 consumer-based criteria. The team spends over 20 hours with each retailer (170 times longer than the average shopper spends on any one site), exploring content, testing functionality, interacting with customer service, buying and returning merchandise, and cataloging communications, screen shots, and photography of purchased goods.

To understand which retailers best meet consumers' expectations, Resource developed a proprietary tool—the Resource Baseline—that measures and compares the total shopping experience as a snapshot in time. An online survey of fifteen hundred consumers is also conducted to assess holiday shopping experiences. It's the most comprehensive analysis of what it takes to satisfy consumers on the Internet that we've seen.

We've worked extensively with Resource, and its president and founder, Nancy Kramer, has graciously given us permission to pass on to you some of the most important findings. In the following pages we cite company practices and success factors as identified in Resource's "E-commerce Watch" and hope that any negative practices mentioned will be corrected by the time you read about them. Consumer criteria have been summarized in this study as Resource Success Factors and can be seen in Figure 6.1. They identify the best practices and breakaway tactics used by e-retailers to deliver superior value to online shoppers. They are summarized, along with our additional comments, in the following pages.

"Consumers want sites that are interactive, easy to use, and don't have so many layers that they get lost. Speed of movement through the site is important, which can be hindered by too many visuals or slow-loading streaming content," says Mooney. "Attractiveness of the site is important, but ease of use and functionality is paramount—consumers want to know if the item is in stock or out-of-stock, when to expect delivery, and how much shipping will cost, and they want most of that information before they complete the purchase," she adds.

Company Policies: Consumers Want to Know Where You Stand

Consumers expect policies that recognize their concern about credit card fraud. That usually means secure socket layer (SSL) protocol and a com-

FIGURE 6.1   Resource E-commerce Watch Success Factors: What It Takes to Satisfy Consumers on the Web

Factor #1:	Policies
Factor #2:	Account administration
Factor #3:	Relationship profile
Factor #4:	Navigation
Factor #5:	Visual merchandising
Factor #6:	Decision support
Factor #7:	Solutions communications
Factor #8:	Shopping cart and checkout
Factor #9:	Postpurchase activities
Factor #10:	Customer acquisition and retention
Factor #11:	Gift services
Factor #12:	Content and community
Factor #13:	International business
Factor #14:	Multichannel integration

SOURCE: Kelly Mooney, *Resource E-commerce Watch,* 2000. Resource E-commerce Watch is an intelligence service and proprietary performance measurement offered by Resource Marketing, Inc.

mitment to cover liability for fraudulent use of credit cards that might occur from a transaction on their site. Consumers expect opt-out abilities for disclosing their personal information and unwanted e-mail and assurance that their personal information will not be sold to third parties or be poached by hackers. E-tailers should clearly explain their policies about cookies, return policies, shipping information, and their guarantees to avoid confusion. Over 85 percent of consumers are concerned with privacy issues, and retailers, rather than protecting their own interests, should use their policy area to be a consumer advocate, build trust, and enhance brand relationships. Our advice is to read the policy section of your website and ask the question "Is this customer-friendly or company-friendly?"

Account Administration: Consumers Want to Be in Control

Delighted consumers expect all kinds of account information at their fingertips—purchase histories, order status, password flexibility and assistance, and convenience in moving between secure and nonsecure areas of the site. Some sites treat every visit and transaction as a new one—making consumers reenter all their shipping and billing information. Making the shopping process difficult doesn't encourage customer loyalty. State-of-the-art sites allow consumers to click from their order to tracking information from the carrier, allowing consumers to know not only when the item is promised but its current status and location.

Relationship Profile: Consumers Want You to Know Them, but Not Too Well

A relationship profile goes beyond account information by collecting data that helps the merchant to serve a customer better, usually with targeted recommendations. If you expect customers to return to your site regularly, you should give them the ability to store favorites in their profile, but above all, customers want to be in control of what is and what is not done with their relationship data.

Knowing customers means remembering them and tailoring both the messages and the products to their needs. Staples.com allows customers to store the items they frequently buy in an easy-to-access purchase history, making reordering items with complicated model numbers, such as printer cartridges, easier and more accurate. Before it closed its cyberdoors, Eve.com sent with customers' orders free samples based on what the customers purchased or their customer profile. A quick visit to the site today results in a simple home page directing consumers to Sephora.com, the online sister of Sephora, a Paris-based bricks-and-mortar cosmetics retailer that sells an extensive collection of some of the world's finest cosmetics and personal care items, including its own brand.

Navigation: Consumers Want Freedom and Choice Without Confusion

Loyal customers, and those you hope to become loyal, want to be able to see quickly where they can go and how they can get there with a minimum of confusion and clicks. Good pull-down menus help customers get to their destination quickly and save retailers precious real estate on the page. There should always be an easy-to-find, comprehensive, click-on site map. Consumers need a clear, dynamic trail that helps trace the location of a product that they noticed three clicks ago and now want to see again. Some of the best sites use Java script rollovers and dynamic HTML to streamline navigation. You can find examples at the Sherwin-Williams site and SaksFifthAvenue.com. When consumers click on the heading "women," a list of departments appears, and when they move their mouse over the apparel heading, for example, additional offerings pop up—from evening to career. This type of navigation tool allows customers to see where in the program they are and easily compare their options. This is one area where the quality of the firm designing your site and providing technical assistance makes a huge difference in the ease of navigation. It's a good reason to outsource with the best instead of inventing your own.

E-tailers need to make shopping easy, fast, and enjoyable, and navigation is a major determinant of whether or not this is accomplished. That includes "little" things like displaying a running total of all items and the dynamic total cost instead of forcing the customer to click back to their shopping carts. It includes "big" things like providing real-time e-reps who can answer questions about everything from policies to products and shipping, a function that should be featured prominently so customers don't have to look far for fast and friendly answers. L.L. Bean does a great job at this—especially during checkout. The simplicity of a site often means that less is more for consumers.

Visual Merchandising: Consumers Want Ambience, but Not at the Price of Functionality

Visual merchandising is transforming e-commerce. And it's doing so by using proven retail strategies to turn transactions into experiences. Done well, merchandising on the Web, as in the store, simplifies things for shoppers, directing them with visual cues, offering information as they need it, and enticing them with relevant goods and services. That's why e-tailers are turning to website developers whose experience includes strong retailing and merchandising backgrounds in addition to technical expertise. Retailers can also fill the role of visual merchandiser. In 2000, Amazon.com announced a partnership agreement with Toys 'R' Us. In addition to toy sourcing and buying, Toys 'R' Us also agreed to arrange the virtual window displays for Amazon.com's online holiday extravaganza.

Typically, e-tailers demonstrate the breadth of their product offering with simple labels to represent each department—men's clothing, women's clothing, home furnishings, and gifts, for example. A few websites go a step farther to position their brands (not just departments) by using language and visuals to communicate assortments. For example, 1-800-Flowers.com added the tag line "Flowers are just the beginning" to its logo to communicate immediately that it sells more than just flowers.

Leading websites must excel at managing visual space by developing visual hierarchies for communicating where, when, and how information is given to shoppers to keep them from becoming overwhelmed. Too often, however, merchants distract, confuse, or annoy customers by interrupting their shopping experience with irrelevant product recommendations or offer related merchandise recommendations in pull-down menus, making add-on sales an effort instead of an option. Some firms, however, do a good job of suggestive selling. When you bought a battery-operated toy from eToys.com, you could expect a prompt asking if you need batteries in the size needed for the toy.

In the visual world, color is important. Black can be boring or it can be elegant, depending on the context. Usually, bright colors are more attractive to most consumers. Some sites still make the mistake of placing black print on dark backgrounds or using red or dark green type on dark screens (perhaps not realizing that about 15 percent of the male population is "color blind," making the latter practically illegible). The point is that visual merchandising is critically important to the "feel" and function of a site. Streaming video, sound for appropriate products, and other features can be attractive, but consumers should always have control over such features. Consumers want options for text only, zooming in for product details and other features that let them shop the way they want to, whether they are just browsing or looking for a specific item.

An important in-store merchandising and sales tool that has aided gift selection and buying in major retailers from Target to Kids 'R' Us is gift registry. This type of service, when placed on a website, acts as an important visual element as well as an information and sales tool. It is important in both the initial sale and postpurchase effect on the recipient. Bridal registries have been in use for decades by traditional retailers, but the Internet expands the value dramatically by allowing them to cross wide geographic boundaries and types of retailers. In one focus group we conducted on this topic, a respondent told us how she bought a tent as a bridal gift because the couple listed it as one of the items they most wanted. "Without a registry," she told us, "I would never have thought of buying a tent as a wedding gift." By placing a variety of gift choices, from the traditional (china and dishes) to the out of the ordinary (tents and hiking gear), in a gift registry, retailers change how and where various items are merchandised. Placing products on a website where consumers expect to look for them is as important online as it is in a physical store.

Decision Support: Consumers Want to Cruise Through the Shopping Process

Many shoppers know what they want to buy before they go online. Just as retailers have discovered, one way to increase loyalty is to allow consumers to get in and out of the site quickly. Good sites must provide multiple paths for fast access, often in the forms of both categorical links and word searches. And once selections are narrowed, it is important that users be able to sort them quickly. eBay does this well, allowing you to sort auction items based on price or date of auction.

Revealing product availability before consumers select an item rather than waiting until checkout or notifying them with postpurchase e-mail confirmations enhances speed through the system. Today's time-starved customers require real-time inventory management and perhaps, especially for business products, substitute suggestions that will fit the task (such as business supplies and components).

Along those lines, speed to screen is vitally important to keep browsers interested. Incorporating visual design elements may make a site "cool," but it may lose customers if graphic-rich interfaces increase the download time users are struggling to reduce. Someday, most consumers will have bandwidth with DSL, cable, or wireless connections that make these factors of less concern, but for the mass market, speed is still a critical factor in developing customer satisfaction.

In-store shopping provides retailers with many opportunities to influence consumers' shopping choices—samples, point-of-purchase displays, and enticing packaging. E-tailers borrow some of these tactics to encourage virtual product sampling for selected products and make virtual shopping closer to the shopping experiences in physical stores. For example, consumers can view sample book chapters at bn.com, listen to CD samples at CDNow, see movie clips at Reel.com, and experiment with cosmetics at gloss.com. Lands' End delivers fabric swatches within ten days to consumers who need to see the fabric before they make a final purchase decision. Look for more innovations that help e-tailing mimic more of the conveniences and strengths of in-store shopping.

Solution Communications: Consumers Want Backup

E-tailers must keep communication channels open, from start to finish. That means recognizing customers' communication preferences and providing many ways for them to talk and get answers, including phone, e-mail, snail mail, and self-help areas. Depending on how live customer service is handled in toll-free call centers, it can build lasting relationships or cost retailers their competitive advantage and ultimately their customers.

When we order flowers online, which we frequently do, it's a simultaneous process, viewing the flowers on the website while talking with a live person on the 800 number. During a recent order, the representative from 1-800-Flowers told us that many customers do the same. That calls for winning sites to design their call centers, training procedures, and software and inventory management systems based on how consumers will integrate all possible help solutions to find the best combination for them. Some sites, many of which have since closed shop, don't provide a phone number for distressed customers to call—probably because the firm is not equipped to handle them. But that's unacceptable for e-tailers who are serious about customer satisfaction and loyalty. Whether customers buy online, by phone, or from a kiosk with the same information in a physical store, the goal is to provide a unified, integrated, and easy communication solution.

Checking Out: Consumers Want Hassle-Free Transactions

Since the introduction of centralized checkout in physical stores, few topics generate more criticism from consumers than shopping carts and checkout lanes. Perhaps it should not be surprising that the same problems are pervasive online. That's why e-tailers dedicated to continuing patronage from valuable customers are working hard to make checkout simpler, speedier, and more enjoyable. Some sites, such as the now defunct garden.com, intercepted abandoned shopping carts to find out why by asking a few questions in a short online survey that didn't compromise privacy.

The best sites now provide controlled viewing of the shopping cart, keeping customers from being taken automatically to their cart each time they add an item, yet they still receive immediate confirmation when they do. The objective is to take merchandise to the cart without pulling customers away from the products each time they add a new find. Also, removing items needs to be as easy as adding them—something that should be much easier in the virtual world than in the physical one.

Checkout procedures are another critical stage that can make or break a sale. Of particular frustration to consumers is payment, often the cause for the high abandonment rates. Supplying credit information is tedious, especially when you visit multiple sites in one shopping spree. Most consumers don't type numbers quickly or accurately, causing delays in checkout. When e-tailers earn the trust of consumers enough to collect credit information just once and keep it, the process is quicker and easier. In fact, consumers feel less like they are paying for products if they don't have to enter the information before hitting that final "buy" button. To do this, consumers need to register for the site, which means they need a password, subject to the forgetfulness of the overloaded human brain. The process of providing hints, receiving a new password quickly, and allowing maximum flexibility about the number of letters or numbers in the password determines if the customer ever returns and transforms from browser to buyer.

Postpurchase Activities: Consumers Want Satisfaction and Restitution

With a click of the "submit" button, orders begin the journey from virtual world to real world. Postpurchase activities are the vital steps e-retailers take to reassure customers throughout the process, beginning with e-mail order confirmations, hopefully within minutes or even seconds of the purchase. Of course the assumption is that what the e-mail says is happening is in fact actually happening. Tracking the package on the FedEx truck or other carrier is a plus that reassures and informs customers. It is so helpful in increasing overall customer satisfaction with the process that it will probably become a best practice of the best sites.

Package presentation is an important way to reaffirm the seller's brand. For starters, shipping address labels must clearly identify the recipient, provide protection in size-appropriate packages, and prominently bear the e-tailer's name. Nobody gets more brand identification, perhaps, than Gateway's famous cowhide, although it also signals to would-be thieves that the package might contain a valuable piece of computer equipment. If the risk of theft is too high for some merchandise, an attractive white box with branding materials confined to the inside may be a better choice. L.L. Bean sends as many of its products as possible in a tough, protective, lightweight fiber bag that is also flexible enough to push through mail slots or fit into mailboxes—meaning a secure delivery even when consumers are not home to accept packages.

Handling merchandise returns is both a challenge and an opportunity for e-tailers. Most e-tailers include preaddressed, self-adhesive shipping labels in case customers or gift recipients need to return merchandise. That's good. Some require customers to call for a shipping label or return merchandise authorization (RMA). That's bad. The best practice, in terms of customer satisfaction and the bottom line, is returning merchandise to a store rather than returning it to the post office or truck driver. In this instance a customer can exchange it for the right size or a similar product, and perhaps buy additional items. And if the exchange is friendly and speedy and a sales associate helps customers find an even better solution than they had, loyalty (the kind that builds a lifetime of profitability) is fostered for the brand. When returns are made by mail, it is important that customers receive an e-mail confirming that the return was received and properly exchanged or credited.

Another feature hot on the Web is loyalty programs. While most reward their customers with dollars-off promotions or free merchandise, others have aligned with firms such as ClickRewards, which rewards customers' online shopping with miles on various airlines. Other firms use automatic entry into contests or include with each shipment special promotions that build repeat sales and brand loyalty. When you receive an order in the summer from L.L. Bean, for example, you may also receive a brochure containing helpful hints on outdoor living, how to deal with insect stings, and a coupon for Campho-phenique and Bactine should a pesky creature bite you. Sending information and coupons closely related to outdoor interests builds good feelings and loyalty among its outdoorsy customers, offers them something they are probably interested in, and perhaps gives the company a little profit from associative marketing with parent company, Bayer.

Emotion and Experience

Retailers can develop strategies for making ordering easy, delivery timely, and returns satisfactory. But in order to capture consumers' loyalty, they need to play to the one thing that makes us human—emotion. Consumers shop for many reasons. For some, shopping alleviates loneliness, dispels boredom, provides escape and fantasy fulfillment, and relieves depression. Others view shopping as a sport, with the goal of beating the system, or a modern form of the primal "hunt," with the shopper acting as "the great provider." Retailers that make us feel good, valued, important, and put smiles on our faces get our business whether they always have the lowest prices or not. E-tailers that recognize and acknowledge consumers when they log on, ask their opinions, and engage them in dialog appeal to the human side of what other retailers consider an order number. In an age of impersonal machines, emotion is an important part of social activity—and remember, that is what shopping is.

Hallmark gets it. Built on the concept of emotion, the company understands the importance of the little things—like including a full-sized greeting card, free of charge with gift items. It also understands the importance of the entire shopping and retail experience customers have when they interact with any component of the Hallmark brand.

Companies would be wise to monitor how Hallmark integrates all of its in-store and online shopping experiences to create a unified image and brand. Kelly Mooney, CXO at Resource, points to the importance of evolving from technology-driven to customer-driven online solutions, a shift that all firms will have to make if they want to satisfy customers at all levels. She explains, "CEOs of retail companies should view the *e* in their titles as 'experience' not 'executive.' Company leaders should be establishing the vision and setting the priorities for a top-notch customer experience in all channels."

Sticky eyeballs are both the cause and result of customer satisfaction. At its best, customer satisfaction is emotional, leading to fun, pleasure, dialog, relationships, and the desire to repeat the behavior that created those feelings. These are some of the critical success factors associated with Web winners. If you'd like to see which e-tailers currently are the best at executing effective e-tail strategies, and more examples of Web success factors, you can find current information and ratings at Resource.com.

THE HAPPY FEET OF SATISFIED CUSTOMERS: COMPLETING THE CYCLE

Not all retailing battles of the twenty-first century will be fought in cyber-space—some of the mightiest battles for consumer loyalty will occur in stores. Even for the best of breed, this will mean diligent focus on the details that are most important to their customers. While sticky eyeballs beckon the attention of e-tail strategists, happy feet demand the attention of all retailers.

If Consumers Like Your Store, They'll Try Your Website

Your best source of new business is your existing customers. For e-tailers, the best sources of new eyeballs are those connected to the happy feet of their existing, satisfied customers.

Customers who love Target will shop Target.com. Conversely, customers who hate Target aren't likely to visit its site anytime soon. Retailers that please their customers inside the store are most likely to capture their online shopping dollars. The store provides the perfect stage upon which to build expectations about the website—the more fun in-store shopping is, the more likely consumers are to expect the same fun feeling online.

What is a phenomenal opportunity to entice consumers to try a website becomes a challenge in execution. Consumers expect the experiences and the level of satisfaction to be the same online as in the store.

Gauging Your Customers' Satisfaction Levels

Early e-commerce advocates often believed the Internet would replace conventional retailing based on the assumption that consumers dislike shopping and want to avoid stores. Yet most studies find that only 20 percent of consumers don't like to shop. While that's a significant number of people who might embrace an alternative, it is far from the majority. Studies also show that 68 percent of items bought during major shopping trips and 54 percent during smaller trips are unplanned, a finding that has remained fairly constant for over thirty years.

It's clear, traditional "walk up and down the aisles and pick what you want" retailing is here to stay, but it doesn't mean that retailing won't change to satisfy customers more and serve them better. To analyze how better to meet consumers' needs and wants, retailers can study the consumer logistics process.

Consumer logistics is the speed, ease, and satisfaction with which consumers move through the retail and shopping process—from the time they begin planning to the time they take products home. It includes seven primary consumer stages: (1) preparation to shop; (2) arriving at and (3) entering the store; (4) movement through the store; (5) checkout; (6) travel home and home-warehousing; and (7) inventory stock-outs in the home, which prompt repurchase. These stages, seen in Figure 6.2, influence store location, store layout, aisle width, point-of-purchase displays, checkout, traffic in the store, customer service and personnel, payment methods, signage, and safety of stores—all from the perspective of the consumer.

Retailers use this analysis to design stores that delight customers, but

FIGURE 6.2   Stages of Consumer Logistics

MOVEMENT OF CONSUMERS THROUGH THE ENTIRE SHOPPING PROCESS					
PREPARING TO SHOP	**ARRIVING AT STORE**	**ENTERING STORE**	**SHOPPING IN STORE**	**CHECKING OUT**	**TRANSPORT & STORAGE**
• Make lists	• Out-store environment	• Getting and separating carts	• Signage, maps and lighting	• Time in line	• Assistance with loading car
• Choose store	• Parking lot	• Entry—clean or cluttered	• Store layout and category flows	• Length of line and speed	• Ease of leaving parking lot
• Clip coupons	• Safety and clientele	• Greeters	• Aisle width and cart movement	• Width of lanes	• Movement of products in car
• Plan route	• Signage	• Security cameras	• Personnel and information	• Unloading cart	• Where and how store products at home
• Bundle stops	• Lighting	• Familiarity with store	• Relocated goods	• Payment methods	
• Perceptions about store and products	• Traffic	• Ability to see through store	• POP/ Promotions	• Monitoring prices and price accuracy	• Pantry loading
• Advertising			• Price and brand evaluations	• Self scanning and checkout	• Disposal
• Past experience			• Size of store and in-store traffic		• Home stock-outs

EXPERIENCES AND SATISFACTION AFFECT SUBSEQUENT PURCHASES

SOURCE: Based on a study conducted for the International Mass Retail Association.

these same elements and their progression can help analyze e-tailing strategies from a consumer standpoint. Surveying consumers on these topics helps retailers determine the best "mix" of services and attributes to offer in their stores and online. This type of analysis answers such questions as: "How well does e-commerce facilitate consumers moving through each of these shopping stages?" "How must e-commerce evolve if it is to complement or compete with off-line retailing?" Knowing what satisfies your customers in each area of consumer logistics can help you design consumer-friendly and satisfying retail experiences on- and off-line.

If the Shoe Fits

Ask anyone who the "king of customer service" is, and they'll most likely answer Nordstrom. In fact, if there were a URL for a firm that owns the best mindspace in retailing, it might be called Nordstrom.satisfaction. This Seatte-based firm was founded in 1901 when John W. Nordstrom used his stake from the Alaska gold rush to open a small shoe store. One hundred years later, that store has evolved into a department store chain with 106 stores and a sizable catalog business grossing more than $5 billion in 2000. Whether it is the live piano music that serves as a prelude for the drama inside the store, the free shoeshines, or the personal service from sales associates, no retailer generates happier feet than Nordstrom.

So, how does a firm with a hundred-year history of customer satisfaction migrate the strength of its brand to the Internet? The answer is by performing the same functions with the same quality standards online that it does in its stores and catalog. In the earliest days of online retailing, Nordstrom struggled with how it would carry out the stylish, high-sizzle fashion merchandising its customers had come to expect. It knew that selling fashionable-quality apparel in this manner took bandwidth. So in the early days of 14.4 Kbps and 28.8 Kbps modems, Nordstrom watched its competitors, whose strength was technology rather than fashion, spend lots of money to sell next to nothing.

Nordstrom management knew that the quality of available online shopping for fashion apparel was under par—not consistent with its in-store experiences and service levels. With only a few errant clicks, Nordstrom's century-old reputation for customer satisfaction could be destroyed. So Nordstrom waited, dutifully letting others test the e-commerce waters. Chastised by some Internet proponents and popular media as having missed the e-tail boat, the company planned and continued to focus on its overriding strategy of superior customer service. By the time enough people had 56

Kbps modems to support the system worthy of the Nordstrom brand, Nordstrom.com was ready to storm the Internet. Timing was everything. By recognizing the dangers of being the first mover, the company protected its brand both off- and online. Speed is not the name of the game for a firm with an established brand; more important is getting it right and satisfying customers. For Nordstrom, the quality of shopping in its stores defines the Nordstrom brand.

A Foot in the Physical World. Nordstrom's blended retail strategy is simple: continually improve on customers' shopping and buying experiences and define and develop online customer service parameters. The ingredients for achieving customer satisfaction have not changed much in the past hundred years—quality, fashion, superior products from the best manufacturers in the world, and unparalleled customer service. But Nordstrom found increased competition from nimble competitors such as May Department Stores, Saks Fifth Avenue, and Neiman Marcus, who also adopted the "customer is always right" mantra.

As other firms focused their attention and committed valuable resources to developing e-tail outlets, Nordstrom revamped its stores. Following several years of stagnant sales, John Whitacre, CEO and chairman, initiated changes from the executive washroom to the stores. For starters, the key women's department was redesigned into two separate areas—one for more trendy items and the other for classic lines. The store added more capri pants and other trendy fashions, featured brighter colors, updated the looks of its mannequins, and reoutfitted its tuxedo-clad piano players with slacks and sport shirts. The company also began its first national TV advertising campaign, touting its updated look. From an operational standpoint, Whitacre wiped out the six-person copresidency (leaving a clear number two position unfilled), created ten executive vice presidents, and created five operating units (department stores, outlet stores, consumer finance, online, and private label). Other changes include a massive update of its computer system to allow better tracking of inventory and centralized purchasing to increase leverage with vendors.

Stepping into the New Economy. Nordstrom's commitment to delighting customers remains a focus of the company, but direct selling requires different skills and processes than in-store retailing. A problem for other retailers who are still focused on transactional accuracy, Nordstrom has already perfected these skill sets because of its catalog business.

In developing its website, Nordstrom went right to the source; it asked consumers through focus groups and in-depth interviews about their shopping habits. It found that many of them remembered seeing something they liked in the catalog, but either could no longer find the catalog or didn't know if the item was still available. Now, when you click onto Nordstrom.com, you'll find an actual catalog—you can flip the pages exactly as you would its paper cousin. The online and catalog experiences are integrated so that consumers can search for an item by scanning the pages or by entering the item number from the catalog. Consumers who like to browse while traveling or soaking in the tub, can move to the computer or telephone to make the purchase.

The key is reinforcing the Nordstrom brand and making it available to customers in the format they prefer. Open a Nordstrom catalog and you'll find mention of its website along with its customer service phone number. Log-on to www.nordstrom.com and you'll find a store locator directing consumers to the store nearest them and announcing new store openings in their area. You'll also find a feature in which customers can e-mail their "wish lists" of Nordstrom items to friends and family for birthdays and holidays, increasing the likelihood that the items will be purchased from Nordstrom rather than from another retailer. With this feature, not only do the brands of the products to be purchased make a person's shopping list, so does the name of the retailer from which to buy it—a brilliant retail branding strategy.

Daniel Nordstrom, Nordstrom.com's thirty-seven-year-young CEO, understands the economics of profitability that we believe will define B-to-C success in the future. Simply stated, it means no unreasonable discounts, no free shipping, and no elimination of tax. Whereas the first wave of online retailers ignored the need for profits and placed themselves in the commodity business, commodities can only translate into profits for companies with superefficient supply chains. The long-term winners of the e-tail wars will rely on profits to fund the customer satisfaction programs to create loyalty among consumers. The random, unsustainable discounts desperate e-tailers are throwing at consumers today will ultimately lead to their demise. Nordstrom believes that when a retailer has the right items, at the right time, of the right quality, and stands behind those items, customers don't need a discount to prompt their purchases.

Judging by its in-store and online success, Nordstrom is right. Nearly fifteen hundred online shoe retailers beat Nordstrom to the Internet punch. But when it entered the ring, the others dropped out. They couldn't compete with its name, reputation, quality of interaction, organization of products, and overall service. And then there's product selection. Because of its strength with its vendors, Nordstrom.com now offers 20 million pairs of shoes, conquering the physical barriers of store-based retailing.

Look for it to apply this model to other product categories with the same intensity and vigor.

Nordstrom is masterful in its integrated approach to retail. This approach allows customers to search and buy any way they like, in ways that incorporate the future but complement the past. This king of multi-channel merchandising has created a closely intertwined marketing and sales strategy that incorporates catalogs, stores, and a website, all promoting each other and working together to promote the Nordstrom brand and ultimately delight customers. Nordstrom, although late to the game, entered e-tailing with a mighty one-two punch of service and selection. The result? Nordstrom quickly became number one in its category and one of the top-rated e-tailers in the evolution of e-commerce.

Multichannel Connections

Multichannel integration is the emerging model used by leading-edge organizations to reach and serve customers no matter where or when they want to shop. The strategy for success is always the same: an integrated experience that guarantees consumers encounter one brand, one level of customer service, one strength of loyalty, and, in most instances, one price, all delivered through multiple outlets. At the store level, it means creating happy feet; online, it means creating sticky eyeballs. But the best of future retailers will create sensations in the heart of the customer, creating an emotional connection between customer and brand.

CHAPTER 7

HOW TO MOVE INNOVATIONS FROM TRIAL TO MASS ACCEPTANCE

MICROWAVES. Computers. Cellular phones. Lights that clap on and clap off. The commerce landscape is littered with innovation success stories from the silly—lollipops with motorized spinners to make licking easier—to the serious—vaccinations for measles and smallpox. With technology on the tip of our population's collective tongue, you can't pick up a business magazine, tune in to talk radio, or hear a business speaker without some reference to innovation. The mantra is the same—innovate, innovate, innovate. Yet for those who are serious about success in e-commerce the mantra should be investigate, contemplate, and, only then, innovate. With the first strategy, you're likely to get a mixed bag of winners and losers, weighted heavily toward the loser side. With the second, you're more likely to increase the proportion of winners.

But don't think you're home free just because you have a great product, a detailed marketing plan, slick advertising, and widespread, efficient distribution. To create an out-of-the-ballpark home run with new products, it takes a process just short of a freakish alignment of planet, moon, and stars. Successful innovations that meet marketing expectations occur about 20 percent of the time; home runs occur once in a blue moon. In this chapter, we describe the process that helps you hit the home runs— an unremitting focus on the needs, lives, and behaviors of your target consumers. You must understand how they shop, why they buy, and how to exceed their expectations. Whether your interests are those of a retailer or manufacturer developing new Web services, a technology firm developing profitable new products, or an entrepreneur evaluating the probable profitability of new Internet services and firms, the process is the same.

The market lures entrepreneurs each day with the most intoxicating bait of all—possibility. Do it right, and you *might* be the next Bill Gates or Steven Case. Many entrepreneurs follow the examples set by the Cinderella success stories of the Internet craze: don't look at the possibilities of the marketplace and just salivate; go for it; innovate. But if you don't do your homework, the only riches you can expect are the experiences you get from having completed the process rather than the monetary riches from long-term, profitable sales. Like other areas of e-commerce, the Internet strategies depend on how well you know the "commerce" side of e-commerce, and there are plenty of lessons available on how to introduce innovative products successfully.

WHAT IS INNOVATION?

If you give the topic of innovation much thought, you begin to question what constitutes innovation. Sometimes it means throwing out the rules of today and crafting newfangled products, management systems, services, operations, and marketing methods the world has never seen. Other times it means altering slightly an established product or solution. We like to think of it as creating better solutions to consumers' life-related problems, needs, and activities. However, the determination of whether something (a product or service) is an innovation or not rests in the minds of consumers. If they perceive something to be new or different—bingo, an innovation is born.

Innovation occurs at many levels. Do you classify the brightly colored iMac as an innovation? Some consumers do and some don't. Those examining it from the functional side of computing would say no. Those interested in design, expression, and marketing would say yes. Vantage point and perception affect how likely consumers are to abandon the products and services they currently use for new ones. And ultimately, the future of any new innovation depends on how many consumers abandon their current solutions and adopt new ones for the long term—otherwise known as sales.

Some innovations win when they enter the marketplace, others lose. A study conducted by EFO Group Ltd., a product consulting firm in Weston, Connecticut, reports that only 8 percent of new product concepts offered by a group of 112 leading manufacturers and retailers reached the market, and 83 percent of those that did failed to meet marketing objectives. For every microwave oven, Nintendo, or compact disc, there are thousands of picture phones, CD-i's (compact disc–interactive), and quadraphonic audio systems. Some of these flops were definitive successes on the drawing board but fizzled in the market. Following suit in the virtual world were Drkoop.com, Boo.com, Toys.com, Reel.com (owned and backed by Hollywood Entertainment, the parent of the Hollywood Video chain), and thousands of unneeded, unknown, and unfortunate dot-com calamities.

Three Strikes and a Hit

When thinking of failed innovations, three distinctive examples come to mind—all bound by a common thread. One was Towlette, a tissue saturated with conditioner that consumers were expected to rub on their hair, which was introduced by innovation-king P & G in the 1980s. Armed with the snappy but meaningless advertising slogan "Towlette? You bet!", P & G took a gamble but lost when consumers rejected the product. Soon thereafter, Pizza Hut introduced Calizza, a pocket-pizza love-child of the calzone and the pizza. Not as weird as Towlette but just as unwanted, Calizza was soundly rejected by consumers despite a considerable advertising campaign, promotional tour, and assumption that because it tasted good, people would buy it. The problem was not that the technology or the product was bad, just that consumers were happy with the round, flat pizza. Finally, there's Control Video, a technology product enabling consumers to download video games off the Internet. It sounded like a great idea and was even backed by super investor Hambrecht & Quist, but it was still a bust.

Besides failure, have you figured out the common element in all these new products? Here's a hint: Rather than thinking of each example as a case in point, think of each as a point in case. The common denominator in each instance was the soon-to-be-famous person who worked on the teams that introduced and marketed these products. His next project would turn out to be wildly successful. That person is Steve Case; the project is AOL.

From his varied experiences, Case learned what he calls the single most important law of business: If you sit down with customers, they will tell you what they want. Today, this is the guiding principle at AOL. While other companies raced to embrace the latest (and usually most expensive) technology, AOL outran them all with the age-old KISS principle: Keep It Simple, Stupid.

Steve Case is first and foremost a marketer. In an admission that should encourage readers who doubt their own skills in computer technology, he confesses that he didn't do well in his college computer course. But he learned marketing very well. Before formal courses on the subject, he learned about marketing as a youngster while selling Christmas cards and other products in a mail-order business, and then later with a number of entrepreneurial businesses while he was a student at Williams College. As technology progressed and the Internet wars started, CompuServe and AOL began to battle. Though CompuServe had a head start and served very profitable segments (techies and financial wizards), Case focused on the masses. With an understanding of what consumers wanted, he and his team developed products that appealed to the masses of technology-challenged but financially advantaged Americans who just wanted a simple way to access the World Wide Web and communicate with each other.

Look at Figure 7.1 and you'll see how Steve Case expresses important principles of making technology successful in his "Ten Commandments for Success in the Digital Arena." His "failures" during his tenures at P & G, Pizza Hut, and Control Video and his "successes" in his own businesses provide lessons for anyone hoping to be successful in e-commerce. When you listen to the customer and make a profit, everyone wins—customers and investors alike.

FIGURE 7.1   Steve Case's Ten Commandments for Success in the Digital Arena

COMMANDMENT #1

The Mass-Market Consumer Is Thy Master.
Technology is a false idol to be mastered, not worshiped. Technology that is easy to use, fun, useful, and affordable will win customers over technological bells and whistles every time.

COMMANDMENT #2

Thou Shalt Not Take Thy Competition for Granted.
No matter who you are or how big your company is, you can never be sure where the next competitive battle will come from. Keep one eye on the known competitors and the other watchful for the next upstart.

COMMANDMENT #3

Remember Economics 101.
A large pool of similar companies competing for the same customers will breed consolidation. All that remains is to separate the consolidators from the consolidatees.

COMMANDMENT #4

Honor Thy Parents, Teachers, Families, and Communities.
We are all responsible to the community that grants us the opportunity to be successful. Breach that trust at your own peril.

COMMANDMENT #5

Thou Shalt Not Spam.
E-mail is a personal and private forum and consumers need to feel that this private space will not be used as just another tool for someone's marketing scams.

COMMANDMENT #6

Thou Shalt Not Launch before the Market Is Ready.
Industry watchers are notorious for salivating over innovations and stirring up interest in technologies before they're ready. Wait until the speed, platform, and price are all in alignment for the customer before you make your move.

COMMANDMENT #7

Thou Shalt Take the Business of the Internet Seriously.
The grace period before companies make the transition to e-commerce and interactive marketing is shrinking every day. This is a bandwagon—either get on or get left behind.

COMMANDMENT #8

Thou Shalt Not Deal with Washington Lightly.
Govern your industry and business dealings effectively and federal regulators won't have to.

COMMANDMENT #9

Thou Shalt Not Compromise Thy Neighbor's Online Privacy.
Consumers have the right to know how you use their personal information so that they can make informed choices. Trust their judgment and you'll reap the rewards of loyalty and appreciation for your integrity.

COMMANDMENT #10

Thou Shalt Improve the Lives of People and Society.
Ultimately, we all need a greater purpose for what we do, make, and sell. If your vision is to help your customers achieve their dreams, then the online world can help make those ambitions a reality.

SOURCE: Malcolm Fleschner, "Open and Shut Case," *Selling Power,* June 2000, pp. 49–52.

PUSHING THE ENVELOPE OF COMMERCE WITH INNOVATION

Tragic failure, runaway success, great product, terrible innovation. Depending on whom you ask, Napster is any and all of these and much, much more. This music revolution, whose following is more dedicated than even the most devoted Deadheads ever were, jumped from underground to mainstream status during early 2000. Napster, which allows users to download free software to swap MP3 music files stored on each other's computers, was sued by the Recording Industry Association of America (RIAA) for copyright infringement to the tune of $100,000 damages each time a song was copied. Frankly, RIAA and its for-profit members felt threatened by consumers' ability to source music from one another, effectively bypassing the sales channels that meant profits to record labels and retailers and royalties to artists. Napster fought tough legal battles as evidence of copyright infringement and licensing issues mounted against it.

Eventually, Napster had its day in court, lost the case on July 26, 2000, and won a reprieve on July 28, only to wind up in bed with one of its "enemies." On November 1, 2000, German media giant Bertelsmann AG became Napster's savior, loaning an undisclosed amount of money to Napster and adding it to its already impressive portfolio, including Random House, bn.com, and CDNow. Since both companies are privately held, not many financial details were released, except that Bertelsmann will have the right to purchase stock at a later date and employ the Web rebel to distribute BMG's (Bertelsmann's music subsidiary) entire catalog of music. But changes in the traditional Napster model were expected. Among them, Bertelsmann's initiated a fee-based membership site using Napster technology that will pay royalties to artists for copyrighted songs. Though BMG dropped its charges against Napster, the other seventeen plaintiffs remained engaged in legal battles, which really heated up in 2001.

Regardless of final outcome, Napster's legacy rests in how Internet business changed because a nineteen-year-old college kid invented a new technology and created peer-to-peer computing. Until Shawn Fanning sent his software (free of charge) to thirty friends he met in a chat room, explicitly asking them not to send the software on to other friends, people searched the Net for MP3 files from a variety of sources. Today, most consumers use computer servers that are easily controlled by one company to search the Internet for information. Fanning's technology of peer-to-peer (P-to-P) computing allowed consumers to share information by hooking up the contents of an individual's computer into a global information index that others can use.

Cheered on and inspired by his roommates and friends, Shawn created a consumer-driven innovation, and people loved it. The reasons were simple: it held great advantages over current solutions; it was free and easy to use; it was compatible with current systems; and anyone could access it. The phenomenon spread like wildfire through college campuses as kids saw their friends downloading music and creating their own collections. With news of its impending shutdown, Napster's Web traffic soared to its then all-time high of 849,000 visitors on July 28, 2000.

Following the popularity of Napster, Gnutella, Freenet, and iMesh are claiming their space in the information-swapping world as well. Gnutella also lets users share digital files; however, with this model, users share directly with each other rather than going through a company to facilitate the swap. (Gnutella has also been acclaimed by many research scientists as the perfect tool for distributed data on massive scientific research projects.) To stop this bandwagon, record companies would have to pursue and sue each user individually. Freenet makes it even more difficult for the record companies—it uses encryption to hide the identities of its users; iMesh simply reminds its visitors to respect copyright law and that compliance is their responsibility.

Undoubtedly, many companies will pursue the P-to-P model, especially in the areas of file sharing, processing, and storage, and there are lessons for everyone about creating successful innovations. The recording industry feels pressure to innovate and move to the next level, but the problem is that they don't have a clear picture of how they should innovate and what their business models should look like once they've finished their transformation. Consumers have voted, and it's clear that they like the Napster model, but it is a model that didn't until recently generate revenues, and has yet to earn profits. While the record industry feels the need to push forward, it is a push to destination unknown. And even if the record companies want to change, they have both artists and retailers to satisfy—without these vital demand chain partners, it loses talent for its products and over 90 percent of its product distribution. At this point, no one is sure of the best solution. It seems a good fit that an entertainment company would buy Napster and figure out how best to fit it into its model. We also believed RIAA could have reaped many rewards had it bought Napster, charged a minimal monthly fee, gotten sponsorships from industry members, and used the medium to promote the entire music industry.

Keeping a close watch on the Napster saga is the film industry, which is just a few short steps behind the music industry in its efforts to curb file-swapping of movie videos. The Motion Picture Association of America filed suit against Scour Inc. on July 20, 2000, claiming it facilitates the illegal distribution of copyrighted movies and material over the Internet. Scour, the world's leading search destination for digital entertainment, denied allegations, but had to file a voluntary petition for reorganization under Chapter 11 Bankruptcy Code because of the lawsuits. Other media, such as books and comic strips, have also been affected by the Napster model and will search for ways to adapt to the new realities of the market.

Regardless of which side you take in this debate, you can't deny the effect Napster has had on the file-sharing world; it forever changed how we interact with each other on the Internet. Napster teaches us all an important lesson: Consumers will ultimately decide the fate of new technologies, and they have already voted that P-to-P is here to stay; companies must find a way to build this reality into their strategies. Napster is the perfect example of how a consumer-driven innovation can change the world without much proactive marketing to create groundswell. As we write about Napster today, we don't know what the final outcome will be. We do know that more than 96 million songs were traded on February 12, the day an appellate court said Napster would likely lose at trial. Napster fulfilled one of the most aggressive of goals of any new innovation—creating upheaval in the market.

WHY SOME INNOVATIONS SUCCEED AND OTHERS FAIL

Successful products are those that become culturally anchored, so inextricably a part of a consumer's life and surroundings that he or she wonders "How did I ever live without this?" Imagine doing without personal computers, cars, or telephones with today's values and lifestyles.

New product failures have and will continue to outnumber the successes, with many successes becoming mere footnotes in the book of commerce champions. To avoid such a fate, diffusion needs to occur. Diffusion is defined in *Diffusion of Innovations*, the classic book by Everett Rogers, as: the process by which an innovation (new idea) is communicated through certain channels over time among the members of a social system.

Any manager trying to rescue would-be innovations that have been pushed prematurely from inventors' minds to the market can forecast their potential using a list of diffusion variables: (1) relative advantage, (2) compatibility, (3) complexity, (4) trialability, and (5) observability. Without acceptable levels of a majority of these top-line elements, most products will fail—never generating enough paying customers (or buyers) to build the bottom line.

Relative Advantage—Give Consumers
Compelling Reasons to Switch

The most important factor determining the potential success of a new product is its relative advantage—the degree to which consumers perceive that it will offer substantially greater benefits than the product they currently use. For a new technology to replace an old one, consumers first need reasons to try this new technology and then reasons to justify switching to it. Sometimes a new product just needs to be a little better than an existing one to capture customers; most times it needs to be a lot better. Relative advantage is often relative to how much money and time consumers have invested in their current solutions, how difficult it is to adopt a new solution into a current system or lifestyle, and how satisfied or dissatisfied they are with their current choices.

Why have debit cards taken so long to be accepted? Major advantages exist, but they're advantages primarily for banks and merchants rather than consumers. Since nearly anyone can get a credit card today, cash-less payment is not novel, and debit cards deduct money from a bank account immediately instead of at the end of a financing or "grace" period. About the only consumers who get much relative advantage from the debit card are those who don't trust themselves to use a credit card or checkbook responsibly. It's not surprising that nearly thirty years after debit card technology was introduced it still has very little market penetration.

When analyzing the relative advantage of a new technology, you must consider the degree to which the new product will be a substitute for existing ones or complement the array of products consumers already own. Complementary products don't need to have as many advantages in order to be successful; however, the relative advantages of substitute products (such as a PC replacing a typewriter) must be greater and address at least one of two conditions—dissatisfaction or obvious improvement.

When consumers are acutely dissatisfied with their existing solutions, acceptance of a new alternative is more likely. After years of frustration with the typewriter, tired of using an eraser to correct typewritten documents and the messiness of making "carbon" copies, consumers were understandably excited by computerized word processing. Had preparing an error-free document been easy and efficient, a substitute product would have been a tough sell. The pathway to technological change is strewn with products that are "better" than existing solutions, but in order to get consumers to throw out the old and bring in the new, simply "better" doesn't cut it. New technologies must be dramatically better if they are to replace existing products.

Innovations must also offer up an obvious perceived improvement in productivity, reliability, or some other characteristic valuable to consumers in order for them to buy. The catch is that consumers, not just the seller, must perceive the improvement as obvious and significant or the product will be quickly forgotten.

Take CD-i for example. Phillips introduced CD-i in the early 1990s, just as CD-ROMs were becoming all the rage in corporate training, computer games, and consumer-educational programs. Phillips improved on the computer-based product by inventing an interactive television-based version that allowed groups to view the program in a seminar format rather than individuals huddled around a computer screen. Users had to purchase a CD-i player (which also played audio CDs) and special discs, but the consumers most likely to buy these types of products were already investing in computers for just this purpose. Despite Phillips's advertising, marketing, financial support, and global distribution system, CD-i flopped. Consumers didn't perceive the advantages to be great enough to change their current behaviors and expectations.

It is possible, however, with coupling or "tying," to gain acceptance of new and improved products even though consumers don't perceive the relative advantage to be large. Simply couple the new product with one consumers already buy, so they don't have a choice but to receive the new product. Microsoft was the master of tying—coupling its Web browser and other products with its Windows operating system—until Justice Thomas Penfield Jackson and the U.S. Justice Department stepped in.

Another strategy, one less likely to incur the risk of antitrust prosecution, is to look for changes in consumers' behaviors or lives that make them more receptive to changes that involve new products. If you are trying to sell broadband Internet connections (DSL or cable-based), getting people to switch from present dial-up connections is tough in spite of the relative advantage. When consumers move to a new home, however, they must make new decisions about phones, cable, electronics, and many other products. Chances are they will be in a "switching" frame of mind, and that's the time to reach them with targeted marketing programs about new products that they might otherwise never consider. Similarly, getting consumers to adopt new appliances that are Web-enabled is tough even though there are advantages to the new technologies. But targeting architects and builders of new, upscale homes may provide an opportunity to sell innovative, upper-income, educated consumers new technologies while building a "home prepared for the future."

Though most consumers are not eagerly awaiting new products such as Net appliances, older consumers may become more receptive to such technology as changes in their lives occur. All it may take is one e-mailed digital picture of the grandchildren to make grandparents get online with an easy-to-use Net appliance. The Net appliances can also be promoted to young technology-savvy parents in the same way for holiday gift giving. *Parents* and *Modern Maturity* magazines might be better advertising media than general-interest publications, but only if based on creative appeals that show very specific ways Net appliances provide a relative advantage for getting photos of the grandchildren and for sending photos to grandparents.

We are always surprised at how few new-product business plans deal with the reality that most consumers would rather fight than switch to new products, even though the new products may offer relative advantages. The hard, cold reality of new product introduction is that only a small group of people, known as innovators in research language and described as techies or nerds by everyone else, actively embrace technological change rather than resist it.

The lesson that you should draw from marketing new technology products is a tough one, but it also explains why the move from bricks-and-mortar retailing to Web-based retailing is slow to happen: Consumer inertia is a cold reality; breaking consumer inertia requires unusually creative marketing strategies and real deliverable added value, which comes from having sound, well-oiled business systems.

Compatibility—Make It Easy for Consumers to Adopt New Products

Compatibility refers to the degree to which a new product "fits" or is consistent with the existing practices, values, needs, and past experiences of the potential adopters. Many computer software and hardware product decisions are based on compatibility of the new product with an individual's existing system, a reason why software developers produced lots of products for PCs and relatively few for Apple.

Compatibility affects the diffusion of Internet business in many ways. One reason we forecast more rapid growth for B-to-B than B-to-C marketplaces is the compatibility of physical distribution for online business purchases with existing transportation systems. In other words, it's easier to move a lot of boxes to stores or warehouses than to dozens or even hundreds of homes. The B-to-B sites that will be most successful will also be those that make the buying process, including navigation on the Web, most similar or compatible with the way businesses already buy off-line.

The strategy of making online business buying as similar as possible to existing business practices is how PrintNation.com took the lead in the B-to-B printing industry, winning such top industry awards as the Upside and Forbes.com B-to-B "Best of the Web." Described as the world's largest printing equipment and supplies superstore, the Irvine, California–based company sells 100,000 paper and printing products as a dealer for Georgia Pacific and some 1,300 other firms. PrintNation.com founders Tony Seba and Freddie Seba had strong technology backgrounds from RSA Security and Ingram Micro as well as degrees from MIT and Yale and MBAs from Stanford. In order to understand the needs and buying practices of the printing industry, the company reached out to the printing trades by hiring industry veterans Kirk Buckham and David Steinhardt and other key executives with strong paper, printing, and distribution backgrounds.

PrintNation reaches customers in traditional ways—by advertising in printing trade journals, attending industry trade shows, and mailing information regularly to printers. PrintNation also operates its warehouses and transportation systems much like successful off-line paper dealers, with the addition of the efficiency that arises from the Web. Most important, however, is the fact that it built (and constantly updates) its website to be highly compatible with the way firms buy paper. Users of the website report that it helps printers save time and money, usually without switching vendors.

Most printers are online and e-literate because much printing content is transmitted electronically, but that doesn't mean the average printer doesn't like talking to a person—the way vendor relationships were traditionally created and fostered. Accordingly, PrintNation.com's website prominently features its phone number for 24/7 access to a live person. In addition to offering all the items a printing firm might need in its business, PrintNation also operates an auction site because it understands the industry well enough to know that nearly every printing firm is either looking to buy a piece of equipment or looking to sell excess equipment. The online auction meets those needs well.

When you develop your strategy for a new technological product, follow PrintNation's lead and ask the critical question "How compatible is it with the way potential customers now buy and use the products we seek to replace?" If the new technology isn't compatible, the risk of failure escalates. PrintNation.com illustrates a philosophy we consider fundamental to attaining success in e-commerce: It's far easier to change a Web business to fit the way people buy than to change the way people buy to fit your Web business. It's no wonder that *Upside* magazine named already-profitable PrintNation as one of its top "Hot 100 Private Companies."

Complexity—Don't Make Consumers Feel Stupid

Complexity describes the degree to which an innovation is perceived as difficult to understand and use. In a nation where it's easy to believe that fully half the VCRs are blinking "12:00," it should be clear that the more complex the new product, the more difficult it will be to gain mass acceptance. Why? Consumers are time-starved and want to spend as little time as possible learning how to use new gadgets. Some tech-oriented consumers may feel that complexity lends credibility to the product, but most consumers get frustrated if products are too complex. If they realize that a product is complex in the store, they may well forgo purchase, or if they don't realize until they get home, they may discontinue using it. Manufacturers also risk alienating consumers with products they can't figure out how to use—confusion makes consumers feel stupid, and they resent that. Microwave ovens, though initially somewhat disruptive to people's cooking behavior, diffused rapidly because they were easy to use.

The complexity principle dictates that consumers are more likely to try products they perceive to be relatively simple to use and understand. Instructions play an important role in creating this perception—the more complex the use or assembly instructions, the less likely the product is to succeed.

Trialability—Give Consumers a Chance to Try; Then Get a Commitment

New products are more apt to succeed when consumers can try them on a limited basis with limited financial risk. That's why P & G and General Foods give away millions of new products each year. Sampling, couponing, and trial-size products all induce trial of new soaps, foods, perfumes, and other low-unit-value, consumer-packaged goods. Creative versions of these methods also work for expensive, complex, high-involvement discontinuous innovations. For example, auto manufacturers use leases and car rental agencies to introduce consumers to new car models.

Trialability is another reason we believe pure-play dot-coms will have to develop some sort of physical presence. People want to "try" a new product before they buy it—and for most consumers that includes any major electronic or computer product. It explains why over 50 percent of Circuit City's online customers elect to select and buy their merchandise at company stores, according to CIO Dennis Bowman.

Similar to Gillette's strategy of giving away razors to build ongoing sales for its razorblades, AOL gave away its software on CDs along with

250 or more hours of free Internet access to allow consumers to try the Internet. AOL couldn't have achieved higher distribution rates if it had dropped the discs from airplanes over America's largest cities. With over 23 million subscribers today, AOL is the leading ISP, with its competitors far behind in the race. Hypernet and Freeride took the free trial one step farther and created a free-use model, giving consumers free Internet access if they agreed to watch online advertising and submit personal information.

More recently, NetZero.com and Juno (which also offered paid Internet access) entered the free ISP arena, with 7 million consumers flocking to NetZero by the end of 2000. But critics wonder about the viability of the model. CEO Mark Goldston says advertisers are responding well to the NetZero model, and he expects to generate enough revenue from advertising to continue supporting free access for consumers. We agree that the research aspect of getting information from a vast online audience is valuable to marketers, but critics wonder how long consumers will give up their time and privacy for an average payback of $40 in free services. Only consumers who value their time as less than the payback will use the service in the long run.

NetZero, however, is not alone in its efforts to entice consumers with free Internet access. Over a hundred free ISPs were in business by August 2000, most of which were backed by real-world companies looking for ways to build brand and lure customers to their sites, such as Kmart's BlueLight.com, created in conjunction with Yahoo!. But dozens of independent free-access providers, including Worldspy.com and Freeweb LLC, have shut down because their advertising revenues couldn't cover operating expenses.

Goldston says NetZero won't be next. In an effort to increase revenues, NetZero has shifted gears, creating a research division offering marketers general, anonymous data about user browsing habits. Skeptics are quick to point out that NetZero users are likely to be low-budget consumers who are less likely to respond to online ads, but Goldston responds by saying it is precisely those consumers who will bring mass-market advertisers to the Internet. The company has also crafted new ventures, joining with companies such as General Motors, that want to create their own free ISP. NetZero remains committed to free access, but Goldston acknowledges the need for a banner-free, nominal-fee service—NZPlatinum. The lesson to be learned is clear: Free trial is an effective way to get people to try a new product, but it is an effective strategy only if the product is valuable enough for consumers to continue using it.

Retailers that want to attract new, Internet-unsavvy consumers to their websites should let consumers try and experiment with their sites while in the store. Setting up kiosks near customer service centers to let consumers try browsing retailers' wares online lets them experiment in a consumer-friendly environment where they can ask for help. Dot-coms may partner with retail outlets, such as Kinko's or shopping malls, to set up kiosks that consumers can explore and search for a wide variety of products and information.

Observability—Create Ways for Consumers to See Product Results

People watch other people using and benefiting from new products, and the more they observe a good product, the more likely it is to be successful and diffuse quickly. Observability (or communicability) reflects the degree to which results from using a new product are visible to friends and neighbors. For instance, a teenager might see the social acceptance and compliments a peer receives when wearing a particular fashion, clothing brand, hairstyle, or fragrance and choose to buy the same product in order to receive the same benefit, a principle that drove the success of Abercrombie & Fitch. Vans plastered with the Webvan logo let other consumers know that someone in their neighborhood is using the grocery delivery service. The use of celebrities often enhances the visibility of products, even on the Internet, which explains why sports heroes like Michael Jordan, John Elway, and Wayne Gretsky teamed up to launch MVP.com.

Microsoft introduced the graphic interface in Windows in part because people saw others use a mouse with their Apple computers. Wherever Apples were in use, people still wedded to the word commands of DOS could readily observe the Apple interface (which it had "borrowed" from Xerox) and the freedom and ease of use it gave users. Apple's improved customer experience coupled with the observability and communication that occurred between Apple users and everyone else forced the inevitable switch to a graphic interface by Gates and company. And with the switch, the mouse-driven technology diffused from a small audience of innovators and early adopters to the mass market.

Apple would rely on a similar strategy of observability to rejuvenate its brand in 1999. The introduction of the iMac in a rainbow of extreme colors created a buzz within computing circles, as everyone took notice of the brightly colored machines. An important piece of the strategy's success was getting lots of people to talk about the product, fueled by the rampant placement of iMacs in movies and television shows. But generating (favorable) word of mouth takes time, not just money. That's a lesson that many dot-com companies had to learn the hard way, after pouring as much as $2 million into one thirty-second Super Bowl commercial to yield negligible name recognition.

Swim at Your Own Risk

These five characteristics—relative advantage, compatibility, complexity, trialability, and observability—should be used by marketers and researchers to rate the likelihood of adoption of a new product in the marketplace. Ignore them, as many people do, and swim at your own risk in the sea of products that flood the marketplace each year. We have seen marketers and entrepreneurs get so caught up in the brilliance or assumed need for their innovation that they introduce it regardless of how it performs on these five characteristics. Most wind up shaking their heads in dismay when the market turns its back or never even notices their innovation.

INNOVATIONS AND MARKETING STRATEGIES: THE GOOD, THE BAD, AND THE UGLY

Innovations fail or succeed for many reasons. For example, failure to perform well in any of the five characteristics just discussed can lead to failure in the marketplace. But beyond the characteristics of the innovation itself, how the marketing and communication programs are implemented mean the difference between a new product's ultimate diffusion or demise. All of these points are relevant to the big strategy—attracting, delighting, and keeping profitable customers. Figure 7.2 summarizes the effects of good and bad marketing strategies on both good and bad products. The most likely outcomes of coupling good marketing plans with good innovations (Schwab.com, Expedia.com, and VictoriasSecret .com) and bad marketing with bad innovations are easy to predict. However, what happens when good things happen to bad products or bad things happen to good products? The outcomes are a little more complicated.

When Good Marketing Happens to Bad Products

Good marketing strategies can make or break the long-term success of an innovation. Promotion programs, including brand strategies, publicity, public relations, and advertising, can aid in the rise and diffusion of a good product through the marketplace, while the same programs can kill a product if it is poorly designed, not ready for mass introduction, unwanted by consumers, or simply doesn't work.

Sometimes good things happen to bad products. Wendy's developed and aired one of the most successful ad campaigns in the history of television advertising in the 1980s. Who can forget Clara Pellar, the small but

FIGURE 7.2   Long Term Effects of Marketing Strategies on Innovations

	GOOD MARKETING OR "GOOD THINGS"	BAD MARKETING OR "BAD THINGS"
	Good	Good and Bad
Good Innovation	Long-term growth following the traditional Product Life Cycle schematic	Sporadic spurts of growth and decline, cycling between good and bad news or publicity
	Bad	Ugly
Bad Innovation	Meteoric rise in levels of awareness and trial, with sudden collapse of sales and attention	Product is dead on arrival

feisty eightysomething customer standing in front of the hamburger counter demanding to know "Where's the beef?" Customers loved the ad and sales increased by 19 percent that year; unfortunately, when those customers got to the restaurants they loathed the experience because of quality issues that developed after Dave Thomas retired as CEO. Wendy's tried to fix its sales slump with great advertising before it fixed its dining experience. Eventually, Wendy's cleaned up its act; today, Dave Thomas's ads and his restaurants are top-notch—as are his sales.

Executives from Wendy's and a host of hotly advertised dot-coms that couldn't deliver in the market will attest to the dangers of creating good buzz before getting their businesses in order. Just ask the folks at CrossWorlds Software, a leading provider of e-business infrastructure software that integrates internal operations and extends these operations over the Internet. CrossWorld's product suite is comprised of business integration modules and related tools that together enable business process integration both within the enterprise and among trading partners over the Internet. Duking it out in the marketplace against tough competitors, such as Oracle, Right Works, and Ariba, meant having to get the CrossWorld name in front of customers—and CEO Katrina Garnett was the person to pull off an attention-grabbing ad blitz. Clad in a black cocktail dress, she appeared in a Dewar's profile-style ad, shot by Richard Avedon and splashed across the pages of trendy fashion magazines. Though the ads got a lot of attention, the product didn't deliver what consumers expected, and Garnett was asked to step down. Since then, under the watchful eye of CEO Alfred Amoroso, CrossWorlds has focused on its business operations and posted record revenues of $17.1 million for fourth quarter 2000 and $51.3 million revenue for the year.

The worst thing a firm can do is create great advertising before getting the product and business operations right. Great advertising only accelerates the demise of bad products.

When Bad Things Happen to Good Products

Sometimes, despite product quality and consumer need, bad things can devastate the future of a good innovation. Beyond product defects or mishaps, such as the Jack in the Box tainted-meat tragedy of the 1990s or the Firestone tire recall of 2000, poor timing and marketing programs affect the long-term viability of even the best of innovations. The fluctuations in the stock market that followed on the heels of the fall of many technology stocks caused problems for even "solid" retail and e-commerce firms.

Think of what happened to the stock market during 1999 and 2000. Wal-Mart, The Limited, and a host of other retailers posted strong earnings and increased same store sales, only to watch their stocks decline. The hype was in the tech arena—no one gave a second glance to the triumphs of traditional retailers (except perhaps astute long-term investors). Many, such as Sherwin-Williams and ServiceMaster, chose to buy back their stock, thereby increasing value for their existing shareholders.

Soon the tide turned and a similar backlash occurred among tech firms, with even strong e-based firms—such as Cisco, AOL, and eBay—feeling the effects of Wall Street skepticism on their stocks. The bankruptcies and lackluster performances of a majority of dot-coms meant dismal stock prices for the entire sector. Viable dot-coms will have to ride out the financial storm that will claim the lives of many of their competitors. Like traditional retailers before them, they will have to take advantage of their time away from the spotlight and concentrate on their operations—controlling expenses, retaining customers, and increasing efficiency.

HOW PRODUCTS DIFFUSE THROUGH THE MARKET

From thousands of studies and the experience of successful marketers, we know that new products (including new Internet applications, new technologies, and new ways of doing business) must go through five stages in order to diffuse through the market—knowledge, persuasion, decision, implementation, and confirmation. First, consumers must learn of and give attention to the new product and how it works. Marketers must consider how to get opinion leaders to use the product, how to stimulate word-of-mouth, and how best to increase awareness of a product and its benefits. Then consumers form favorable or unfavorable attitudes toward the innovation, sometimes giving it a "vicarious trial" in their minds. During persuasion, individuals consider the potential gains from adoption against the potential losses of switching from the product now used.

Consumers then decide between adopting or rejecting the innovation. When Windows 2000 was introduced, some potential adopters studied and bought, while others rejected it because it was NT-based and not as compatible with their existing operating systems. Yet some consumers rejected it without ever really considering it, dispelling the assumption that "everyone wants to try something new."

Finally, consumers implement and put an innovation to use, which leads to confirmation, the process by which consumers seek reinforcement for their decision. But consumers sometimes reverse previous decisions, especially when exposed to conflicting messages about the innovation, causing dissonance. Those who adopt products can reject them after short or long periods of time, and vice versa.

As individuals move through this process, they affect the rate of diffusion of innovations through the general population. This process is shown in Figure 7.3. Organizations influence consumers with marketing and com-

FIGURE 7.3   How Consumers Decide the Fate of Innovations

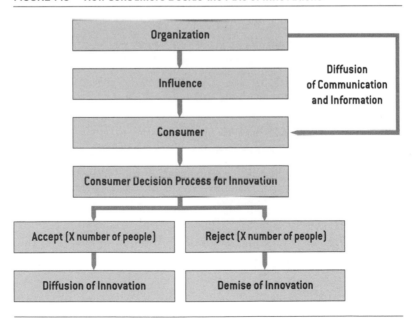

munication programs, while peers and other opinion leaders exert their own influence. Consumers (or end users in the case of B-to-B e-commerce) then proceed through the diffusion decision stages and ultimately accept or reject an innovation, though they can vacillate between these two options. Depending on the number of consumers that accept versus reject an innovation, the product either diffuses through the population or dies in the marketplace.

DISCONTINUANCE: WHAT HAPPENS WHEN CONSUMERS CHANGE THEIR MINDS

The enormous deficits incurred by firms such as Amazon.com and others to induce trial would be justified if sales and customer retention continued in the long run. But what if people try buying on the Internet a few times, find a few applications that they repeat, and discontinue most of the others? It's a possibility that, for the most part, was ignored by early e-commerce entrepreneurs. Today, though the number of people on the Internet continues to increase, the proportion of people shopping online is declining, a process we call the "Pringles Problem."

Pringles, the quirky modern version of the old-fashioned potato chip introduced by P & G in the 1980s, was by all initial accounts a huge success. Consumers plucked canisters off the shelves of their grocery stores and sales boomed. The cool canister kept the chips fresh, took up less space in kitchen cabinets, and prevented crushing and spilling. But as quickly as consumers tried Pringles, they dropped them. After purchasing Pringles several times, consumers went back to bagged chips—the old chips simply tasted better. Yet for every consumer who discontinued use, a new consumer tried the product. With strong sales and word-of-mouth, P & G invested millions in marketing and in building additional manufacturing plants before it detected the very real trend toward product failure. With a recent revamp of the product—a "new, better-tasting" product and an upbeat marketing campaign appealing to younger consumers— P & G has rejuvenated the Pringles brand, but still claims only a small portion of total chip sales.

Could this same process be happening to B-to-C commerce?

"Surfing the Web" became a phrase of modern language in the late 1990s. It describes well what nearly everyone does when they first experience the Internet, especially the technology enthusiasts who drove the great increases in Internet usage during that early period. But you don't hear the phrase much anymore. Why? Because after a few virginal months in cyberspace, consumers usually settle into a groove, returning only to the sites where they find real value. All evidence indicates that consumers derive value from information and communications—e-mail being the most valued application for most consumers. But there is no clear indication that shopping is one of the applications with little more value than Pringles. There are situations where Pringles is clearly a better choice than bagged potato chips, but it is the choice of only certain segments of the market, resulting in a small proportion of total potato chip sales.

It's possible that a new technology can be accepted by the masses only to be discontinued later by everyone except a small, dedicated minority. The CB radio comes to mind. Driving on the highways of America in the 1970s and early 1980s meant talking to fellow travelers on a CB radio, keeping track of "Smokey," getting information from truckers about traffic, creating "community" on the road, and just having fun while driving. Today, there is still a dedicated core of CB radio users, but most consumers have discontinued its use.

Fast forward to today. Chat rooms offer benefits similar to the CB radio and may follow a similar life cycle, in which people initially spend a lot of time but decrease or discontinue after the initial thrill is gone. Similarly, many early purchasers of digital cameras found them so time consuming to use that they returned to analog (film) cameras, except for special uses and professional needs.

As long as new users of the Internet are increasing, the sales curves will also increase. At some point, however, the innovation reaches maximum penetration, and sales level off and often drop among former users. Today, over half of Americans have bought online and the percentage is rising fast in other countries as well. Whether or not they like shopping on the Internet determines whether they "adopt" it for the long run. We recently interviewed a young man who, at eleven years of age, is nearly a straight-A student and as Internet-savvy as any, searching the Web for any facts he needs to know. We asked this typical member of the "click and drag" generation what he likes to buy on the Internet and his answer, surprisingly, was "nothing." When we asked him if lack of a credit card was the problem, he replied most revealingly, "No, it's just easier to buy most things in a store." He added, "The more I get to know about online [shopping], the less I trust it to get things right."

From the mouths of babes! Analyzing whether consumers, including today's generation who grew up on the Internet, will adopt e-tailing and for what types of products or services requires research. Remember, even though today's kids are learning on the Web and communicating with friends, they are also going to stores with parents and grandparents, learning through good old consumer socialization the skills of buying and shopping off-line. This is a generation that will do many things alone, online, sitting in front of their computers. How will they get their socialization? How will they feel a part of the community? How will they want to spend time with their families? These are all questions that must be analyzed in order to determine the size of the adopters market.

To prevent consumers from abandoning e-tailing, dot-coms should consider the following strategies:

- Develop personal relationships with consumers through e-mail or other individualized communication.
- Offer consumers reasons to visit your site and buy, such as new offers not found in stores or points in a loyalty program.
- Offer consumers specials available only online.
- Give consumers updates on new fashions, products that compliment previous purchases, and warranty or recall information.

The environment will provide dozens of reasons for consumers to abandon use of any new technology; a retailer needs to provide convincing reasons to continue use. Taking a page from traditional retailers' play books, e-tailers will have to shift from attracting customers to retaining customers.

INCORPORATING CONSUMERS' INFLUENCE ON DIFFUSION INTO STRATEGIC PLANS

From a strategic perspective, one of the most important forecasts a marketing manager or executive can make when presenting the marketing plan for the latest, greatest innovation since sliced bread, is market size. And an extremely important variable in determining initial and potential market size is the diffusion rate. Though discussed thoroughly in Chapter 4, accurate segmentation analysis is required to forecast potential market size and rate of diffusion. Given the fact that a new product must first satisfy customers' needs, wants, and expectations rather than the dreams of a management team, understanding a segment's level of innovativeness and adoption practices leads to a bankable sales forecast. If marketers know that a segment is likely to adopt a new product slowly, meager initial sales and slowly upward trending early sales trends won't be disappointing.

Forecasting How Consumers Will React to the Innovation

While formal analyses of why products fail might point to product life cycles, poor performance, or failed communication plans, often the bottom-line issue is lack of understanding of the intended market. For example, firms don't always understand how targeted consumers are likely to react to new products and why.

Remember "push" technology (in which companies sent information to consumers)—it was going to make "pull" (in which consumers directed individual information flow) obsolete by revolutionizing content delivery with reversed data flow. PointCast became this paradigm's poster child. Customers indicated their areas of interest, and PointCast compiled and disseminated the latest news on those topics, regardless of file size, whether they wanted it or not. What sounded like a great idea lacked understanding of individual consumers and the reaction of employers to the innovation. Massive amounts of information coupled with bandwidth limitations brought company systems to an information-overload-inspired halt. PointCast was subsequently banned from corporations around the country as individuals and organizations collectively gasped "e-nough already!"

Consumers' reactions to new products and technologies depend on consumers' individual characteristics, from educational background to degree of innovativeness. Different consumers possess different levels of innovativeness (how averse or receptive they are to trying and adopting new products and innovations), affecting which advertising and positioning strategies will be most effective in recruiting and retaining them. For example, highly innovative consumers (early adopters) attach more importance to stimulation, creativity, and curiosity than less innovative consumers do. Marketers can highlight these characteristics to target product offerings and advertising to specific segments. Less innovative consumers usually react better to messages that focus on a new technology's ease of use and compatibility with current equipment or consumption behaviors.

Marketers need to determine who is most likely to buy the new product, a condition determined by individuals' personalities, their aversion to or acceptance of risk, social status, and education level. In addition to individual characteristics, the role within the family also affects adoption behavior. The decision maker for home products and food, for example, is more likely to try new products in those categories than in categories in which he or she does not have much experience or is not likely to make final decisions. Although 80 percent of the early adopters of Internet technology were male, today the majority of new users are female, a fact that may explain why male-developed websites of the past are increasingly unsuccessful with today's majority of female consumers. Understanding these characteristics are the "commerce" skills that are found among executives of today's successful retailers and consumer goods manufacturers. Executives of e-commerce firms must possess or acquire those same analytical skills if the products and services they create on the Internet are to succeed.

Forecasting How Long It Will Take to Diffuse

Managers often ask "What is the single biggest mistake executives make when introducing new products?" Our answer is "Failing to understand the time it takes to gain acceptance of new products." Many managers, entrepreneurs, and investors believe that when a new product or service is introduced, the masses either buy it or they don't. Yet rarely, if ever, does the market work that way.

As with most things, timing is everything—sometimes causing an innovation's performance to lie somewhere between success and failure. In an era where instant gratification is expected, some innovations are grounded before they ever have a chance to fly. Sometimes products emerge on the scene ahead of their time but manage to establish enough of a following to survive the lean years and remain poised to take off when the market catches up to the innovation.

Home banking, for example, was introduced in the early 1980s, remained on the back burner for two decades, and is just beginning to receive market acceptance (how widespread that market acceptance will be has yet to be determined).

In fact, the Internet falls into this category. What many have categorized as a meteoric rise in acceptance and popularity got its humble beginnings in 1969 in government and academia. Its evolution has really followed the traditional product life cycle schematic of growth; its diffusion to the masses is what's caused all the recent ruckus. Contrary to the beliefs of some analysts, the Internet did pass through the traditional diffusion stages and was adopted first by early adopters (innovators). These first sales made to computer techies kept the innovation going until popular applications, such as chat rooms, information search, and e-tailing, spread through traditional early majority, majority, late adopter, and laggard classes of consumers as the technology became increasingly easy to use and more goods and services became available to the growing number of users.

Introducing new products successfully almost always involves directing marketing efforts to those few buyers they know hold the key to reaching many, as CompuServe did by marketing its services to computer-savvy consumers in the early 1980s. The Internet didn't arrive overnight and e-tailers shouldn't expect e-tailing to capture a significant portion of consumer dollars overnight either.

Gathering Information from the Marketplace

New product development requires coordination between marketing, engineering, research, and other parts of the firm along with extensive knowledge about the end user. Important to the innovation development process is research and there is a wealth of research available to enable managers to understand how consumers decide to try and adopt new products. In addition to formal research, marketing managers need grassroots ways of understanding consumer reaction to new products.

The following companies provide examples of using effective tactics to gather information from the market in forecasting diffusion rates:

- *Silicon Graphics, Inc.* It turned to heavy graphics users for knowledge about their usage behaviors and needs and used it in designing a new generation of (now very popular) graphics supercomputers.

- *Sony.* It requires its managers to talk with dealers and consumers on a constant basis to get their reactions to new products from Sony and its competitors. It can use this information to analyze future diffusion rates and sales as well as to influence future designs of products.

- *Campbell Soup.* The company has its managers do their own grocery shopping. This type of knowledge helps management understand how consumers choose brands and shop for various products, including Campbell's products.

These types of tactics help explain how consumers evaluate, accept, and reject new technologies and how to capitalize on consumer behavior to market and sell more effectively.

THE EFFECTS OF INNOVATION

When you learned about inventors in school, you undoubtedly heard the stories about Alexander Graham Bell and Henry Ford. The lessons often focused on how their inventions changed society—how the telephone allowed people to communicate in real time and how the car allowed people to move their bodies more quickly from one place to another. Life would never be the same.

The lessons to be learned from most innovations of the latter half of the twentieth century, however, should focus on the effect of the innovation on the company and its creator—look at what the innovation means to the firm's bottom line. Though innovations from CDs to voice mail have created a potential high quality of life for society, many of them have solved the same problems other previous inventions addressed, and actually affected society in a largely cosmetic way. For example, the microwave oven allowed consumers to cook faster, thus freeing-up time for the new wave of working women who had to cook dinner for their families at the end of a long day on the job. The focus here was what the product meant to the company that sold it (profits) and to a lesser degree what the product did for individuals.

To examine an innovation or invention from a societal point of view requires understanding what it means for those who adopt it and for those who don't. Consumers who didn't buy the microwave oven didn't suffer severe consequences. We would argue that in this light, the Internet forces consumer behaviorists and social anthropologists to revisit the lessons of the telephone and the automobile. Policymakers and CEOs need to address how the digital divide will change the structure and behavior of society. They will have to monitor the expanding gap between the haves and the have-nots, which may lead to a society in which the haves work to take care of the have-nots.

Marketers collectively salivate at the thought of a global community—one in which they can reach customers from around the world. But consumer behaviorists interested in more than just increasing sales for their companies must also concern themselves with the masses of people not included in this global village. The connectivity chasm almost ensures that today's undesirable market segments will be tomorrow's technology casualties. Corporations around the world will have to unite their efforts to bring jobs and connectivity to these forgotten pockets of people. Expect these types of social issues to rise to the forefront of international political debates in the next few decades.

CHAPTER 8

THE RISE OF E-COMMERCE IN THE BUSINESS WORLD

TRAVEL FORWARD IN TIME for a moment if you will. The year is 2016. There's a young girl, Josette, poised in front of a Web camera celebrating her sixteenth birthday with all her friends and relatives around the country. She opens her e-cards, one of which instructs her to click on her WebPad to make an eagerly awaited purchase—her first car. Clicking past several websites, she chooses Daimler.com, preferring this brand over the several generic Build-Your-Own-Car.com versions.

In a process that reminds you of your own youthful experience putting together a Dell computer (component by component, feature by feature) during your first major online purchase almost twenty years earlier, you watch Josette pick the most recent Chrysler brand. She clicks and chooses her own variations—Honda seats like those in her parents' car, a Bose audio system, and an HP built-in computer/television screen—instead of the standard Chrysler components. After selecting Sherwin-Williams's custom metallic blue exterior paint, Ralph Lauren designer fabrics, and adjustable cup holders, Josette confirms that her grandfather has transferred enough cybercurrency to her account to buy the birthday gift of her dreams, and clicks "submit." When the e-mail confirmation arrives telling her the car will be delivered to her home by a local dealer next Wednesday, she takes her first bite of birthday cake, not realizing that today also marks the sixteenth birthday of the B-to-B venture that made her cybershopping experience possible—Covisint.

Covisint was born February 25, 2000, and lived its first months as Newco (the commerce world's equivalent of Baby Doe). Finally, on May 16, 2000, its proud parents, General Motors, Ford Motor, Daimler-Chrysler, Renault, Nissan Motor, and later Toyota (which since has questioned its participation), agreed on the name Covisint—described as the largest Internet business ever born. The name (pronounced ko'-vis-ent) is derived from the roots of many words used to describe the parents' vision for the future of the child. "From the concepts of connectivity, collaboration, communication, and cooperation to the visibility that the Internet and the integration our solutions will provide, as well as the integrity with which we will conduct business and our international reach and resources, 'Covisint' is a succinct expression of our promise to our customers," the proud parents declared. (Let's hope the committee that designs the systems works better than the committee that created such a name!)

When Giants Unite

Covisint is a new breed of e-commerce giant that offers the unprecedented opportunity—and threat—of changing every firm in the supply chain of one of the world's most important industries. The ambitious parents' goals for Covisint are to use the power of the Internet to speed the flow of material through the supply chain, increase response to consumer demand, and deliver new products to market faster than ever before. These goals embody what the Internet can do for the B-to-B world.

In 1991, we presented a paper predicting the birth of this baby at a J.D. Powers conference, based on research about how cars were sold in Japan. Even then, Japanese auto dealers took orders in homes for most cars, permitting dealers to operate with only two or three cars in their space-constrained showrooms. The order was transmitted to the manufacturer and the specified car was pulled from the distribution system, delivered to the consumer by the dealer, and replaced with a new car made to the specs of the sold car. This practice reduces costs of carrying inventory and "floor plan" financing charges, both major expenses associated with carrying hundreds of cars on lots and showrooms of American car dealers. Manufacturers used the term SOMO (sell one, make one) to describe the manufacturing process; we used it to describe the function of the entire supply chain that we envisioned for the future. This semi-custom ordering system helps explain the emergence of specialized, short-run vehicles aimed at very specific market segments, such as the Plymouth Prowler and the PT Cruiser. With the addition of Internet technology linking all major suppliers and manufacturers (if it truly works), Covisint has the potential of becoming an extremely efficient demand chain, delivering

built-to-order capability around the needs and desires of consumer preferences and behavior.

How far off in the future is the reality of the Covisint model? From
a consumer standpoint, it still resides in dreams of what possibilities lie
ahead, but from a business standpoint, the reality is here today. B-to-B
transactions and partnerships housed on the Internet define the cost and
labor savings that will be required to remain viable in an era focused on
increased efficiency, growth in profits, and reductions in cost. Today's
B-to-B models are the foundation for tomorrow's B-to-B-to-C strategies.
While the consumer aspect may be publicly touted as the ultimate goal of
developing these fortified models, today it is a mere by-product of the efficiencies that supply chains are experiencing almost immediately after
implementation. Josette may in fact order and receive her car as described
by the year 2016, but more important, partners of Covisint or other to-be-
created exchanges could experience supply-chain efficiencies and cost
savings much sooner once the players and transactions are in place.

Why B-to-C E-tailers Need to Understand B-to-B E-commerce

Winning in the future marketplace depends on the efficiency of the supply
chains of which you are a member. In the case of a retailer, the supply chain
will make or break your organization's long-term viability. Wal-Mart is great
for many reasons; foremost is its tremendously efficient supply chain. Try
as they might, competitors can't beat its channel efficiencies, which it
passes on to consumers in the form of price reductions, in-stock merchandise, and enhanced customer satisfaction. Retailers, take note of
what's happening in the B-to-B cybermarket. As boring as it sometimes
seems, the insights you capture may be the best ways to make retail buying more efficient and less costly, which means more to your bottom line.

THE KILLER APP

If B-to-C commerce is the tip of the iceberg, then B-to-B commerce is the
rest of the glacier. All firms, regardless of their position in the supply
chain, are positioned to reap the rewards of technology when applied to
B-to-B selling and transactions, making B-to-B the killer application of the
Internet. While firms struggle with how to apply the technology successfully to B-to-C commerce, others are profiting from new applications in
the B-to-B world.

You've heard the predictions—$2.5 trillion of B-to-B e-commerce
sales by 2003 (forecasted by Merrill Lynch) and $7.8 trillion by 2004

(forecast by the Gartner Group). Compare these to the forecasts in the $100 billion range for B-to-C, and even the most savvy e-tailers have to admit that today's greatest applications lie in the B-to-B arena. The key for retailers is how to profit from the potential successes.

How Do They Get These Numbers?

One reason B-to-B e-commerce will be so much bigger than B-to-C is the number of transactions on each side of the business equation. While the B-to-B side consists of transactions between manufacturers, distributors, retailers, and various facilitating organizations, the B-to-C side only consists of the transaction between consumer and seller. Iron ore, for example, is sold to steel companies, which sell steel to appliance manufacturers, which sell to distributors, which sell to retailers and ultimately consumers. Even in this limited example, chalk up four transactions for the B-to-B side and only one for the B-to-C side. Even the finished product typically goes through at least three levels of sales, and most of the inputs for making that product will also have three or more levels. Once you understand the number of transactions that might switch to e-commerce transactions, the estimates might be reasonable after all.

The other reason the proportion of B-to-B sales is so much higher than its consumer counterpart is because there is less need to change behavior in order to use the technology. Whether in homes or offices, people don't like to change their behavior—it is the exception rather than the norm. When consumers buy online, their buying patterns are changed, as are product delivery (unless they are switching from catalog purchases), product returns, and customer service.

B-to-B requires fewer changes in how people do things. The purchase is often made from the same firm or one with the same operating characteristics and, in the case of technical products and services, with the same need for assistance from a salesperson or technical consultant. If the prices are different, they may be lower—reflecting transaction cost savings and perhaps an auction process. Delivery of products often occurs the same way as before, utilizing established delivery and distribution systems. In short, B-to-B in its most typical applications requires little fundamental change in the buying and selling functions, confining most changes to peripheral areas of order processing and tracking information.

Moving Business Functions to the Internet

Performing business functions efficiently, a major downfall of the B-to-C e-tail model, is actually an advantage in the B-to-B arena. While the functions remain the same, usually the only required change is the method of carrying out tasks in the basic areas of procurement, payments, supply chain management, inventory management, and data collection and sharing.

Just ask the folks at Eastman Chemical in Kingsport, Tennessee, about how the Internet provides revolutionary increases in efficiency. Switching from paper catalogs, phone calls, and faxed orders, this chemical pioneer today transmits orders on Commerce One's BuySite, allowing it to slash average purchase order costs from $115 to less than $30 according to *Business 2.0*. And Microsoft reportedly saved $16 million the first year it converted to digital purchasing.

Here's the format that underlies such savings in the new economy. In the old economy, a worker needing a new computer submitted a paper form to a supervisor for approval, forwarding it to the purchasing department where a person checked budgets and, if approved, submitted bids from a list of approved vendors. Days later, or perhaps weeks if you worked in a university or the government, the forms were sent out to vendors for delivery. In new-economy firms, an e-mail is sent by the employee to the supervisor; when approved, the purchase order is charged against preauthorized budgets and instantly submitted to the vendor for delivery—probably before the requisition reached the purchasing department prior to converting to a digital process.

We have seen studies in companies of all sizes, calculating the cost of old-economy paper-based purchasing, where the low-end cost was $20 per transaction and where estimates over $100 per transaction were common. Compare those figures to digital purchasing costs falling into the $1 to $5 range, and you'll quickly understand how potential savings of this magnitude provide compelling reasons for the trillion-dollar forecasts.

Potential transaction savings alone make B-to-B e-commerce strategies useful for every firm that wants to increase its efficiency. Online buying is increasing, albeit at mixed rates between industries. For example, the fastest growth is occurring in highly fragmented industries and among commodities that are frequently traded on the "spot" market, with energy and agriculture being among the leaders. However, firms of all sizes should be prepared to adopt this form of buying in order to play with the big boys in major supply chains.

MIGRATION OF THE SUPPLY CHAIN TO THE INTERNET

In the 1980s and 1990s, electronic data interface (EDI) was the big buzz. Large firms like General Electric, General Motors, and Wal-Mart built systems to increase efficiency and decrease costs through supplier/vendor electronic ordering and communication. These corporate giants pioneered e-commerce with their supply chain partners, achieving fast growth, improved profits, and big payoffs in asset management that still work fabulously today. Mostly, the advances possible with EDI required dedicated terminals and lines that were cost efficient mostly for a few large firms and their trading partners. By developing software and integration processes for basic commerce functions, they paved the way for an information highway on which small- and medium-sized firms can now travel alongside corporate giants. Instead of EDI, however, they run together on the information superhighway made possible by the Internet.

Beyond migrating functions to the Internet, retailers, distributors, manufacturers, and other supply chain members are all banding together for a unified migration of the supply chain to the Internet. The Internet allows the efficiencies that EDI brought to a few large firms to be brought to millions of medium and small firms. What once were supply chains comprised of elite, large firms able to invest big bucks into the development of EDI systems, are now open to small firms with Internet capabilities.

The Auto Industry's Internet Baby

Whatever it means to the long-term health and survival of the auto industry, in the near term, Covisint expects to handle as much as $750 billion in annual purchases by automakers and suppliers by linking the makers of engines, tires, steel, glass, and all the other components needed to make a car via the Internet. Major component manufacturers such as Delphi Systems and Dana Corporation have joined the exchange with letters of intent from Meritor Automotive, Johnson Controls, Federal-Mogul, and many more. Covisint's goal is to reduce overall costs by streamlining the procurement processes between buyers and sellers, possibly expanding the reach for some suppliers of auto components, and achieving greater reach for the buyers. Covisint promises compelling services along three fronts: procurement, supply chain management, and collaborative product development.

The ultimate goal is eliminating the "back them up against the fence" effect of current auto marketing. Today, manufacturers make cars based on their attempts to predict consumer demand. When they don't do it well, they are strapped with excess inventory, which dealers "back up against the fence" (of the lot) until price cuts, interest rate deals, and promotions move them out. With Covisint, a true picture of demand and supply will be available to all levels in the supply chain in the form of current available inventories, supplier capacities, accurate customer demand information, and alerts when demand exceeds supply. Shared information throughout the channel fosters accurate demand and supply levels and leads to better fore-casting and supply planning, as well as collaborative production planning and scheduling. Through Internet-based collaboration, supply chain part-ners will be encouraged to participate in the development of new products and processes—sharing information and ideas freely. This is expected to increase speed-to-market and decrease the risk of creating products that the market doesn't want. The pie-in-the-sky final outcome of this demand chain is expected to be greater customer satisfaction, monumental loyalty, and lower prices.

Will it work? It depends on many variables, including how readily competitors will share information, the interest the Federal Trade Commis-sion has in the "independence" of the arrangement, the effect of state fran-chise laws that regulate how cars are sold, and the degree to which security and confidentiality agreements are enforced. Ultimately, the success will be determined by whether consumers like buying cars on the Internet. But the rewards are immense, even if this model only replicates and improves speed and transaction costs in the existing supply chain.

Juergen Schremp, the analytical, innovative, and outspoken CEO of Daimler-Chrysler, put the pedal to the metal in speeding the German giant to become an active participant in Covisint. When questioned about the potential of this e-commerce venture, he told us that when implemented, it has the potential of reducing the cost of manufacturing a typical vehicle by $1,000. Multiplied by the millions of cars sold around the world and the increasing global demand for the independence and pleasure people obtain from their cars, there is plenty of incentive to make Covisint work.

But don't brand him a devout believer in the philosophy that the Internet will take over the consumer side of the business anytime soon. With a dry sense of humor and intense understanding of his customers, he explains that the Mercedes-Benz dealer still plays a vital role in the sat-isfaction of the Mercedes customer. While consumers may search for cars on the Web, he's not convinced that his customer base will buy many cars electronically. For a business that has spent decades building special ser-vices provided by the dealer to the consumer, it seems unlikely that the dealer-customer relationship will give way to an informal electronic one in the near future. As Schremp so rightfully points out, it is all in the hands of the customer.

Power in the Supply Chain

The migration of supply chains to the Internet is significant for several reasons. If you were a supplier to any of the partners involved in Covisint, you would quickly have to get your operations and systems online and compatible with those of other supply chain members in order to remain an active member of the channel.

An example that may hit closer to home for many retailers is the Wal-Mart supply chain. If Wal-Mart wants its suppliers to adopt certain order processing or delivery systems, suppliers usually reply with a mighty "yes sir" and make the requested changes. The customer, Wal-Mart in this instance, is king. But even Wal-Mart has another higher power to which it must answer—the consumer. As B-to-B models evolve into B-to-B-to-C models, as Covisint plans to do, the survival of the entire channel depends on the consumer. If consumers don't buy what the channel offers, it doesn't matter how efficient the channel is—the business will fail.

Migration to the Internet will also affect those large firms that have established EDI systems. After years of investment in both time and money, look for these firms to resist moving to the Internet because they will not want to give up their legacy systems and market advantages to other, smaller firms. So while small firms might feel they are in the hot seat of having to develop new systems, they also will gain access to supply chains with which they might previously have not been able to partner. In essence, the Internet levels the playing field and gives an advantage to small and nimble companies that may have even been in the game in the past.

As you read about Covisint and read the remainder of this chapter, you might be concerned about where your firm fits in the new business paradigm. You are not alone. If you manage a bank, a logistics firm, or an advertising firm, or provide accounting or engineering services, it's difficult to envision a future without adopting some new e-commerce applications. If you are a wholesaler, retailer, construction firm, or trades person, you can easily see power shifting—ebbing and flowing between consumers and various members of the supply chain. Perhaps you are wondering about your position within the channel and the future of your business. Perhaps the best way to prepare for the e-based B-to-B future is to remain in constant contact with your customers and monitor your competitors. You should also learn as much as possible about various technologies, B-to-B players and potential partners, and cost-saving applications. Or you might want to complete an exercise Jack Welch pitched to management teams throughout GE.

Dyb.com

In the battle for growing profits among bricks-and-mortar firms, no leader shines brighter in the B-to-B world than GE's Jack Welch. He may look better in a suit than the jeans worn by so many e-entrepreneurs, but he is a true hero in leading an "old" firm into the "new" economy. With sales over $111 billion, net income increasing 15 percent a year or more, a return on equity of 27 percent, and the stock market rewarding GE with a 30 p/e ratio, Welch's insights are certainly highly valued. In fact, when he signed a contract upon retirement to pen a book of his wisdom, Time-Warner paid him a $7.1 million advance, the highest advance ever paid by a publisher for a business book.

How did Jack Welch prepare his troops and forge into the B-to-B revolution? With a preparation tool he coined "destroy your business.com"—an exercise in which business units at GE created a new Internet firm with the mission to destroy the team's existing business unit. It forced management to brainstorm strategies, recognize their weaknesses and strengths, and understand the Internet and how to compete in the new economy. But even occasionally Welch doesn't get it completely right. When GE later dropped the "dyb.com" exercise, we had the opportunity to ask Mr. Welch why. He explained that dyb.com was too defensive—gyb.com (grow your business.com) is a much better exercise, he explained, recognizing that new technologies should be embraced if they can help grow an existing business.

As we watch Jack Welch speak to executives, two things impress us that should inspire and instruct every business leader. First, Jack Welch "gets it." He understands the importance of the Internet and the necessity of adopting it into GE's business strategies. Second, he's having fun matching the best of the new with the best of the old. As a leader in your organization, you've got to walk the walk—just talking about e-commerce doesn't cut it. Your organization has to see you use it, embrace it, and really understand it. That begins with understanding cyberspace geography.

MAPPING B-TO-B CYBERSPACE

The first task in mapping the terrain of cyberspace is to identify which entities are having the greatest success and impact on B-to-B e-commerce. Though you have undoubtedly read about hoards of flashy B-to-B facilitating firms and e-commerce marketplaces, keep in mind that the money is often made in the mundane.

The Jeans and Shovels of the Internet

"Go west young man" was the motto that lured American dreamers to the California Gold Rush in the 1800s, in numbers that would not be exceeded until the Silicon Rush of the 1990s. For the great majority, the dream did not pan out. The numbers who actually found gold were small. But some saw beyond the streams and mines and realized that the highest probability for wealth was not in the mines but in making or selling shovels, tents, pans, and the other equipment needed for mining. Perhaps the most successful was a Bavarian immigrant, Levi Strauss, who knew all miners needed durable clothing. Soon he had stitched together a very profitable business of making and selling jeans.

It's much the same with the Internet and the dot-com world. The greatest successes are more likely to be found in the "jeans and shovels" of the Internet—the companies that make hardware, software, systems, and services without which the Internet does not function. That's why some of the greatest stock market successes have been the "four horsemen of the Internet"—Oracle (which dominates software to manage databases), Sun Microsystems (which provides the servers), Cisco (which sells communication and network essentials), and EMC (which dominates storage of the bits that need to be stored and retrieved instantly). You'll find the technology leaders—firms such as Cisco, Oracle, IBM, NCR, Microsoft, EMC, i2, and a host of others—concentrating their activities on building the railroad tracks for the e-commerce locomotive. You'll also find many other B-to-B firms providing Web design, ISP services, advertising, freight forwarding, and other activities that keep the railroads of B-to-B e-commerce running.

Getting a Lay of the Land

A space map of B-to-B e-commerce is beginning to evolve into several major areas of activity, although with many variations to fit each type of business. The principles we discussed in market segmentation, brand development, obtaining sticky eyeballs and happy feet are fundamentally the same in the B-to-B world, whether the issue is marketing to consumers or marketing to organizations.

When Cardinal Health or McKessonHBO, both major drug wholesalers, established a website for e-commerce, they usually dealt with their smaller customers in pretty much the same way they used EDI with larger customers years earlier. These sites are sometimes called "sell-side sites" in which one supplier uses the Internet to sell to many buyers, controlling products, prices, and other conditions of the business. Prototypical examples of how to do this well include Dell.com. Michael Dell wrote the book, literally, on how to create a "one-to-many" sell-side portal. If you haven't read *Direct from Dell* by Michael Dell, there's no better place to start in learning e-commerce and how to build your firm around the Internet.

The Internet unites buyers and sellers either through a firm's website or through PLPs (private label portals) that allow firms to share technology but retain their identities. When multiple firms are accessed through a portal, you'll find them called a variety of names, such as hubs (or e-hubs), hubs and spokes, exchanges, marketplaces, or various forms of portals—sell-side, buy side, horizontal, vertical, and so forth. Some exchanges (or "marketplaces") are sponsored by suppliers (sell-side) and some are sponsored by groups of buyers (buy-side), as Covisint illustrates. Some are sponsored by trade associations or industry groups and some are owned and sponsored by commercial organizations in the business of establishing and operating these exchanges and perhaps selling the software, servers, and other "solutions" needed to operate them. Increasingly, they are organized by a combination of the above.

What are the ways to move your firm into the world of Internet exchanges? Here are some of the major categories of hubs or market exchanges emerging in B-to-B cyberspace. Some may be crucial in creating a successful e-business strategy, but keep in mind that they are constantly changing and often defy classification into neat, mutually exclusive categories.

Sell-Side Portals. Just as Dell, Applied Industrial Technologies, and GE become effective as e-commerce portals, groups of suppliers see the advantage of joining together to provide their own portal. Their goal is to reach many buyers, including, hopefully, some new ones, for the benefit of the group's members. Often the impetus arises in a trade association, hoping to perform sales functions at lower costs for its members and perhaps generate revenues from sales for the association. Some portals are owned by a single firm just hoping to make a lot of money aggregating catalogs from a group of suppliers to attract a larger audience. These catalog hubs work best in fragmented industries where this type of information consolidation is helpful to the customer.

Chemdex was a prototypical catalog hub of firms selling to over 26,000 registered users from major pharmaceutical to biotechnology companies, as well as academic institutions. Chemdex described itself as a "distribution portal uniting life science enterprises, researchers and suppliers" hoping to streamline business processes, enhance productivity, and reduce costs. Owned by the Ventro Corporation, it offered more than 1.4 million products from 2,200 suppliers. In addition to its award-winning website design, it offered electronic procurement, systems integration, and comprehensive customer support programs.

Ventro, based in Mountain View, California, hopes to make money by developing these systems for a variety of industries. The software and devel-

192

opment might cost hundreds of millions of dollars, but the company's plan is to spread those costs across multiple industries, thereby making it possible for an individual industry to purchase a superior system at an affordable price. In addition to the Chemdex marketplace, Ventro developed Amphire (food service), Broadlane (high-volume hospital and medical supplies), Industria (process plant equipment in a broad range of industries from chemical to power generation), Promedix (health-care professionals buying products such as pacemakers, catheters, heart stents, and hip replacements), and Ventro Life Sciences (provider of B-to-B e-commerce solutions for the life sciences industry in Europe).

Ventro's strategy seems sound. Focus on market segments that sell technical products requiring buyers to have intensive technical knowledge and have healthy margins (usually 30 to 40 percent gross margin for suppliers). One insurmountable problem, however, was profitability. By March 2001, Chemdex and Promedix had ceased operations, and Ventro stock had plummeted from its January 2000 high of $228 per share to under $1.00, leaving many wondering if sell-side exchanges could survive. With "restructuring" plans underway, Ventro CEO David Perry announced a new focus—a marketplace service provider model that partners with bricks-and-mortar companies.

Buy-Side Portals. When buyers in an industry get together to organize an exchange, they are called buy-side, or "procurement," portals. They are usually organized by relatively few firms to obtain price advantages and perhaps expand the reach to additional suppliers. Fortified by "strength in numbers," it may be difficult for suppliers to decline participation in this type of buying consolidation program, especially in the "many to one" purest form of a buy-side portal or the "many to a few" portals such as Covisint.

PaperExchange.com is an example of a typical buy-side portal that offers its member-buyers in the pulp and paper industry direct access to broader supply sources on a global basis. This type of model works best with replenishment contracts that are typical of the paper industry. PaperExchange.com enables buyers to access sellers directly, thereby dislodging paper distributors from the supply channel and, in theory, reducing costs and transaction fees.

PaperExchange.com offers other advantages to its members as well. Credit approval is shifted from the sellers to PaperExchange.com, enabling the buyer to buy from multiple sellers without having to be approved for credit by each seller. Since transactions are simplified, buyers are more likely to search a wider base of suppliers, thereby giving sellers access to a larger base of customers. In addition to credit efficiencies,

PaperExchange.com members are able to obtain real-time logistics quotes and track shipments via the website.

PaperExchange does not charge buyers for its services, but receives a 3 percent commission from sellers on transactions conducted through the site. Only firms with a website can be listed as resources. Among its strategic partnerships is a leading logistics provider, a quality-assurance firm that can test product quality of online purchases, and VerticalNet, Inc., the provider of website software and services. Other alliance partners and investors include Staples, a large buyer of paper for its 1,100 office-superstore chain, and The Kraft Group, a large buyer of packaging and corrugated containers. Without the right partners, these organizations can't win in the marketplace. The right partners are just as important as the right software and technology.

And here's a bit of e-commerce irony. Officials of this exchange state on their own website that "reduced administrative costs are achieved as buyers are able to consolidate invoices and replace existing paper-based functions." Isn't it a little curious that the paper industry is trying to save money on transactions by reducing the use of paper? Go figure.

Market Exchanges

If you're having difficulty making a clear distinction between "sell-side" and "buy-side" portals, don't worry. The distinction, although pertinent in understanding how your firm can benefit from involvement in each, is negligible in the long run because it takes lots of both genres to make a portal or hub effective. B-to-B sites not only vary by origination but also by depth. Some offer only procurement (Chemdex), while others expand into industry content (VNET), supply chain management (i2), integration with legacy systems (Ariba), and ASP software (My SAP). Because of these expanding characteristics and complexities, it is easier simply to group these sites as market exchanges.

The significance of market exchanges is that they allow all firms up and down the supply chain to buy most anything they need or want on the Web. Some markets are vertical, buying and selling products of interest to a specific industry, while others are horizontal, cutting across a wide range of industries and products. The most common application in both is MRO (maintenance, repair, operating) products, such as sprockets, paint, and conveyor belts, which tend to be low-value goods with relatively high transaction costs. You'll find a wide array of such goods at MRO.com, Grainger.com, BizBuyer.com, and ProcureNet. These are products that while used by nearly every business may not be core products for a company's operations.

The hope for exchanges is to cut out the middleman (or intermediary), especially for products where technical information is low, transaction costs are high, and third-party shipping is feasible. If you are a wholesaler or distributor of these peripheral, or noncore, products, the threat of being eliminated from the channel is higher than in almost any other area of e-commerce because these products are more likely to be commoditized. With commodities, the buyer is willing to buy from anyone with the lowest price. But if you are a manufacturer thinking about selling through exchanges, remember that your largest distributors may decide to cut your products from their offerings because you have, in effect, become a competitor rather than a trusted supplier.

How to Succeed in Exchanges. There are some areas in which exchanges work well, such as energy and advertising, which fluctuate greatly in capacity of supply and volatility in demand.

Need an oil tanker quickly diverted to your refinery? Enron, the Dallas-based energy giant, has developed one of the largest e-commerce websites for petroleum, natural gas, electricity, and telecommunication products. Click on EnronOnline and find spot prices for these commodities from around the world, purchase them, and arrange transportation. Within eight months of operation, over 200,000 transactions were executed on EnronOnline with a face value exceeding $100 billion. In that same time frame, the unit grew from 0 to 60 percent of Enron's total trading volume, with the company gaining revenues from transaction fees as well as profits on goods traded. EnronOnline allows existing employees and infrastructure to increase transactions from 30 per day to 30 per hour. It is on its way to becoming the world's largest, and perhaps most profitable, Internet site of any kind.

If you need ads to reach your target audience quickly and cost-effectively, check out AdOutlet.com. While it started out brokering unsold Internet ads, it now handles almost all media ad-space that begins to perish as the publication or broadcast date nears. If a retailer needs to liquidate goods or advertise a special sale, it can source excess ad-space quickly and inexpensively from AdOutlet.com, similar to last-minute or cost-conscious travelers needing to access an airline flight on Priceline.com. Buyers and sellers of advertising connect through AdOutlet.com, which gets a transaction fee for connecting the two entities.

Exchanges generally work best in industries that are highly fragmented and deal with commodities, such as energy and agriculture. A kilowatt is pretty much a kilowatt regardless of who generates or uses it. The same is true for many agricultural products, and that's why e-Merge, an exchange for beef, was developed to serve cattle raisers and processors. But e-Merge offers an extra advantage—ability to track the source of the beef (with a patented process that starts in the ear of the cow) through processing and into the supermarket or restaurant. That provides cattle raisers the possible advantage of adding value to their product and taking it out of the commodity category. Tracking may also help assure the quality of the beef to buyers, who might want to know on which ranch it was raised, what types of medicines were used, and whether it was organically raised. Exchanges that provide proprietary software or advantages such as e-Merge add value beyond even traditional methods of commerce. In the case of e-Merge, it overcomes the objection of many sellers that exchanges tend to "commoditize" their products or brands.

Why Exchanges Fail. In most instances, exchanges are missing the mark of early expectations. One example is an exchange in the financial arena organized by one of America's best-known giant corporations. One of its executives, who asked to remain anonymous, talked to us about the e-venture enough for us to report its results and share with readers the valuable lessons the company learned. The company developed an Internet exchange to link buyers and sellers of mortgages (a product that can easily be transmitted digitally). Nearly all of the buyers and sellers in this particular product category are seasoned professionals in medium and large financial institutions and are connected to the Internet.

Initial response was good   good enough apparently to justify the capital investment, world-class software, and expansion of staff needed to develop the exchange. But after the "low fruit" of buyers entered the exchange, sales stalled. When future growth became questionable, the company studied the problem and discovered the reasons for its sputter. The enthusiastic Internet supporters quickly joined, but the great majority of well-educated, financially successful, mature professionals didn't like to use the Internet for any purposes other than e-mail and other limited applications. Although technologically competent and financially able, they just didn't like the Internet. That may be the most important lesson to be learned about exchanges and e-tailing in general: If people don't like the Internet, they won't readily adopt it.

Although the number of buyers in this industry is large and fragmented, the number of sellers is much smaller. The company found that the sellers, although technologically savvy, actively avoided the exchange because they did not want their prices easily compared with competitors.

The company assumed sellers would have no choice but to join the exchange; however, without force from the buyers to get on the Internet, the sellers wouldn't join and reveal their prices openly.

The company still operates the exchange but has reduced both its investment and staff, realizing that growth will be slow. While you can understand why the company does not want us to disclose its identity, we are able to disclose the lessons learned from this and many other companies' experience:

1. Exchanges most likely to be successful are in industries in which buyers force sellers to enter the exchange. The more concentrated and powerful the sellers, the less likely they are to enter the exchange.

2. Management must understand the motivations and behavior of the industry. If industry members don't like Internet-based exchanges, they won't use them, regardless of how compelling the reasons are to join.

3. Exchanges that provide proprietary software or other technologies that can add value beyond the existing methods of commerce are most likely to succeed.

The Future of Exchanges. Similar to the consolidation among retailers in the 1980s and 1990s, you can expect a similar consolidation of market exchanges from about two thousand in the year 2000 to less than two hundred within a few years. Why? Because since the value of the site increases with the number of buyers and sellers using it, members migrate to the most dominant sites until only one or two of each type remain.

Future cash flow and profits of these exchanges depend on human behavior. Many exchanges survive on commissions from online sales, but after a buyer finds a good supplier and becomes a satisfied customer, there is a big incentive for the seller to suggest they go off-line and save the commission on future sales. Where the traditional sales model often depends on the development of a "personal" relationship between buyer and seller to create a sale, the new model promotes a sale first and then an off-line "personal" relationship for ongoing transactions. If humans succumb to the financial temptations of moving subsequent sales off-line, exchanges will lose commissions and revenues associated with ongoing business.

How are exchanges most likely to affect your business? First, if you sell MRO items as a manufacturer or distributor, exchanges may help you find new customers. Second, if you are a seller of MRO or core products, you may have no choice but to migrate to exchanges if your customers want to buy at least some of their products that way. Third, if you are a

retailer or other type of buyer, you may use exchanges to find new suppliers on a global basis or reduce transaction costs with existing suppliers.
Whether you are a buyer or seller, plan on gearing up to follow the migration of your current and potential customers online or plan on being left
out of future transactions.

E-commerce at this level sounds great, but there is a glitch. The problem is that there is a missing link in connecting buyers and sellers wanting
to complete transactions through exchanges or through online ordering
channels. Connectivity, to replace humans taking an order from a buyer
and placing it with an exchange supplier, may mean adding new software
that will connect your legacy systems for accounting and enterprise
resource planning (ERP) to the exchanges. That's why Frontstep (formerly
Symix), an ERP software firm selling to thousands of small- to mid-sized
manufacturers and distributors, developed "e-suite" software products. In
essence, they let buyers' and sellers' systems talk to one another, connecting their legacy systems to e-commerce entities and exchanges.

Some exchanges can't deliver service as well as traditional bricks-and-
mortar firms because of lack of experience in the areas of logistics, buying, selling, and other essential business functions described in Chapter
2. When this happens customers go back to their tried-and-true traditional suppliers. Expect exchanges that provide genuine value, but lack the
resources to develop or maintain the most sophisticated sites, to be
merged into one or two exchanges per industry. The survivors will make
strategic alliances with other exchanges, be acquired, or buy software and
solutions from one of the rising stars in B-to-B cyberspace, such as Ariba
or Commerce One.

Star Wars

Perhaps no movie grabbed the attention of a generation growing up in the
1970s as Star Wars. Little did the youngsters watching that movie know it
would foreshadow the galactic battle fought in cyberspace in the year
2000. Unlike the Star War's battle between good and evil, the modern-day
epic revolves around the battle between Ariba and Commerce One for
control of B-to-B marketplaces. Fortified not with laser beams but with
differing software, servers, and business models, Ariba CEO Keith Krach
plans his next move from his Mountain View, California, headquarters,
while Commerce One CEO Mark Hoffman does the same from his headquarters just across the San Francisco Bay in Pleasanton, California. As
the battle heated up, these competitors gathered armies of support from
the universe's most powerful alliance partners to join them in their battle.

Both Ariba and Commerce One sell software and systems to B-to-B clients and "stick around" after the sale to support the systems they've created. One distinguishing difference exists, however, between the two competitors. Ariba acts as an "arms dealer," willing to sell products to any firm ready, willing, and able to fork over the necessary funds, including competitive firms within an industry. Commerce One, on the other hand, sells to and forms an alliance with a particular company, in effect "taking sides" and doing whatever it can to help that client win in the marketplace. Commerce One also takes an active role in managing the exchanges it helps to create.

To date, Ariba has some of the strongest alliance partners in e-commerce, including IBM, Arthur Anderson, and Bank of America through which it establishes competitive advantages in the marketplace. For example, with IBM, it gains access to IBM customers around the world. Its key competitive advantage, however, came with the announcement that Ariba made a profit in the first quarter of 2001.

Ariba already has twenty of the Fortune 100 leading companies as clients and is signing deals with firms and exchanges almost daily. Typical of these deals is the WorldWide Retail Exchange (WWRE), one of the world's leading retail e-marketplaces. It's a member-owned, neutral organization permitting participating retailers to conduct a full range of food, nonfood, textile, and drug e-commerce transactions with individual suppliers. Consisting of leading retailers from Asia, Europe, and the United States, the WWRE is designed to facilitate and simplify trading between the retailers and their more than 100,000 suppliers. The retailers include Albertson's (U.S.), Auchan (France), Best Buy (U.S.), Casino (France), CVS (U.S.), Delhaize (Belgium—and the owner of Food Lion in the U.S.), Kmart (U.S.), Target (U.S.), Tesco (U.K.), Walgreens (U.S.), and others that together represent sales of over $450 billion.

Commerce One can't boast the sales or profits of Ariba, but it does have bragging rights to snagging one of the most important alliances of all: a contract to power the TradeXchange portal of General Motors, forerunner of Covisint. By offering a complete e-procurement solution, Commerce One is selling solutions to global organizations to bring their purchasing operations onto the Internet. In addition to the Covisint relationship, Commerce One has SAP, the German software giant, as its alliance partner, providing "front of the house" capability to ERP software of SAP, used to manage the "back of the house" operations in firms around the world.

Who will emerge the victor in this B-to-B star wars? Each company is growing at very rapid rates and can boast impressive cash flow; yet to date, only Ariba has become profitable, with a $14 million net income for its first quarter of fiscal 2001. Both have strengths in their software and systems and both have impressive lists of customers and alliance partners. What do you think? How will your company, your competitors, and your supply chain be affected by these firms in the next few years. Watch them closely, as Wall Street certainly will, to see if they are on a path toward mutual destruction or mutual dominance of the B-to-B marketplace. Perhaps one day we'll see the winner called "Ariba One," "Coriba," or some other combination of the two.

THE DISINTERMEDIATION DIVIDE: WHAT WILL THE SUPPLY CHAIN OF THE FUTURE LOOK LIKE?

Willy Loman, the protagonist in Arthur Miller's *Death of a Salesman,* worried about the threat of disintermediation—a threat that continues to weigh heavily on firms evaluating the effects of B-to-B e-commerce on their futures. The explicit reason for many of the market exchanges described earlier is to bring buyers and sellers together, cutting out the wholesalers (or distributors) that currently handle two thirds of the commercial transactions for physical products. But if disintermediation occurs in the proposed exchange-based B-to-B marketplace, who will perform the various business functions discussed in Chapter 2? Are you ready to operate in a new, abbreviated supply chain, or will the traditional retail channel survive and thrive as it has throughout the evolution of commerce?

The Distributor—Mighty or "Might Be"?

The wholesale industry has gained might in the supply chain by performing functions that other companies either couldn't or wouldn't perform as efficiently as the distributor. Despite its precarious position in the supply channel, lying between manufacturer and retailer and dependent upon each, today there are over 150,000 wholesaler-distributors, accounting for more than $4.4 trillion in sales. Most sales (59 percent) are made by merchant wholesaler-distributors—people who take title, take risk, and in most cases take possession of goods. The rest of wholesale sales are handled by manufacturers' sales branches (31 percent) and agents, brokers, and commission agents (10 percent). About 6.5 million people work for distribution firms, handling everything from ball bearings to baseballs, with most (51 percent) in firms with sales below $1 million.

A superficial examination of B-to-B exchanges and e-commerce often causes analysts to wonder if this mighty entity "might not be" in the future. In a contrarian view, we believe the wholesaler will remain alive and well in the future for two primary reasons: first, distributors help keep the prices of goods down, and second, exchanges can only perform a fraction of the functions performed by the distributor in the channel.

Why Distributors Won't Die Anytime Soon

Distributors exist because they increase efficiency of supply channels and reduce the costs of products. If they did not, they would quickly cease to exist. Specifically, the reason distributors and wholesalers exist is because they reduce the costs or increase the efficiency for other members of the distribution channel by reducing the number of transactions required to get products from manufacturers to users.

Figure 8.1 shows an economy without distributors on the left side of the diagram and with distributors on the right. To make it easy to see, we've drawn a small "economy" with only five sellers and five buyers. On the right side of Figure 8.1 you see what happens when the economy has a distributor. Each seller needs only one contact (with the distributor) to reach five buyers, rather than contacting each one individually. Similarly, every buyer needs only one contact to reach multiple suppliers. Without distributors, every seller would need to contact every buyer and every buyer would have to contact every seller, a very expensive endeavor in terms of labor, packaging, transportation, distribution, and supply chain management.

If "transactions" were just a matter of placing and receiving orders, that function could be easily replaced with an e-portal, but transactions include much more than that—just think of what Applied Industrial Technologies and Manco, discussed in Chapter 5, do for their supply chain partners. Wholesalers' functions include gathering information about the needs of the buyer, making a sales call or contact, picking and

FIGURE 8.1

Life Without Wholesalers   **Why Wholesalers Exist**

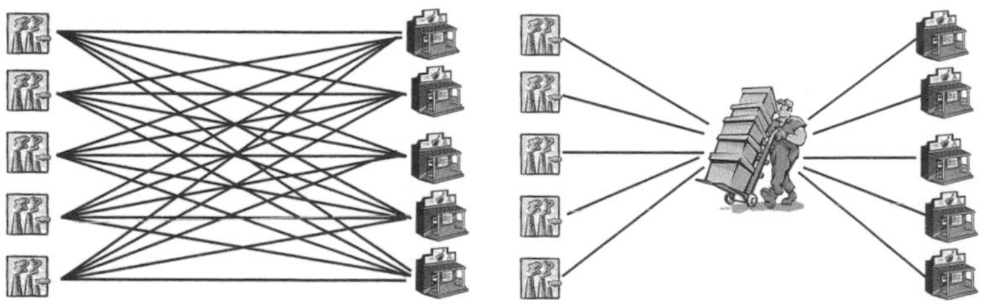

storing products for each buyer in the assortment that fits an individual buyer's needs, and packing the goods to ensure they arrive in good condition. The transaction also means sending a truck (and maybe a rail car or airplane) to the buyer to guarantee that important goods arrive at the precise time they are needed—often with a "window" of only a few hours in today's "just in time" economy. It also includes assessing the credit worthiness of the buyer, assuming credit risk, providing technical information on products, and standing ready to correct problems or accept returns if something goes wrong with the transaction. Even a well-known brand is likely to be manufactured thousands of miles from most buyers, making parts and service dependent upon a local distributor.

When you examine the role of "e" portals or market exchanges from the perspective of functional analysis, it is painfully obvious that e-exchanges can perform only a few of the functions that occur during a typical transaction. E-commerce can bring buyers and sellers together, which performs some parts of the selling/advertising/buying functions digitally that formerly required paper or personal contact (which really can't be replaced in industries that sell complex, information-laden products). E-commerce cannot, however, transport goods, store them in warehouses, or perform other costly functions. At best, e-commerce may help in scheduling those functions more efficiently.

Given that the functions of marketing can be shifted but not eliminated, are retailers or manufacturers ready to take over some of these functions? And if so, will they cost more to perform at a less efficient level than at the distributor level? How well can Ariba or Commerce One or any of the other exchanges perform each of these functions? Remember, the degree to which portals will replace distributors depends on the savings that accrue when moving some of the functions from the present system to e-commerce. Exchanges do best in the "marshmallow" part of the B-to-B world—catalog scanning, order processing, and so forth—but those are the least costly functions involving the least important products bought by a business.

It's Not a Marshmallow World

Traditionally, many of the "marshmallow" functions were provided "free" or bundled with the sale of the product in the past. If price reduction and margin erosion becomes commonplace with the rise of open exchanges and auctions, however, you can expect distributors and manufacturers to start charging for services that were formerly provided free.

For example, if you buy a product at a low price from a market exchange and then expect the seller to deliver it, expect a higher cost than previously. And if you ask for technical knowledge, don't expect that knowledge to be bundled in with the price of the product when you buy on the Internet. You'll probably receive little information or an invoice for consulting services. Expect also to receive a "willco" (for "will comply") part or component rather than a trusted brand for which manufacturers spent millions to develop and support with a network of authorized dealers and distributors. And if your plant is down with a busted bearing, don't expect the manufacturer or distributor with whom you canceled your long-term relationship to get up at 2:00 A.M. to deliver the part you need to get the factory running again.

The next few years will find firms experimenting with e-commerce, sorting out which functions can be sourced online through exchanges and which functions will be sourced off-line with the websites of trusted manufacturers and distributors. It's the most valuable (and costly) functions that are the most difficult to shift to direct channels, and that's why disintermediation may be minimal among bricks-and-mortar distributors and manufacturers. The existing bricks-and-mortar manufacturers and distributors will thrive only *if* they continue to perform with excellence the functions that don't migrate well to exchanges *and* develop their own websites and portals to perform the functions that do. Some companies will have the vision to take their supply chains to the next level; others won't.

WHERE DO WE GO FROM HERE?

As much as exchanges want to change supply chains, visionary firms, such as Hewlett-Packard (HP) and Cisco, want to keep the supply chain intact but use the Internet to make it more efficient and cost-effective. These traditional bricks-and-mortar mega-stars had already mastered the lessons of commerce before they began pushing the frontier of how to use the Internet to perform business functions better. The reason these firms are e-commerce leaders today is directly attributable to the vision of their CEOs. They serve as examples of where firms must go in the future.

It Takes Vision to Move into the Future

A leading contender for the title of ultra-visionary is John Chambers, CEO of Cisco Systems, seller of "Internet ecosystems" and leading producer of network software, hardware, and technical support. At the behest of Chambers, Cisco moved its internal functions to the Internet before migrating its supply chain of customers and vendors to the Internet. With this move it achieved greater efficiencies internally and created the plat-form where today approximately 85 percent of its transactions are con-ducted on the Internet. These transactions account for more than $1 billion in sales per month. But the Chambers vision extends way beyond sales and that of many executives. He's pushed Cisco to use the Internet to integrate voice, data, and video throughout the firm; to create Web-based consulting and technology support groups; and to handle employee benefits, accounting procedures, and other administrative processes both internally and with strategic partners.

Another visionary leader, selected to lead HP into the new millen-nium, is Carleton S. Fiorina. Taking the reins in 1999, she was given the challenge of creating a new vision for a company that had all but missed the Internet age. Once one of the foremost computer innovators, HP had recently been mocked by Sun Microsystems chairman Scott McNealy, who called it "a good printer firm."

Armed with success in building a $20 billion business at Lucent Technologies, Carly Fiorina arrived at HP with a mission to transform the company into an Internet force. HP turned to another B-to-B visionary firm, USi, to develop one of the most comprehensive websites in the busi-ness. How comprehensive is it? Well, you can even calculate what you would have earned if you invested $10,000 in HP stock in 1980. (The answer is $324,063.58 when this book was written.) It definitely gave the company "presence" on the Web, foreshadowing the imminent changes on HP's horizon.

A big turning point was nabbing Amazon.com as a customer for 90 percent of its new software and equipment, replacing products from Compaq and Sun. Besides new products for online businesses, Fiorina led HP back to the garage, where the company was started by founders Hewlett and Packard, and made strategic investments in many start-up firms. Those investments include Silver Tech (www.silvertechnic.com), a builder of a secure sub-Internet for kids; SpinCircuit (www.spincircuit.com), an online service for electronics design engineers; and Primus Knowledge Solutions, an online customer relationship management firm. Sound risky? You bet—but these moves represent a new vision for an old-economy firm that many, including Wall Street investors, thought had passed its best days. "It sounds risky . . . count me in!" is often the motto of visionary leaders!

The E-volution of Supply Chains

The best supply chains are built on long-lasting relationships from years of service and working together. HP and Cisco didn't disrupt their supply chains; they strengthened them. They understood the advantages the

Internet could bring to their channel partners and had the vision of how to make it happen. They also prove that the better company portals are, the less likely exchanges are to capture significant market share of B-to-B commerce.

Retailers such as Wal-Mart and The Limited have worked for decades with their supply chain partners to develop efficiencies and cost savings for each channel member. In turn, they have been able to pass those advantages on to customers in terms of lower prices, in-stock merchandise, and greater levels of customer service. The Internet provides new opportunities for capturing even more advantages up and down the channel. Yet some firms will resist migrating to the Web even today, which is OK if the supply chain operates as efficiently off-line as it would on the Internet. But when competitive supply chains or channel members experience lower costs and enhanced customer service levels because of online efficiencies, firms not willing to change will be left to sell to and partner with other remaining competitively disadvantaged firms. Eventually, the most efficient supply chain will win in the marketplace.

CHAPTER 9

BLENDED STRATEGIES FOR COMPETING IN THE REAL WORLD

SINCE THE RISE IN POPULARITY of the Internet, retail executives, consultants, and marketing firms alike have jumped on the e-commerce bandwagon, proclaiming the beginning of the end of retailing and business as we know it. Let's face it, that was the "exciting" place to be; authors, consultancies, and lecturers made millions speculating about the meteoric rise in e-tailing. It wasn't exciting to point out how the realities of the marketplace—human behavior, logistics limitations, financial constraints, and limited market penetration—would threaten the long-term viability of the pure-play dot-com model, so we didn't hear much about that. It was even less exciting to talk about how the tried-and-true retail strategies that brought success to Wal-Mart, Home Depot, Victoria's Secret, Target, and other retail greats would be the key strategies for dominating the future. Yet these were always our positions in the e-commerce debate—that customers rule, that eventually they will decide and determine how business will be conducted.

Many retailers and e-commerce firms have been chewed-up and spit out by the tumultuous tornado of Internet speculation that swept the nation from 1998 to 2001. While fly-by-night Internet schemes made millions for brazen investors, others watched from the sidelines, eventually demanding traditional retailers get in the game or watch their stocks get hammered in favor of a more innovative breed. Many firms spun their wheels trying to race to the Internet with half-baked branding, fulfillment, segmentation, and integrated marketing strategies, but enjoyed, nonetheless, a temporary boost in stock prices. Others, such as Wal-Mart, Kmart (with BlueLight.com), and Nordstrom, took a lot of criticism for stepping cautiously into the new frontier.

Suddenly, Wall Street came to its senses, much to the chagrin of most Internet players. Employing the financial analysis models of the past (namely profitability measures), shareholders and analysts started talking about the dreaded *P* word, forcing even the most gung-ho consultants to take a realistic look at the dot-com business model. As for traditional retailers who squandered shareholders' dollars on money-losing e-ventures, their stocks took a beating because they couldn't make their overall numbers. After spending millions on developing financial Internet flops, Drug Emporium sold off DrugEmporium.com for next to nothing, and Consolidated Stores axed its KBkids.com venture after a reported $80 million investment, even though it was hailed as a website extraordinaire.

We believe that, after the dust settles, many firms will find the secrets to success in the new economy by revisiting the strategies that brought them success in the past. Strategies that deliver better shopping experiences to customers, provide better value, and increase customer satisfaction and loyalty will create the best-of-breed blended businesses of the future. The key will be, as it has been in the past, to adapt and update these strategies to meet the changing needs of customers—and today, that means exploring the avenues technology has to offer. Gearing up for the future mass adoption of the Internet and predicting the right mix of retail strategies to meet customers' wants are very important, but not at the peril of profits and growth in the present. It is subject to the same principles observed in the e-volution of commerce for hundreds of years.

Whether online or off-, retailing is not about technology; it is about solving customers' problems better than current solutions and competitors. And though we don't believe that e-tailing is the end-all, be-all of traditional in-store shopping, incorporating the Internet into your arsenal of strategic weapons is a must. We believe that all businesses, whether they are retailers, manufacturers, or service organizations, must develop aggressive e-commerce strategies because the Internet is here to stay and its adoption rate is still growing. This doesn't mean, however, that retailers have to focus on selling online. Some businesses choose not to sell online, and for now, that's OK. But every firm will have to develop a strong online presence to provide information about their stores, products, hours of operation, and company information. This presence is vital in communicating with customers and exchanging information. Any business that fails to complete these minimal prerequisites risks becoming roadkill on the information superhighway.

For B-to-B firms, developing e-commerce strategies means employing e-technology to enhance customer and supply chain relationships, decrease inventory and operations costs, enhance purchasing efficiencies, and reach new customers. For retailers, understanding e-commerce means using the B-to-B portals and exchanges described in the previous chapter to decrease buying and operations costs, just as any other business must do. But for retailers, e-commerce also means developing technology-based methods for enhancing marketing, communicating with specific segments of consumers, providing information to the marketplace, and selling to profitable segments of the consumer market. Both entities must understand how e-commerce will change their supply chains—one of the ultimate determinants of who wins in the new economy and who loses.

The previous eight chapters focused on how best to accomplish each task and blend the advantages and lessons of bricks-and-mortar firms with the world of possibilities associated with the Internet. The result is the e-volution of today's business models into new fortified ones focused on the customer and ready to dominate in the new economy—a healthy marriage of the best of the old and new economies. Though we don't believe the Internet will serve as a replacement of traditional retailing and business-to-business marketing in most industries, we champion the notion that it is an important tool for retailing and business marketing.

The following strategies summarize how we believe retailers or dot-coms with e-commerce operations can formulate operating strategies to help them succeed in the new economy. These ten strategies draw on the concepts and cases we have described in earlier chapters. We hope you read them reflectively and consider the lessons that will place your firm at the forefront of profitability with e-commerce. Even if most dot-com firms fail along with many of the e-tail strategies of traditional retailers, some will succeed. These are customer-based strategies we believe winning firms will employ to succeed in a blended retail environment.

STRATEGIES FOR DOING BUSINESS IN A BLENDED WORLD

Before a firm can develop an effective e-strategy, it has to develop a clear vision of what it wants e-commerce to accomplish for the firm. It also needs to identify measurable objectives for the technology. Does it want the Internet to become the primary vehicle for selling to current customers or does it want to use it primarily as a brand-building device or in-store traffic builder? Without a clear vision supported by measurable objectives, firms often employ a slew of tactics to create online activity; however, a collection of Internet activities does not a vision make.

Famed baseball player Satchel Paige said it best: "If you don't know where you're going, you might end up someplace else." Jack Welch, Carly Fiorina, John Chambers, Lee Scott, and other famed business leaders who have taken their firms headfirst into the new economy have one thing in common: great vision of where they wanted to go, knowing their customers would be better off for their actions.

Strategy 1: Develop a Physical Presence for Your E-tail Operations

Strategy number one for pure-play dot-coms should be to develop a physical presence—and top of the list for traditional retailers is to leverage their physical stores with their e-tail customers. Early dot-coms missed the importance of having a bricks-and-mortar presence because they assumed that e-tailing would replace in-store retailing, rather than just enhance it. For the most part, consumers are still leery about e-tail's give-your-information-to-a-machine-and-hope-for-the-best model. Customer concerns are minimized when they know they have a "place to go" when there is a problem with the transaction. For a pure-play, developing a physical presence, which doesn't necessarily mean opening a store, allows it to:

- Give customers a place to try merchandise before they buy (eBay bought a real auction house to showcase select merchandise).
- Provide customers face-to-face contact with a person to help them make a selection or solve a problem (Gateway developed mini-stores inside OfficeMax).
- Give customers a place to return products and walk away with exchanges in hand (Barnes & Noble provides immediate exchanges that Amazon can't).
- Gain customers' trust that you'll be there for them tomorrow (WalMart.com is backed by the world's largest retailer).

We predict more alliances between e-tail concepts and traditional retailers, similar to the Gateway-OfficeMax relationship. What will Dell do—follow this type of strategy or stay on its own? A master of online e-commerce, Dell has focused on partnerships with universities, government organizations, and large businesses, where it gets most of its sales. It understands the importance of a physical presence for these organizations, with its substantial personal sales force to promote and supplement online transactions. Would there be an opportunity for Dell to develop a similar presence at the retail level with a nationwide chain of local stores? Staples might be a logical partner, but choosing an existing retailer that has excess capacity, great locations in suburban and small-town malls, and needs additional store traffic might lead Dell to someone like JCPenney. It would be a different type of product for JCPenney, but the combination would attract a new, young, affluent customer base, which Penney needs, and a broader, not yet "connected" consumer market, needed by Dell to continue rapid growth in the future. We are not suggesting that Dell and JCPenney have any deals in the making; we are, however, suggesting that a useful "out of the box" strategy for any e-tailer is to develop an "into the box" marketing and channel strategy.

Recognizing the need for a physical presence, one e-entrepreneur pulled a fast one on his e-tail backers. Shortly after receiving millions in funding for Gazoontite.com, an Internet site focused on selling allergy remedies and hypoallergenic related products, founder Soon-Chart Yu took some of the cash and started retail stores, first in San Francisco, then in New York and Costa Mesa, to complement his online venture. He also started a physician-direct catalog, offering specialty allergy and wellness products, giving Gazoontite a multichannel physical presence.

By planting its feet on terra firma, Gazoontite made enough money to cover some of its losses from its unprofitable Web store. Eventually, despite good consumer response, the site remained unprofitable, declared Chapter 11, and was eventually shut down in October 2000, but its physical store doors remained open, continuing to serve customers. In early 2001, an investment group headed by Craig P. Womack, former president of The Sharper Image and Gazoontite's new CEO, rescued the brand. The goal is to open ten to twenty stores beginning in 2002 and treat the website as just an additional distribution outlet. The future of the company now remains in the hands of customers—if enough allergy-stricken people wanting to shop for health-related products exist, Gazoontite might be on its way to a clean bill of financial health.

Blended retailers must overcome the obstacles e-tailing presents to creating mass acceptance and profitability. These daunting characteristics of e-tailing include:

- Higher acquisition costs to attract online customers than store customers

- Greater difficulty in delivering an overall shopping "experience" to customers

- Higher product return rates and difficulty facilitating returns satisfactorily

- Inability to touch, feel, and try on merchandise
- Inability for the consumer to leave with product in hand
- Inability to re-create the social aspects of shopping that appeal to consumers' desires to be with people

All of these issues are barriers to long-term success of selling online. Paramount among them is returns, which often can run as high as 30 percent for online and catalog sales. Bricks-and-mortar firms, such as the Gap and Target, are poised to solve this challenging and frustrating issue more efficiently than e-only retailers. By having locations around the country, consumers can return gifts or damaged products to the store, talk with a person, avoid shipping charges, and walk out of the store with a new product. Firms with e-tail operations will have to create "reverse logistics" networks of physical facilities to which customers can return goods or get help in assembling them properly. Implementing this strategy mirrors somewhat the service centers established throughout the nation by appliance marketers such as GE and Westinghouse to repair faulty products.

Selling and shopping are social experiences—most people want some level of social interaction with others, whether they admit it or not. That is one of the reasons traditional retailing will never disappear, nor will most other businesses where personal relationships are important in the selling process. Blended retail concepts fulfill some of these social needs, not to mention also increase customer trial of e-tailing and overall satisfaction with the experience.

Strategy 2: Focus on Solving Customers' Problems Better; Avoid Adopting Technology for the Sake of Technology

The most important strategy in e-commerce is one that is often the most ignored—focusing on customers and their problems, wants, and needs. Perhaps an unpopular notion in the technology arena, the truth is that unless a new technology provides a knock-their-socks-off advantage to what customers currently buy, they are likely to pass on it. The same goes for buying methods. If consumers are happy with traditional retail stores (and for the most part they are), they will continue to purchase a majority of their products through them. When e-tailing satisfies them more, they will switch.

Retailers must study consumer behavior to identify opportunities to satisfy their customers better. Marketers can use the Consumer Decision Process model described in Chapter 3 to analyze how consumers are likely to evaluate, search for, purchase, and use the Internet and e-tailing. It can also be used to predict the likelihood of success within specific segments of consumers and also for the mass population. We urge firms to use the model to:

- Understand how consumers buy products and determine how satisfied or dissatisfied they are with their current shopping solutions.
- Understand for which products and in which situations e-tailing (or online buying) is a better solution to in-store retailing (or current sales methods) and develop applications accordingly.
- Predict the level of acceptance of online applications and develop marketing and communication programs.

A few years ago, an Internet entrepreneur showed us a technology for a milk carton equipped with a microchip that would automatically reorder milk over the Internet when the empty carton was dumped into a specially equipped trash can. It was neat. But our question to him was simple: "How many people have difficulty knowing they are out of milk, and how many want to wait for Internet delivery?" Stopping by a convenience store seems like a pretty good solution. Our technologist friend had ignored the realities consumers inject on the acceptance of even the snazziest technologies. His thinking is common; more times than not people believe that when technology is possible, it should be introduced to the marketplace.

It's time for technology buffs to get their heads out of the sand and look at the facts—and the facts lie inside the lives and minds of consumers. The role of a good marketer, involved early in the innovation process, is to inject the realities of consumer behavior into the design and communication processes. Identifying and developing consumer-driven products (solutions) rather than technology-driven products can be condensed into four basic steps:

1. Understand how significant the problem faced by potential users really is.
2. Estimate how many potential customers "feel the pain" or perceive this problem to be significant enough to pay for a better solution.
3. Analyze how satisfied consumers are with their current solutions and why they are likely to accept or reject the technology.
4. Develop or change the technology to reflect consumers' behavior rather than try to get consumers to change their behavior to adopt an innovation.

These steps will help identify when the market is ready for a new technology or new solution and indicate when to pull the plug on a new or existing innovation.

Consider the most successful of the new economy companies: Microsoft. Even though it competes in the technology arena, it grew to its present status because it focused on solving computing problems rather than inventing technologies and finding applications for them. It didn't invent DOS; it bought the operating system from a small tech firm when it recognized the growing consumer demand for IBM PCs and IBM's need for an operating system. And when consumer demand showed a clear preference for graphic interfaces using a mouse instead of word commands, Microsoft adopted the format quickly, even though it was invented by Xerox and pioneered by Apple. Microsoft also recognized the growing demand for spreadsheets by business customers and cashed in on the diffusion to the masses of its easy-to-use, compatible version. It became one of the most productive applications ever invented for the computer, giving millions of business customers their first major reason to buy a PC.

After careful examination of how to solve customers' problems better, retailers and industrial firms may recognize the need to beef up sales efforts online. Others may realize they can better satisfy customers by investing more in their stores—enhancing employee training, streamlining checkout, or making products easier to find in the store. To enhance the shopping process both online and off-, retailers should focus on how people search for products, what characteristics cause them to choose one over another, where and when they purchase them, and what problems they have with consuming them and divesting of them.

For example, eBay built its business around two of these areas—search and divestment—thereby offering a better solution with its Internet auction site. Consumers in search of rare, old, out-of-circulation, autographed, and used items had a difficult time finding these types of treasures; garage sales and antique shows were sporadic solutions, but didn't cover the vast array of items available from one central auction house. The result: eBay became a collector's dream! In addition to helping find "stuff," eBay also helps consumers get rid of "stuff" without organizing a garage sale or advertising in the classifieds. It also solves a lot of problems for small businesses by helping them sell excess inventory online and reach the vast audiences eBay has built by attracting with collectibles and keeping them with an ever changing array of offerings.

Many firms fail trying to invent new technologies, instead of adapting existing ones to changes in people's preferences or buying habits. Every innovation passes under the scrutiny of consumers who collectively vote yea or nay on its acceptance. If marketers want to increase the like-lihood of mass adoption of a new technology (including e-tail applica-tions), they must:

- Give consumers a reason to try the product.
- Give consumers access to try the technology.
- Don't make things so complicated that consumers get frustrated and abandon their efforts.
- Make the new technology compatible with consumers' current life-styles, behaviors, and equipment.
- Let consumers see the product being used by peers, family, or people they admire.

Designing new technologies without understanding consumers is much like scientists seeking to discover cures for diseases people don't have. But make no mistake about the need for corporate commitment to technology. Microsoft, HP, Cisco, GE, and other technology leaders clearly spend massive amounts of R&D dollars, but they pay off most when focused on major problems faced by significant numbers of customers. This book is filled with dozens of examples of such customer-driven appli-cations. The real payoff in the new economy accrues not necessarily to peo-ple and firms that invent new technologies but to those who solve old problems with the help of new technologies.

Strategy 3: Don't Strive to Be the First Mover; Strive to Be the Final Victor

Many pure-play dot-coms rushed into e-commerce armed with little more than a fancy website, Internet technology, and a venture capitalist's funds. Strategists touted their first-mover advantage. First on the scene, they hoped to write the book on how to succeed on the Internet. Rather than penning such a work, many are starring in the final chapter of the book—Chapter 11.

First-mover advantage, when coupled with efficient execution in the market, can stifle the success of those that arrive fashionably late to the party. A great example is eBay. First to the online auction party, it rapidly attracted customers to its complete, easy-to-use auction site, and it retained them with vast product offerings and attentive customer service. Even against formidable competitors Amazon and Yahoo!, eBay boasts 90 percent market share of all online auction business. Core to its strategy is the special attention it gives its "power sellers," the 20 percent of sellers (many of which are small businesses) that provide 80 percent of its sales. But more important is how efficiently it performs the business functions required to succeed in the long run.

While eBay emerged as a king, other first movers, such as CDNow, Homewarehouse.com, and Boo.com, failed. Without systems that deliver consumer-driven products in the right condition, in the right quantity, and at the correct time and place, first movers gain little more than brand awareness and reputations. Being first often means more mistakes than the firms that wait long enough to observe mistakes of the first mover and deliver a better product. CompuServe, The Source, and Prodigy were the first movers in online services for consumers. AOL came along later and fixed what consumers disliked about the first movers, emerging as the clear final victor serving over half the nation with Web access and owning both CompuServe and Source. If customers try the new brand first and are disappointed, they probably won't return to the site. First movers that don't have quality customer service systems and efficient operations often turn out to be "first losers." The first movers for personal computers included Atari, Commodore, Kaypro, Tandy, and Osborne—not exactly in the same category today as Dell and Compaq.

Traditional retailers that joined the e-tail bandwagon before they could deliver the same quality shopping experience their customers had come to expect suffered the same fate as some of the ill-fated first movers. ToysRUs.com and DrugEmporium.com moved quickly but failed because their systems were not up to speed with their websites. Other successful retailers, who watched as first movers received glory and attention from the media, waited to launch their e-tail sites until they could deliver the same quality as their customers had come to expect. If established retailers such as Hallmark move too quickly, they risk losing not only their e-customers but their store customers and retail store owners as well.

Retailers that waited to get their systems right, such as Nordstrom, Kmart (with BlueLight.com), and Wal-Mart, may still end up as final victors in their categories by buying remnants of failed first movers. Reminiscent of a Filene's Bargain Basement for deflated dot-coms, bricks-and-mortar bargain hunters are likely to buy up dot-com brand names (such as Petstore.com) for pennies on the dollar. In the mix, they may find a few bricks-and-mortar cousins that spent too much on their Internet strategies.

Consolidated Stores, best known for its close-out stores operating under the names Odd Lots, Big Lots, Pic 'n' Save, and MacFrugal's, had a big run on Wall Street during the 1990s, approaching $50 per share in late 1997. Premier in the areas of logistics and operations, it provides consumers with bargain-basement prices on a variety of brand-name products while still gleaning significant returns. In the late 1990s, Consolidated bought KB Toys, the number two toy company in the United States. Drains on profits from acquisition costs and growing pains dropped the stock below $20 by the end of 1997. But news of KBkids.com, a consolidated effort between KB Toys and Brainplay.com, would catapult the stock back above $30 on speculation and high hopes.

But even this logistics-savvy retailer couldn't avoid the logistical terrors other retailers faced during its first e-Christmas season. Though sales volume was good, order fulfillment was poor and profits nonexistent, leading the company into a loss position for 1999 and a stock price that plummeted to $11. Consolidated announced in May 2000 a delay in the KBkids.com IPO (due to market conditions), a 30 percent reduction of KBkids.com staff, and the termination of its CEO. Eventually, KBkids .com, an award-winning website, and the entire KBToys division was sold.

Our strategy recommendation for firms with earnings, effective management of the basic commerce functions, and access to capital is simple: Analyze carefully where "e" methods can expand markets, build brand, and increase customer loyalty; then start studying the landscape of technology firms that have assets that might be valuable to acquire for your long-term strategy. Make sure your board of directors understands the scope and costs of your Internet strategy, and be ready to move fast, as Ahold did in its acquisition of Peapod and Wal-Mart did in its acquisition of Homewarehouse.com.

The acquisition of first movers like these can add volume at little marginal cost to the last survivors, providing they have the economies of scale to handle extra business effectively and can move at Internet speed. The assets listed on balance sheets of bricks-and-mortar firms are bricks and mortar, of course, but on the balance sheets of new-economy firms, intellectual property usually dwarfs the bricks and mortar.

The asset of greatest value when acquiring a faltering dot-com is its list of customers—complete with e-mail, street addresses, and probably information about their buying patterns and interests—giving acquirers the "high-ground advantage," to borrow a term from military strategy, over future competitors. Just how much information is available for liquidation is a matter of concern, however, to both the FTC and organizations concerned with privacy. Toysmart, which filed for bankruptcy, listed its customer list containing information gathered about 250,000 customers as a saleable asset. Its intent to sell this list to the highest bidder violated its own privacy policy, which pledged to customers that personal information "is never shared with a third party." The courts maintain that if information is gathered under this premise and cannot be sold during operation, it cannot be sold during bankruptcy either—that would violate state consumer fraud laws.

Other important assets that might also be acquired are software and systems that are worth more than the purchase price, possibly a great domain name, and a good group of e-commerce specialists. If these assets provide a high-ground advantage, final victory may go to the bricks-and-mortar firm that waits to buy the high ground at bargain basement prices when the dot-com firm falters. Though Homewarehouse.com could not accomplish its goal of becoming the "Home Depot" of the Web (a lofty goal under any standard), its technology assets became a sound acquisition for Walmart.com, as did its addition of several members of the failed dot-com's engineering and design teams.

The best opportunity of all for acquisition potential, however, might be the best of first movers: Amazon.com. First in vision, first in brand, first in customer service, first in distribution, and first in software and computer systems, Amazon does every part of e-tailing well, except for one. After five years of "success," it still doesn't make a profit. The bankers who made loans of $2 billion to Amazon expect to get paid $2 billion, plus interest, on the agreed-upon date—beginning in 2003. If they can't pay, bankers can take the company. And renegotiating the terms of the loan doesn't work well when you are increasing the amount of money you lose every year.

In addition to unprofitable sales, Amazon made a critical strategic move when it invested in several pure-play dot-coms that promised to pay hefty fees to be Amazon's online partners. Count among them Living.com, which agreed to pay Amazon $145 million to be its furniture store, but Living.com died in August 2000. In similar deals with Wine.com, WineShopper.com, Pets.com, and Drugstore.com, Amazon faces losing up to $500 million in revenues over the next five years of partnership "fees" should those companies suffer a similar fate. Likely to join Pets.com and Urbanfetch.com in failure is Kozmo.com, a Web-based home delivery company, actively shedding employees and cutting costs to avoid the chopping block.

In August 2000, Amazon.com and Toys 'R' Us announced the formation of a strategic alliance. Toys 'R' Us knows how and why people shop for toys. It also performs well the commerce functions associated with sourcing, pricing, inventorying, and selling them. The company readily admits, however, that the technology it used to run its e-tail operations stinks. Amazon.com, on the other hand, has the best technology on the Web and excellent customer care systems. When each entity tried to sell toys online, disaster hit. Amazon lacked expertise in understanding and predicting consumer demand and identifying good sources. In the strategic alliance,

Amazon exits its money-losing e-toy business and is paid a commission to provide the e-services of handling Web marketing and e-fulfillment for ToysRUs.com, which can now provide state-of-the art Web technology and level of customer service that it could not afford on its own.

Is its partnership with Toys 'R' Us a step in the right strategic direction? It could be, if the physical retailer can bring costs down and make individual customer transactions profitable. One only hopes that it is not just a marriage of convenience to "buy time" and improve the image of each entity in the market and on the street—Amazon gaining credibility in physical distribution and retailing from aligning with a giant retailer, and Toys 'R' Us getting a shot in the arm from aligning with the glamorous, e-savvy Amazon brand.

Partnerships aside, only time will tell whether customers will support (at profitable margins) Amazon enough to keep it afloat. But if not, it has a boatload of assets that Wal-Mart, Sears, Carrefour, or other major bricks-and-mortar firms would find very attractive, especially at the right price. Take, for example, Borders, the third largest bookseller. Had Borders decided to concentrate on delivering an experience in its stores rather than invest time, money, and energy into developing a losing online store, perhaps it would be in the position to buy Amazon—a deal that would surely have crowned it king of book and related e-tailing. A clearance sale on Amazon might even attract the shopping center real estate managers that Jeff Bezos hoped to replace with his virtual shopping mall. Amazon's demise would start the sale of the century for bricks-and-mortar firms looking for bargains in their evolution to the world of e-commerce. If Amazon, the best of the best, goes under, imagine how many other dot-com boats will also sink in the Amazon river of debt.

Strategy 4: Develop an "Octopus" Brand

With the increasing need to attract and retain customers and carve out an image in the minds of consumers, brands skyrocketed in importance during the 1990s and are destined to rise even more in the new economy. Marketers bombard consumers every day with a barrage of messages through a multitude of media. To distinguish themselves from myriad also-rans, successful firms need to develop "octopus" brands, whereby each tentacle represents a different method of reaching consumers. While the message is always the same, extending from the same beast (in this case the brand), each tentacle provides additional strength in penetrating potential customers' sensory processes. In this branding strategy, methods from in-store promotions and advertising to sales persons and the Internet work together to create a unified promise and personality.

The dawn of the dot-com brought boom times to advertising agencies, commissioned to create images for a breed of virtual unknowns. Who can forget the 2000 Super Bowl, remembered primarily for its glut of multimillion-dollar dot-com ads, including Computer.com, which spent $3.2 million—more than half of the $6 million it received in first-round funding—to hype a company with little more than a good name. But without efficient operations positioned to satisfied customers, good advertising only accelerates the demise of bad products.

Smart firms are recognizing that one of the killer applications in the B-to-C e-commerce world is building brand. The Internet can be used in a variety of ways to build brand, including:

- Promote personality of the brand with graphics and interface similar to those appearing in advertisements, brochures, in stores, and on packaging
- Promote relationships with customers with interactivity and communication features
- Position brand to individual consumers with personalization features, such as personalized greetings and e-mails
- Create an online shopping experience similar to in-store shopping
- Create a human dimension to the brand by giving consumers information about the CEO, company philosophy, company social endeavors, and policies
- Give customers information on stock purchase and performance

Recognizing that some sales will come from the Internet, the most profitable strategy may be developing an Internet presence to build a brand with a presence in the physical and virtual world.

If your corporate strategy for developing an octopus brand is plagued with strategic gaps, perhaps buying a brand rather than building one from scratch will be more efficient. That's what Proffitt's did to develop an online brand with a healthy dose of "Saks"-appeal. Although well known and respected in the southeastern states, Proffitt's was relatively unknown in the rest of the nation. So it bought Saks Fifth Avenue, a worldwide respected brand, to create its online presence. Today, the online business operates as Saks Direct, which includes the catalog business (helpful in e-fulfillment) as well as saksfifthavenue.com.

If a company brands itself successfully, it may choose to develop its own line of branded products. In recent years, traditional retailers have spent millions on developing store brands because of their higher margins, price value to consumers, and their ability to build consumer loyalty and increase store traffic. Online retailers are poised to introduce their own brands of products for two primary reasons. First, they have to invest in creating a brand for their companies anyway; introducing their own line of product is a naturally bigger bang for their buck and a way to prevent direct price comparison. Second, consumers often want more information about private brands, including their comparability to manufacturer's brands, which can be explained well online.

The challenge for many e-tailers will be overcoming the experience and consumer trust inherent to established brands and bricks-and-mortar storebrands. Traditional retailers, however, may find long-term opportunities by using the Internet to offer specialty, private-label products not yet available in the store. They may also test new products, registering consumers' reactions to packaging and other attributes, before they launch a full-scale product release.

For most bricks-and-mortar firms, there is a natural advantage in migrating the store's name to the Internet, saving the cost and time new dot-com firms face in building credibility and trust for their brands. Target, Wal-Mart, Gap, and Victoria's Secret have such strong brand appeal in their stores, they are wise to leverage their names on the Web. Kmart, on the other hand, has had some problems in its stores, with stock-outs, cluttered floors, and customer service problems at the top of the list. *If a store's brand lacks positive image and doesn't bode well with consumers, a retailer may consider developing a new brand for its online presence.* Though we can't say that this is *the* reason Kmart elected to name its online retail business BlueLight.com, we can say that the new name lends itself well to developing a new, brighter, and "hipper" image. The BlueLight name draws on the nostalgia of the past, yet promotes a new upbeat image with help from its partner, Yahoo!. It also allows the firm to distance itself as far from the store image as managers and executives see fit. Partners such as Yahoo! bring a younger, computer-minded consumer group to Kmart, while MarthaStewart.com attracts female segments. New to the job, Kmart CEO Chuck Conaway plans to rid the chain of its in-store problems, creating a more shopping-friendly environment and experience. Who knows, if BlueLight's online business and image catch on, perhaps Kmart will rename some of its newer upbeat, efficient stores BlueLight.

Strategy 5: Change from Free to Fee

Charge a fee or do it for free? That is a question many e-based firms have grappled with since the inception of their models. In the early days, when getting hits was *the* Internet success indicator, dot-coms did anything to get a customer. They gave away products, gave away cash, offered free shipping, and discounted products to below cost just to reel in some fish. The problem is, the bait cost more than the fish were worth. Also, unfortunately, the dot-coms created a consumer mind-set that expected discounted prices and minimal shipping charges from e-tailers.

What was a great way to attract customers will create a retention nightmare for many—once you give away something, how do you then tell customers they have to pay for it? But that is the reality. For more and more e-commerce firms, creating a long-term, profitable Internet strategy means charging for something that used to be free. Bricks-and-mortar firms have a leg-up on their e-only competitors in this instance. Retailers can provide information and Web services for free if these activities help increase sales and profits off-line. Pure-play dot-coms don't have the same revenue safety net. Advertising was supposed to be the underlying way to pay, but that paradigm is fading fast except for a few dominant firms like Yahoo!.

AOL and eBay make money with a "make a little on a lot" philosophy. They understand what consumers value enough to pay for, but keep the prices low enough to attract millions of customers. That is Wal-Mart's ace in the hole strategy: It maintains low prices but creates its profits with unprecedented volume and rapid turnover. Online auctioneer eBay has charged a modest fee of 1.25 to 5 percent on each sale from its inception, and customers are willing to pay it because they value the service.

AOL, which did give a lot of free online access away, did so on a limited-time basis, just long enough for customers to get an e-mail address, communicate it to their friends, and become "hooked" on chatting. It mastered switching consumers from free to a modest fee to maintain the service, building a profitable business for AOL. And the astonishing fact that 54 percent of all Internet users in the United States access the Web through AOL gives it such dominance that it can also charge hefty fees to advertisers for "pop ups" when consumers sign on to AOL.

AOL is so good at the free-to-fee game that it often gets paid for its free service. When customers sign on for free access, many of them also sign-up for a 480-page book AOL sells to show enthusiasts how to "get the most from your online adventure." Just click "accept" and your credit card will be charged a mere $24.95 (plus $3.95 shipping charge)—and AOL is well on its way to recouping the lost fees of its "first-month free" offer.

If you offer something of value, a better solution to what is currently available, don't sell yourself or your concept short; people will pay for it. And those who don't probably don't represent profitable customers anyway. SAMSClub.com is banking on the fact that its customers will pay a membership fee to shop its online store similar to the fee people readily fork over to buy from warehouse clubs. The classic example of charging a fee for valued services lies in the dark side of the Internet—pornography. Consumers pay significant fees to view pictures of naked bodies and watch sex videos. It is the most successful retail industry on the Web, generating over $1 billion of revenue for hundreds of highly profitable sites.

If they'll pay to look at dirty pictures, consumers would surely pay to send their friends and family electronic greeting cards, right? Bluemountain .com provides a hundred ways to electronically say thanks, happy birthday, and I'm thinking about you for free, as do its retail competitors Hallmark .com and AmericanGreetings.com. While the latter two perhaps can absorb the costs of free e-cards from profits obtained when customers shop at the many retail stores carrying their cards, Bluemountain.com hopes to make money from the products consumers buy when they click on ads appearing on its site, a fading paradigm for profitability. Hallmark and AG also offer gifts on their sites, but they often act as the primary or exclusive retailer for these gifts or own these brands, and therefore collect more than just a transaction fee.

Implementing a free-to-fee conversion strategy requires an analysis of the types of customers that will pay a fee. Often, it's not the Internet user. Look at E*Trade, Charles Schwab, and other online brokerage firms and the minimal fees they charge for online trades. The real "fee" they receive is the income they earn from bank accounts where idle funds are held when not in stocks and from mutual funds paying commissions on some classes of shares. Traditional brokerage giants, such as Schwab and American Express, also make money by generating funds held on deposit in its customers' accounts used to support highly profitable loans. But that strategy doesn't work well if customer accounts average only $25,000, as many of the online brokerage firms are finding. American Express's online brokerage service puts a spin on the free-to-fee strategy. It earns its "fees" from customers by requiring them to maintain a minimum balance of $100,000, making it possible for American Express to provide its customers "free" trades.

Going from free to fee sometimes requires creativity. As an example, Priceline, the online pioneer of patented pricing processes, borrows one of its tactics from the "traveler's check" model. For years, Citibank, American Express, and other financial institutions have sold traveler's checks for a few dollars per hundred dollars face amount, which usually covered only the commission paid to local banks to issue the checks. The money was made on the "float"—earning interest on money from the time it is collected (before the vacation) to the time it's paid to merchants (weeks or months later or sometimes never if the checks weren't cashed). After seventeen years at Citibank, developing its consumer banking services, it's not surprising that Priceline's chairman, Rick Braddock, figured out how to do the same thing with its airline and travel services.

Strategy 6: Add a Human Dimension to E-commerce Strategies

Some of the earliest and most useful marketing studies were based upon principles of sociology and anthropology. They revealed decades ago what marketing studies still reveal today, that buying and selling is about human behavior much more than about products and prices. *The human dimension of consumer behavior helps us conclude that e-commerce strategies that provide human interaction, whether through a retail store or a salesperson operating from an office, have a major advantage over firms with e-only strategies.* This is not exclusive to the B-to-C arena; B-to-B firms must recognize that industrial products are sold to people in organizations rather than to the organizations themselves.

Strategies that add the human dimension close sales more effectively, cross-sell related products better, and have higher product and distribution accuracy rates. They therefore increase customer satisfaction as well. If you are an e-tailer, there are several tactics that you may want to consider to bring the human factor to your technology.

Add a Human Dimension to the Web-Buying Experience. Winning online strategies provide ways for customers to interact with real people. For example, 1-800-Flowers.com lets customers see the flowers and gifts they want to buy online and either order from the site or go off-line and order by phone, similar to talking to a customer service rep at your favorite catalog retailer. Most consumers like being able to see the products on the website, but they also like having someone to answer questions, assure them about delivery, and simply to talk to. LivePerson.com provides these services for e-tailers on an out-sourced basis, supplying live people answering questions about how products work and suggesting other products that work with it. L.L. Bean has found a way to coax customers through the Internet buying experience with human interaction via real-time e-mail. The option to see products online and buy via phone (similar to catalog shopping) also calms fears of submitting financial data online. Although more costly for retailers than Web-only solutions, one way to make Web-buying more human, is to make humans more available on the Web.

Combine Customer Intimacy with Market Vastness. Small firms, many of which already have an inherent advantage of customer intimacy, are now able to increase their market reach through the Internet. The premier Canadian clothier Harry Rosen, for example, has developed a detailed consumer information data collection and communication program that prompts sales associates to call customers when specific apparel matching previous purchases arrives in the store. The Internet now allows Harry Rosen to do this beyond Canada's borders—reaching consumers in the United States and Europe—yet maintain the same level of intimacy created with in-store customers.

E-tailers should follow Harry's footsteps, offering customized merchandise and special promotions depending on their shopping patterns or specific interests captured in sophisticated data programs. But these Web-based solutions must truly satisfy human needs and behavior patterns, rather than demonstrate the capabilities of technology and customer relationship management (CRM) software. The so-called one-to-one approach may turn some consumers off—unless they've indicated they want this type of intimacy. Software that presents consumers products and offers based on past behavior may also be less effective than letting people make their choices based on changing and future interests.

Reexamine Customer Service Tactics. In an age in which too many retailers, wholesalers, and manufacturers are chasing too few customers, the decisive strategy for success focuses on customer service. Wal-Mart, Target, Banana Republic, and Home Depot, as well as other traditional retailers, have worked diligently over the years to train their sales associates to be helpful, knowledgeable, and courteous. For example, Bath & Body Works achieves higher sales per square foot than The Body Shop, partly because BBW trains its associates to interact extensively with potential customers, demonstrating the products personally. Traditional retailers depend on their associates to increase customer satisfaction and customer retention. But retailers who fail to improve sales associates' effectiveness will lose one of the most effective weapons against electronic sales they possess—their people.

Customer service rules are not repealed just because you operate on the Internet. The key to enabling a firm's sales associates to provide better customer service is to link internal information technology systems with the outside world of the Internet. Customers want to know whether products are in stock, order status, return policies, payments in progress, and parts needed to fix products. Today, customers have little choice but to ask a store employee, and though the store's internal computer system will likely contain the information, it's often difficult to retrieve. Connectivity software linking the firm's "back room" with its customers and suppliers allows information to be accessed instantly by a firm's employees or customers. And instantly means just that. During the Christmas 2000 rush, many Amazon customers discovered that items that were in stock when they put them in their shopping carts were out of stock by the time they checked out. The problem was that they didn't learn this until after their order shipped, which meant another shopping trip and, perhaps, another shipping charge.

Increasingly, the Internet will solve many customer service problems without the need for a firm's personnel to be involved. Either way, firms win when they use the Internet to solve routine customer service problems, saving the firm's most important resource—its people—to interact with customers in out-of-the-ordinary glitches or in need of personal attention.

Strategy 7: Use Multichannel Marketing to Sell to New Segments and Extend Product Offerings

Marketers need many ways to reach customers effectively and the Internet allows them to expand product offerings, sales methods, and customer segments. There exists a variety of ways in which the Internet can help companies reach both current customers and new segments with existing products and analyze how new products might be developed to augment sales. For marketers seeking ways to reach customers, the Internet has become one of their best friends, although not their only friend. Here are some ways it's useful.

Firms can use the Internet to sell their existing product lines more effectively to existing customer segments. You saw in Chapter 4 how Sherwin-Williams is employing this strategy to sell paint more efficiently to its existing segments and possibly new ones. Chris Conwell, the CEO of Sherwin-Williams, told us, "In addition to receiving over 6 million hits per month, the Sherwin-Williams website helped us reduce labor costs in our stores while increasing service levels to our customers." Sherwin-Williams currently doesn't sell to do-it-yourself (DIY) consumers on the Internet, but it uses the technology to increase efficiency of its DIY sales process in its stores. Other firms might actually turn to Internet sales to sell more effectively to existing customers, as Staples.com has, with its online catalog and delivery service to area small businesses.

The Internet can also be an effective way of increasing sales by reaching new segments of customers with current product lines. The Internet breaks the geography barrier, making it possible for small retailers, who might otherwise only sell to local customers, to reach a global audience. Their degree of success depends on how prominently they are featured on other websites and how easy they are to identify on search engines. Similarly, if a customer doesn't have a Target store in his or her area, he or she can buy from the company online, regardless of physical location.

The Internet works well for small customers in search of products sold primarily through a personal sales force. Companies often forgo sales to low-volume customers because the potential sales revenue doesn't justify the cost. But even low-volume, low-purchase-frequency customers can order the products they need on the Internet—providing the company a low-cost method of reaching new segments for existing products. This is a key to the appeal of many B-to-B sites, including PrintNation.com. It's also important for major retail sites. For example, Circuit City can offer big-city product availability to rural or small-town segments not large enough to support a store, let alone the costs of personal selling and inventory typical of one of its stores. If the costs of logistics and distribution are manageable, the Internet can be a powerful tool in growing profits by selling to new segments.

Bricks-and-mortar retailers can also use the Web to extend their product offerings. That's why Sears started business with a catalog a hundred years ago—to offer even rural consumers an extended range of products impossible to stock in the stores of that time. Taking a page from the century-old Sears catalog theory, retailers can offer products on the Web that they might otherwise not be able to sell in stores, either because of their large physical size, high costs, seasonality, or low turn rates. Examples range from bulky items such as wine cooler–cabinets and designer home furnishings to shoes and apparel in unpopular sizes. Nordstrom.com can offer a much wider array of sandals, wedgies, and pumps in sizes 4 to 14 online than it ever could in a single store. The result is more choices for the consumer and enhanced brand loyalty without increasing costs or lowering inventory turn rates.

Strategies that target various consumer segments with specific product offerings can draw consumers into stores and entice them to try the website. Firms may also use the Internet to:

- Introduce new products online and test reaction of frequent buyers before offering them in the store.
- Offer select seasonal items year-round (coats during the summer for people going on an Alaskan cruise).
- Offer special online discounts on slow-moving inventory.
- Sell closeout merchandise and odd lots directly to consumers.

In short, the Internet allows large firms to tailor offerings to specific customer segments and even individual customers, thereby making a large, seemingly impersonal retailer more intimate. It does the opposite for small firms—giving them a "larger than life" presence that expands their reach and potential customer base.

Strategy 8: Sell and Source the Global Marketplace

The Web allows firms of all sizes to operate efficiently on a global basis—just as consumers can source products from stores around the world, so, too, can businesses source global suppliers. Currently, the e-tailers with the greatest global presence are the same ones that hold star status in the United States: Amazon, eBay, and CDNow. According to a study released by Ernst & Young, Amazon claims the title of "most popular e-tailer" in Canada, Australia, the U.K., Italy, and France. Its customer-centric approach in Japan, for example, has led to a customized site promoting Japanese literature and culture. Though Amazon's business model is a great example of growing sales globally, its profitability woes are still a concern. Expanding globally means employing costly customer attraction strategies (perhaps reminiscent of those used in the United States in the past) and incurring the expense of expanding its bricks-and-mortar warehouse facilities in countries with smaller populations and lower volumes.

Selling globally may be a better strategy for small, niche retailers, wholesalers, and manufacturers than it is for the global bricks-and-mortar giants. Noggintops.com, the global seller of chapeaus and top hats, sells to an eclectic cadre of customers as far away as Japan and Europe from its tiny Congerville, Illinois, headquarters. It serves its hat-obsessed niche of consumers by sourcing hard-to-find hats from around the world. Noggintops performs the business functions required to source, sell, and ship these specialty products at costs consumers are willing to absorb. Small firms that attract customers throughout the world willing to pay premium prices for them to source, procure, and ship specialty products are likely to find success on the Internet. But these firms must concentrate on performing commerce functions even more efficiently globally than domestically if they are to generate acceptable profit margins.

Though global e-tailing is filled with opportunities, it is also filled with challenges. Developing a global strategy requires careful planning to attract potential buyers in other countries, as many search engines are English-only and potential buyers spend a lot of time with local country domains (.uk, .jn, .de, and so forth). Global e-tailers must overcome customs and tariff regulations for each country and expensive and frequently unreliable transportation and delivery. E-tailers must also organize payment systems for customers without credit cards, which is a much higher proportion of consumers in Europe, Asia, and Africa than in the United States. Finally, firms will need to help potential customers gain access to the Internet. Some retailers accomplish this by setting up kiosks in their stores and helping consumers place orders, as 7-Eleven does successfully in Japan for a host of online merchants. Ford and Bertelsmann CEOs Jacque Nasser and Thomas Middlehoff placed computers and Internet access in the homes of all their employees to prevent them from falling behind in the digital divide.

When these obstacles are overcome and strategies are executed well, global e-commerce means big opportunities to sell products, source solutions, and build brands. VictoriasSecret.com, discussed thoroughly in Chapter 5, now sells around the world, without the costs and risks of building and operating stores outside the United States. This nonstore approach can yield better profit margins than those of competitors that place a lot of resources into their global network of bricks-and-mortar stores. The Internet can also be used to set the stage for entrance to a new market. An online presence that says "look for our new perfume in your local XYZ store" can increase interest in a new brand launch in a new market. Perhaps more important, the ability to source on a global basis online may yield the greatest area of profit improvement for retailers and many other firms that truly understand and develop strategies to exploit the global capabilities of e-commerce.

Strategy 9: Develop Strategic Alliances to Perform "E" and "Commerce" Functions Better Than Competitors

During the early days of e-commerce, marketers, media, and executives focused almost exclusively on the "e" portion of e-commerce, forgetting, in effect, that it was the second part of the equation that would most likely make or break a business. Although developing a user-friendly and complete website is extremely important, it is the commerce functions—logistics, transportation, inventory management, and delivery, to name a few—that must be mastered to succeed in the world of e-commerce.

Mastery of the commerce functions is difficult alone, especially for small- and medium-sized firms; that's why dot-coms need to create strategic alliances to create their sites, run their logistics functions, and build their physical operations. A strategic alliance involves more than just finding a supplier; it means finding a firm that understands your strategic intent and is willing to partner with you for the long term to attain those goals. No entity needs strategic partners more than the dot-com to increase credibility among consumers and other potential partners and gain the experience of established bricks-and-mortar commerce firms.

Small- and medium-sized firms need to find strategic partners to develop e-solutions that rival the advantages and efficiencies of large, established firms, without the hefty price tags. With over fifteen hundred website designers and specialists ready, willing, and able to create the perfect site, the "e" portion of e-commerce has approached commodity status with many firms available in almost any city ready to build and maintain sites inexpensively. A few firms stand out, however, such as Usinterworking, Inc., the leading ASP delivering e-commerce and enterprise software. USi has captured 35 percent market share because of the value it adds to sites such as www.hpshopping.com. For many small- and medium-sized firms, the best place to look for finding strategic partnerships in the Internet sector is their trade association.

Trade shows play an important role in introducing new products, building relationships between buyers and sellers, and exposing firms to new technologies and services. As some questioned the future of the traditional trade show in the wake of the Internet craze, ExpoExchange partnered with hundreds of associations (ranging from the National Retail Federation to the National Spa and Swimming Pool Institute) to develop extensive e-solutions they would have not been able to develop alone. With expertise in expositions, ExpoExchange designed systems to increase trade show efficiency by registering guests, planning travel, and making appointments with vendors and exhibitors through an association's website. The company, in effect, operates websites for association members to continue relationships started during the trade show, making e-commerce accessible to member firms of all sizes and tailored to the needs of specific industries.

In addition to building the "e" side of the business, dot-coms must develop the "commerce" side of doing business online. Every e-commerce firm selling molecular products must address the very difficult question of how to achieve effective warehousing, distribution, and e-fulfillment. Unless they already have established systems from store or catalog operations, dot-coms must make win-win strategic alliances with logistics providers if they hope to turn a profit. Why? Because when deciding between various brands and whether to shop electronically, consumers consider:

- How quickly and safely will the firm deliver the ordered items?
- How likely is the product I want to be in stock—and if it's not, how long will it take to tell me it is out of stock and how long will it take to get it?
- Will I get what I ordered, and if there are problems, where and how can I exchange it?
- If I need the product now, can I go to the store and get it?
- How much will delivery cost and when will it occur?

We believe logistics capabilities will become one of the most important attributes of e-commerce brands. If your logistics systems aren't cost effective and swift, and if they can't relate critical information to consumers about their orders, your firm is plagued with competitive disadvantages that could kill the company.

To plan and develop these types of strategic partnerships, we suggest these basic steps:

1. Define the functions that must be performed to satisfy customers with an e-commerce solution (described in Chapters 2 and 8).

2. Determine which functions can be developed more efficiently internally than if outsourced.

3. Analyze which functions are "core" to your business and should be retained internally (both immediately and in the long run).

4. Analyze which firms can perform functions you require to be outsourced.

5. Determine what you can offer to induce the highest rate of cooperation from capable partners, and create trust in the channel.

The new economic model for strategic partnerships has become an equity stakes model, in which firms pick their partners based on speculation of their future profitability. In return for providing their services and allowing their names to be used to promote new companies, established firms are getting stock and royalties on future sales. *National Geographic* magazine, for example, recently agreed to license its name and graphic resources to a dot-com firm, retaining editorial approval rights and 30 percent of the dot-com firm. Another example is the strategic alliance between Purchasepro.com and Sprint, a deal in which Sprint received 23 percent of Purchasepro.com stock and a percentage of future sales (not profits) in exchange for agreeing to be the telephonic and communication provider to Purchasepro.com customers. Rather than paying for advertising, traditional firms are paid for letting someone else market their brand, sell their services, and reach new customers.

Perhaps the best evidence that such alliances can be very profitable for bricks-and-mortar firms is the deal signed by Delta Airlines giving available seats and instant credibility to Priceline.com and about 28 percent of Priceline's stock to Delta. A year later, Delta reported profits of $175 million from operating its airline, but it earned $575 million in "nonrecurring earnings" from the sale of a portion of its stock in Priceline.com—a tidy sum to fund the development of Delta's own website. Still, many firms will get burned in these deals, as would Delta had it held on to its Priceline stock too long. *As more e-businesses falter, getting cash upfront to provide services might be safer in the long run than getting a piece of the "action," especially when there is no action.*

Strategy 10: Use the Internet to Create a Lean, Mean Demand Chain

Down with stores and up with e-tailing was the battle cry of the late 1990s, while farther back in the supply chain, the battle was positioned as traditional distributors and manufacturers versus electronic exchanges. Equally shortsighted, as we described in the book *From Mind to Market*, is viewing competition as retailer versus retailer, distributor versus distributor, or manufacturer versus manufacturer. Successful strategies in the twenty-first century are based on the recognition that competitive battles are increasingly fought supply chain versus supply chain, with the most efficient quickly choosing up sides.

Further, winning supply chains are no longer constrained to a left to right progression from manufacturer, to wholesaler, to retailer, and finally to customers, who sit passively at the receiving end of the channel. *The paradigm for the twenty-first century is one in which supply chains begin with customers' needs, wants, and lifestyles, progress through channel members, and end back at the customer level with execution in the marketplace.* That's what we call a demand chain—serving the ultimate master, the consumer.

When all is said and done, individual firms can do a lot to increase their efficiency and effectiveness in the market, including implementing successful e-tail, marketing, branding, and sales strategies. But ultimate victors of the next century will be those with the most efficient supply chains—taking a page from Wal-Mart's, The Limited's, and Carrefour's strategy books. E-commerce can help create lean, mean demand chains. Just look at Dell's Internet-facilitated demand chain, which lets customers design their own computers and then assembles and ships them while maintaining an average inventory of only six days. Compare that to the six months average inventory of competitors who forecast what customers will buy and then push them through distributors and retailers, hoping they sell at a profit before becoming obsolete. Dell doesn't make computers until they've been sold, presumably at a profit.

Covisint plans on transforming the traditional auto supply chain into a consumer-driven demand chain. Starting with a consumer configuring a car on the Internet to his or her specifications, progressing to the creation of the car, and ending with delivery to the consumer, Covisint is banking on increased efficiencies in the supply chain to create lower prices and higher satisfaction for consumers, and higher profits for channel members. More than a vision for the future for cars, this could be a model for future supply chains, meshing both industrial and consumer goods, beginning with the mind of the consumer. Though this vision may take decades to accomplish, it is nonetheless the dream driving supply chains toward demand chains.

Designing leaner, meaner demand chains rests on the performance of major commerce functions through the channel—from predicting and interpreting consumer demand and sourcing products to managing logistics functions and conducting marketing research. These functions will not be eliminated in the new economy; they will, however, shift to the most efficient levels in the supply chain, performed with the use of EDI and the Internet.

At the end of the day, the supply chain that can deliver what consumers want, to the right place, for the least amount of money and in the quickest time frame will win. How consumers order and buy their products is but a small part of the process. The e-tailers with the most efficient and cost-effective supply chains will beat their dot-com competitors, and physical retailers will do the same. When you begin to weigh the odds of e-tailing taking over a high percentage of retail sales, look at the supply chain issues. Unless the e-tail supply chain (which shifts many functions that consumers do for free in the traditional model to a supply chain member) becomes more efficient than the traditional store-based channel, e-tailing's prevalence is limited.

CUSTOMER-DRIVEN BUSINESS EVOLUTION

All business involves people, with human emotions and instincts. Superceding the strategies and advancements in technology discussed throughout this book, business leaders must remember that their customers are living, emotional, social beings who for the most part thrive on relationships and interaction. Collectively they make the mightiest of powers—society. Bob Tobin, CEO of Ahold North America, points out that "Since the Stone Age, gregarious humans have seen fit to 'join' other humans in tribes, religions, Elk Clubs, political parties, fraternities, and, now, computer networking groups (which in most cities meet off-line as well as online). Shopping is a social experience, not just buying a product."

Bob is right. The immediate implications of his comments affect how we might analyze the scalability or totality of e-commerce. But the more we think about his comments, the more we realize that as marketers and executives we help form the future of society—constrained only by the behaviors innate to people after centuries of living. Just as surely as the industrial revolution invaded every sector of society in the eighteenth and nineteenth centuries, the Internet is creating changes so pervasive and profound that they have the potential of invading every avenue of life in the twenty-first century—work, leisure, education, communication, government, and values.

The danger we see lies within the possibility of industry's mass disconnect from the realities of society. Remember, if you are reading this book, chances are you are not "normal." If you own a computer, have more than a high school degree, or live in a household earning over $45,000 per year, you are not a "normal" consumer. We talk about the possibility of creating a single world marketplace, but the reality is that the vast majority of global citizens will never get computer access in our lifetimes. Even today, 42 percent of the world's population over fifteen years old has never made a phone call—and even in the United States there are millions of people who dangle on the poverty line. These forgotten consumers will be further isolated and segregated from the rest of the world as the digital divide expands. While marketers talk about the need to have the latest technology to keep up with their competitors, there will always be a need for companies who sell to consumers who don't have technology and probably never will. And yet they buy the most food and basic products, have more votes, provide more workers for companies, and reproduce the most consumers of the next generation.

The future of business will be decided by people and the degree to which new sales and marketing formats fit consumer behavior and lifestyles better than existing ones. In the end, customers rule—they decide what the future retail and business landscape will look like by adopting some technologies and changes and rejecting others. The future of business-to-business e-commerce rests on its ability to execute on the promise of more efficient supply chains and more satisfied customers. As blended strategies become the mainstream, e-commerce will be absorbed into the all-encompassing, umbrella definition of commerce.

The predictions of many have spelled out doom and gloom for traditional retailers. We disagree. In fact, we believe retailers would be wise to continue improving upon their greatest strength—the shopping experience in their stores. Look for improvements in the areas of store atmospherics, return policies, customer service, automated checkout systems, phone-in ordering, shopping hours, and special product offerings. After getting the stores right and increasing customer retention rates, retailers should focus on the e-offerings. The goal should be to shift consumer mood and attitude toward stores from "I have to shop here" to "I am shopping here because I want to." And chances are, if they like the store, they'll like the website.

The more things change, the more they stay the same. There are fundamental business strategies and tactics that have worked over the years for bricks-and-mortar firms. They will work as well, if not better, today and tomorrow when coupled with the appropriate new technologies. Will the majority of dot-com firms fail? Probably so, as will many e-commerce-based strategies implemented by reputable companies. But this book shows what it takes to be among the minority that succeed. We realize our message, though pro Internet for certain segments and for certain applications, is different from all the hype and hope that has been written about e-commerce in the past. We believe in the institution of marriage between traditional firms and e-commerce. We just don't believe that all of these marriages will last.

Much media attention has fallen on the Internet as a new selling tool. We like to think of it as a marketing tool. If you want to build brand and market your company and products, go online. If you want to build profits, go off-line. That principle applies to firms as small as Gazoontite and as large as Wal-Mart. We believe e-commerce will occupy a place in the business books of the next century, not as the final chapter but as a catalyst to another stage in the evolution of commerce—one in which customers continue to rule.

INDEX

ABOUT THE AUTHORS

ROGER D. BLACKWELL is professor of marketing in the Max M. Fisher College of Business at Ohio State University, president of Roger Blackwell Associates, Inc., and author of *From Mind to Market*.

Professor Blackwell was cited by the *New York Times* as one of the top speakers about global business on the lecture circuit and heralded as a marketing and retail "guru" with the ability to mesmerize his audiences. His depth of knowledge, energy, and humor make him a favorite among students and business audiences. He was named Outstanding Marketing Educator in America by Sales and Marketing Executives International and Marketer of the Year by the American Marketing Association. He also received the Alumni Distinguished Teaching Award, the highest award given by Ohio State University.

Roger Blackwell is considered to be one of the founding fathers of consumer behavior and is coauthor of one of the leading books in this field—*Consumer Behavior,* now in its ninth edition—which is used by business schools throughout North America, Europe, Asia, and Africa. He has also written twenty-three other books on marketing strategy, research, and global marketing.

Roger Blackwell received his B.S. and M.S. degrees from the University of Missouri and his Ph.D. from Northwestern University. He also received an honorary doctorate degree from the Cincinnati College of Mortuary Science. He resides in Columbus, Ohio, and serves on the boards of numerous NYSE, NASDAQ, and privately held corporations, including Airnet Systems, Applied Industrial Technologies (formerly Bearings, Inc.), The Banc Stock Group, Checkpoint Systems, Flex-Funds, Max & Erma's Restaurants, Intimate Brands, and Anthony and Sylvan.

KRISTINA STEPHAN is vice president and partner of Blackwell Associates, Inc., through which she works with many companies on consumer behavior, logistics, and strategic marketing issues. She is coauthor of *Contemporary Cases in Consumer Behavior* and numerous articles on consumer behavior, retailing, and supply chain management. She has also been a contributing author for *Consumer Behavior, From the Edge of the World,* and *From Mind to Market.*

Kristina Stephan received her M.B.A. from the Max M. Fisher College of Business at Ohio State University. She is a director of Daymark Group, a privately held logistics solutions company, and the United States Figure Skating Association.